NEMESIS

NEMESIS

ANTHONY RICHES

An Aries Book

This edition first published in the UK in 2021
by Aries, an imprint of Head of Zeus Ltd

9 7 5 3 1 2 4 6 8

A CIP catalogue record for this book is available from the
British Library.

ISBN (PB) 9781801100106
ISBN (E) 9781800248984

Printed and bound by CPI Group (UK) Ltd,
Croydon, CR0 4YY

Typeset by Siliconchips Services Ltd UK

Aries
c/o Head of Zeus
First Floor East
5–8 Hardwick Street
London EC1R 4RG
WWW.HEADOFZEUS.COM

For Helen, as always.

1

The black Loake boots, Mickey decided. A perfect match for black Wrangler Arizonas, and freshly resoled in rubber. A midnight-blue shirt, and that was him ready. Externally, at least. Looked in the mirror and got a quizzical stare back. Michael James Bale. Age forty-three, no distinguishing marks. A nondescript face, nothing to make him stand out. Not the tallest of men at six foot one, but solid. One hundred and eighty-five pounds of gym-toned muscle honed at his local boxing club. Good genes too. Strong, and in good shape. In his prime, pretty much.

Roz met him at the bottom of the stairs. The usual examination, before letting him out for the night. Looking up at him with that expression. The all-knowing, all-commanding, straight-to-the-point woman who'd charmed him over a decade before. And who still had him in the palm of her hand after all that time. With her dark hair that she wished was blonde. The all-seeing brown eyes that she wished were green, like Mickey's. And a body that she kept very, very well toned. 'Giving you no excuses, Mickey Bale,' as she frequently told him. Not that Mickey wanted any excuses. A childhood spent watching his friends struggling through the debris of their parents' failed relationships had taught him the value of holding on to what worked. And not letting go for anything.

'Shaved? Sure there's no-one waiting for you?'

He grinned in the way that always disarmed her.

'Oh they'll be waiting all right. Empty glasses and "where you been all this fucking time?" looks.'

She laughed with him. Knowing his friends well enough.

'You will keep drinking with that lot. What do you expect?'

He let his face assume what she called his chump look. Lips pursed, eyes rolled up. Waited a moment, timing being the secret of comedy. Then face-palmed and shook his head.

'Now you tell me?'

'Don't think I don't know what you're doing.'

'Wait… what? You've seen through my plan?'

A swift prod in the breadbasket to reinforce her point.

'You come it the poor me, but really you love it. Talking shop with the boys, playing up to the image. Flash Mickey. With the guns and the cars and all that.'

He shrugged. 'Beats the alternative, doesn't it? Beats actually working. You know how that would have gone.'

'Yeah.' She turned him round and pushed him to the door. Slapped his backside for emphasis. 'Go on. Back by eleven though; you've got an early start.'

He grinned at her again, accepting the heavy-lipped kiss. The door closed behind him as he stepped out into the early spring night. Down the Crescent and out onto the High Road. Warm enough in his black Belstaff jacket that had cost a fortune the previous month. Strolling under the streetlamps, he zipped it up to his neck. Clicked the placket pop-studs shut. Checked that the wrist and pocket studs were closed too. Knowing they would clatter if left unfastened. Then fastened the neck strap, not wanting the buckle to flap around.

He paused on the corner with Jervis Road. Looked up at the CCTV camera above his head. Frozen, lifeless on its gimbal mount. Still out of action. Just the way Warren liked it. Mickey quietly slipped into a doorway and squatted down. Affecting to fiddle with a bootlace. Peeped round the corner, looking down the pavement. The club opposite Warren Margetson's pitch would still be nine-tenths empty. Its drinks too expensive while the pubs were open. But Warren was already on duty. As any good dealer would be. A professional, of a sort, Warren. And there was more than one sort of client in his line of business. Some of them dabbling. Some of them hardened recreational users. Some of them functioning addicts. And some just victims. Like Katie.

Mickey got back to his feet and turned away. He walked casually down Jervis Road for a hundred yards, then turned left into Nelson Road. Still strolling, in no rush. The street empty, other than for a single passing car. Flickering screens behind lace curtains told their story. People settling down to a night of delivered takeaway and on-demand. No-one to see a black-clad figure pause for a moment, at the top of the alley that led back to the High Road. He ducked into the shadows, immediately lost in the darkness. The streetlights didn't illuminate the cut-through, never had.

His heart rate was elevated, he reckoned, but nothing drastic. Just a touch of nerves. On with the balaclava, silk smooth. His face freshly shaved to avoid stubble drag. Then the gloves. Black latex, thick enough to be durable. But still with enough feel for the trigger. And out with the weapon, untouched by his skin at any time since he'd picked it up. A Ruger .22 automatic. Black metal, boxy-framed, but small enough to be hidden in a hand. Its protruding muzzle screw-threaded. Ugly but functional. The suppressor glided down onto the threads with a well-oiled absence of any sound. As recommended by Martin. Which, given his expertise, was good enough for Mickey.

'It's not what you might have imagined, I get that. But you'll thank me when you're doing the job, I promise you that. Fires .22 sub-sonic ammunition. As quiet as a nun's fart. All you have to do is put a round into his head from a foot away, right? Physics will do the rest.'

He'd frowned at his old schoolmate, looking hard at the small automatic nestled in its foam-lined case. A twenty-four-hour loan to Martin from a fellow dealer. The intra-library loan of the illegal gun trade. Picked up on his way home from Lambeth Road that afternoon.

'Physics? Isn't it all physics?'

Martin had shaken his head. Grinning like the conscienceless fixer that life had made him. Life, and, of course, his Auntie Steph.

'This is *special* physics, Mickey my son. And, I should add, physics with a proven track record. This pistol's already done three jobs and never yet been identified. Because when you put one of these...' holding up the tiny bullet '...into a bloke's head from a foot away, it doesn't have the power to break out the other side. Not enough energy. But it will keep moving, and so it goes round, and round, and round. Turning his brain into soup. Until it stops. Battered out of all recognition, just a lump of metal that can be sussed for a .22 all right, but without barrel striations.'

He'd known what those were, of course, but allowed his friend to keep talking.

'No barrel fingerprint, in simple terms. So no-one will ever link the hit to the pistol. Or the pistol to the bloke I got it from. Or him to me. Which is a good thing. Because he'd give me up in a heartbeat to get a TIC, and a few years off his sentence, right? And I'd be talking on the way to the nick, if they were to pick me up for it. And then where would you be?'

He checked that the suppressor's short tube was firmly attached. Pulled the slide back against the spring, feeling the tension inside the weapon. Released it, to snap forward and chamber the first round in the stubby magazine. And then stopped for a moment, to think. Remembering his school friend's last question.

'But are you *sure* you want to do this? *Really* sure. Because this is major league shit, Mickey. Not like anything you ever did. *Ever*. You sure you got the stones?'

'He supplied the stuff that—'

'Killed Katie. Yeah. We all hate the bastard for that. Fuck, I'd kill him, given the chance. And he knows it, right? Lives in fear of exactly what you want this for.' Raising both the weapon and an eyebrow. 'But are you really... *really*... fucking... sure?'

And that had been choice point number one. He could have said no. Knew he should have. Just walked away, nothing lost. The nasty little Ruger returned to its owner, and no questions asked. Some hard-faced gun dealer would have shrugged. Probably had a laugh with Martin about lost bottle. And no-one would ever have known. But this was the last chance to back out. Unscrew the suppressor.

Slip the pistol back into the bag in his pocket. Peel off the gloves. And the balaclava. And forget the idea of revenge. Tell Nemesis he was out.

He made sure that the mask was all the way down his throat. No white skin to reflect light. Walked slowly, carefully, down the alley. Stepping carefully, silently, over the inevitable detritus of the urban landscape. Fifty yards. He could see Warren now, lit by the lights behind him. His back to the alley, half-hidden in the shadows. Surveying his domain. His little kingdom.

Other dealers wanted the pitch, but none of them would stand against him. Warren carried a knife, and his face told you he'd use it happily enough. The same hard face he'd turned on the police investigating Katie's death. *Nothing to do with me, Officer*. Find Warren in possession of either blade or merch? Not likely.

Thirty yards. Warren turned, made a cursory scan of the alley, seeing nothing. Eyes accustomed to the streetlight. Head to foot black, Mickey could have been within arm's reach and probably still been invisible. But the quick turn and look told him it was time. In thirty or so seconds the dealer would do it again. Warren worked instinctively, to some rhythm only he could hear.

He paced silently toward the other man's back, raising the Ruger. Ready to take the shot, if needed. Twenty yards. Not impossible at that range. He knew that from long practice. But the bullet, slowed by the weapon's fat little suppressor, would be inaccurate. Not like a 9mm. He could have put a 9-mil round into Warren's head from thirty yards away. But where would the subtlety have been in that?

Fifteen. Better. The chance of a kill shot doubled.

Ten. Properly inside killing range. Common sense said to do it now. One round, back of the head. Put his target down, never even knowing what hit him. One second alive, vital. The next, dead. Already on the other side. Discovering whether there was more. Or just eternal darkness. The common-sense option. But not the one Mickey intended taking. Not the safest way. Not the most fitting either. Five paces. He leaned forward, putting the gun's barrel a foot from the back of Warren's head.

Pitched his voice softly. Words for one man's ears only. The last words he would ever hear.

'All right, Warren?'

'Jesus, you scared the *fucking*—'

And as his sister's killer turned, eyes widening, body starting to react...

Thup.

Louder than a discreet cough, quieter than a sneeze. Warren's eyes suddenly shot through with blood, as the bullet went in through his forehead. Twin bloody orbs staring sightlessly at his killer. He swayed for an instant, like a puppet with loose strings. Mickey leaned forward. Grabbed Warren's coat and pulled hard. Stepped back smartly to let the falling body crumple into the alley's shadows.

Done. He bent, retrieving the spent cartridge case from the ground. Then tucked his calling card up under Warren's coat collar. Where it wouldn't be found by anyone searching the corpse for valuables. Let the forensics crew find it in a few hours. Not even Martin knew about the card, Mickey's own little secret. Him and Nemesis, of course. An untraceable rectangle of white cardboard. Letters and a symbol traced on using a kid's plastic template bought in a toy shop. A message to one very special man.

He stood, walking quickly but quietly back up the alley. Unscrewed the suppressor and dropped it back into the thick-walled ziplock bag in his pocket. Along with the spent round. Then the pistol. Gloves peeled off, balled up and into the same bag. Balaclava pulled off and tucked in on top. He closed the seal tightly, then refastened the pocket.

At the alley's end he turned left, adopting a brisk pace. Just a man on his way to the pub, walking with purpose. But no urgency, nothing to catch the eye. Rejoining the High Road two hundred yards further up at a steady pace. Restraining his eagerness to get to his alibi. They were waiting for him in the pub, of course. Pints half-empty while his sat untouched. Calling at him to 'come on, you lightweight, have some of this!' as he crossed the saloon bar towards the gents'. He grimaced, miming urination. Waving away their jibes that yeah, he'd better make some room.

The toilet was empty, its single cubicle's door yawning wide. Mickey grabbed a handful of paper towels. Ducked into the lavatory and bolted the door. Opened the thin top window and passed the ziplock out to Martin. Who took it and was gone. Pulled a small spray bottle from another pocket, aiming the nozzle at his coat. Disinfectant, a brisk squirt and rub. Paper towels went into the pan stained light brown, gunshot residue from his sleeve. Scrubbing and dumping fresh towels into the water until they came away clean.

He flushed, dipping the rest of the wad in the water and rinsing off the cleaner's scent. Sniffed the arm and nodded. Good enough. He'd shot fifty rounds of qualification that afternoon, so any residual trace could be put down to that. He flushed again, waited to be sure the paper was gone.

Opened the door and examined himself carefully in the mirror. No blood specks on his skin or clothing. No obvious trace of having used the gun. Nothing to indicate he'd just shot a man point-blank in the face. And then stared back into his victim's bloodshot eyes without a hint of remorse. Turned to the door, bracing himself for abuse.

'*Here* he is!' Deano held his pint up for inspection, theirs all empty. 'Get this fucker down you and get back to the bar, tight arse!'

Mickey grinned and strolled over to them, nodding knowingly. Drank the pint in one long swallow, resisting the urge to gag. Just another quiet Friday night out with the boys. Right?

2

'Hello, there it is. The Friday night symphony.'
The other three men smiled reflexively at Deano's sardonic observation. They were all veterans of hundreds of Friday nights in their time. A well-established routine. Relative calm in the early evening, boring almost. Good-natured banter as the punters made their way from pub to pub. A wary eye on each other's backs, even before closing time. Just in case.

And then from midnight to dawn, a bloody war zone. Vomiting drunks. Abusive drunks. Violent drunks. Assaults, provoked or just out of nowhere. Sometimes right under your nose. Talking sense into the aggrieved. Nicking the violent, team-handed. Taking no chances, and, metaphorically at least, no prisoners. Clocking off in the early daylight, shagged out and ready to drop. JAFN. Just Another Friday Night. Other F's being available.

A single siren, an area car on fast response most likely. A bit early to be coming in loud. But Friday night, right? They exchanged knowing glances and sipped at their pints, Deano carrying on with whatever it was he'd been quacking on about.

'He ain't getting the best out of what he's got, right?

As long as he's playing Garcia in the holding role and not letting him get forward—'

A second siren in the distance, perhaps half a mile away. An ambulance, to the experienced ear. An early street assault, most likely. And then, just as they were exchanging knowing looks, a third siren joined the chorus. The first car dopplered past the pub and pulled up. Noise dying away, rotating roof lights tinging the windows.

'Three on the blues, that's a decent—'

Another siren joined the momentarily reduced cacophony. Raising eyebrows around the table. Unprecedented, to have such a big shout so early. They looked at each other speculatively. After a moment Deano went over to the window, just as a second police car joined the first. He came back with a knowing look.

'Something big all right. And it ain't just the area cars. There's a pair of uniforms just come down the High Street like they're after Usain Bolt. Looks to me like they've found something in the alley.'

He shot a glance at Mickey, knowing what they all knew about who did business in the alley. He shrugged. Gave them the studied imperturbability he'd practised in the mirror earlier. And every day for the last three months. Practised, polished, perfected. Saved for this moment.

'Margetson got himself a kicking – I'll buy the bloke that did it a pint.'

Nods around the table, a muttered 'fucking right' from Deano. More response vehicles arriving, and the sound of shouted orders. The big man stood up again and looked over the frosted section of glass.

'Looks like every woodentop in town. Bosses trying

to look like they know what they're doing, incident tape around the alley entrance.'

'Serious, then.' Steve took another mouthful of his pint. 'You fancy joining in?'

That got him a disparaging grin from the self-proclaimed king of the short-timers.

'Do I look fucking stupid? I've got less than a year of my thirty left, *and* I'm off duty. And the first rule of off duty is…?'

The answering chorus was immediate.

'Keep your fucking head down!'

Except none of them really believed him. Deano, the last of the old-time street coppers. A throwback to a bygone age. Put simply, a warrior. A man you knew would have your back, no questions. A man who would instinctively front up to even a hint of a scrap like a black-clad jack-in-the-box. A man who would sprint fifty yards and rugby-tackle a belligerent drunk just for the hell of it. And swear blind to the desk sergeant that the poor guy had slipped and fallen badly. And in the early days, that had worked. Most times, at least.

But not anymore. Six-foot-four thugs with cropped hair in uniform weren't the zeitgeist anymore. Not even if their motives were mostly pure. Now it was all body cams and reasoning. Management oversight and Professional Standards, the Met's version of AC-12. With the occasional chance to shoot some stupid bastard with a Taser. If you got lucky. No life for a warrior like Deano. So when he denied the urge to get stuck in, it was mainly due to lack of opportunity.

'Exactly. Keep your fucking head down. So they can have it, whatever it is. Right, come on, Den, it's your round.'

Den's round was the last of the four, all Mickey was able to stay for. He shrugged at their good-natured jibes, standing up and pulling on the Belstaff.

'Time and tide, boys, time and tide. Got an early one tomorrow. You know the rules.'

'We know Roz'll have your nuts off if you don't get home!'

He grinned at Deano, shrugging.

'I resemble that remark.'

Tapped fists with each of them in turn. The ritual salute of the street coppers from times long past. What he used to be. What they all used to be. What Deano still was, the only one of them.

Den, his thirty years done, installing windows to supplement his pension. Average height for the Job, greying hair and a deceptively strong jawline. Never really a copper's copper. Always a bit stand-offish, like he wasn't quite sure what he was doing there. He'd done his time with a perpetual vague air of mystification. Seemingly a bit confused as to what the whole thing was all about. Deano reckoned Den would go to his grave still not quite sure what it all had been for. Although to be fair Deano had an opinion on everything and was never knowingly wrong.

Steve, in his penultimate year as a detective sergeant. Squat and muscular. Still powerful despite the years. His curly hair fading from ginger to silver at the temples. Wondering what to do next. Although where Den had always been uncertain, Steve never really worried about the meaning of his existence. Five years as a soldier before joining the Job. After a tour in Bosnia as a nineteen-year-old lance corporal. Where it was pretty obvious that he'd grown up fast. And seen things that had scarred him for the rest of his life.

Consequently, no room for any doubts in Steve's mind. He knew it was all meaningless. Knew his place in life was simple. To protect the good people. And to put the bad people down, just as hard as they deserved. Simples.

And Mickey? Mickey had always been the baby among them. Initially under their collective wing. The youngest by years, but now a long way from his roots nicking drunks on a Friday night. A very long way. And they all knew it.

He strolled out of the pub and down the High Road towards home. Looked across the road with just enough interest as he passed. They had the tent up already, blocking the pavement. Forensics techs pulling on Tyvek suits, preparing to do their ghoulish work. He shrugged for any watching camera and walked on, getting home dead on time. Enjoying Roz's approval.

'You finally growing a brain there, Mickey?'

'Might be. But don't—'

'Hold my breath. I know. I heard the sirens.'

With that look. Like he ought to know what had caused them. Pricking at Mickey's guilty conscience. Even if that wasn't even remotely what she was thinking.

'Looks like a serious one. The locals have got a tent up in the High Street. Tyvek suits and a fingertip search.'

She shrugged and switched the searchlight of her attention to making him a cup of tea. Herbal, of course, to help him sleep.

'You're up at oh-stupid-hundred, so you need all the—'

The doorbell interrupted her. They both looked over at the video feed that he and everyone else in Prot used.

Best to know who's knocking before you open a nice thick armoured front door.

'Isn't that Jason Felgate?'

He nodded. It was. Went into the hall and opened the door. Receding hairline, brown eyes, big sideburns and stubble you could strike a match on. Combined with a snub nose and slightly wonky jawline that had mapped his career as effectively as phrenology or palmistry. A certain degree of photogenicity; a major assist in the climb to senior ranks these days.

That, and what the evaluators now labelled emotional intelligence. Or common sense, in old speak. A genetic trait which, Mickey had known since those early days, Jason had never been overly blessed with. That Jason had made it as far as DI was testament to a metric fucktonne of hard work. And, it was clear to all around him, the limit of his realistic ambition.

'Evening, Jase, we were just talking about you.' The plain-clothes inspector looked back at him levelly. A uniformed constable was lurking at the end of the path behind him. 'And one of the ugly sisters to keep you company, I see. I suppose his twin's waiting at the back gate?'

Another moment of considered silence.

'Good evening. And yes, since you ask, there is an officer at the back. SOP.'

He grinned back knowingly.

'Yeah, SOP. So... I'd invite you in, but I've got an early start.'

'We could always talk down at the nick.'

'Really? *That* old line? Come on then.' Looked past the inspector as he wiped his feet. 'You want a cuppa, sunshine?'

Got a big smile back from the uniform on the gate. 'I'll do a couple. NATO standard, right?'

Led Felgate through into the kitchen and reached for mugs.

'NATO for you?'

'No sugar, thank you, Sergeant Bale.'

'Sergeant Bale? I remember the days when we were Mickey and Jase. The two daftest kids on the relief, always fucking something up.'

'This is serious, Mickey.'

'It's Mickey now, is it? That's something, I suppose. And yes, murder usually is quite serious.'

His former beat buddy levelled the stare again. Waiting in silence for anything more. After a minute of watching Mickey fill cups with boiling water he spoke again.

'Who said anything about murder?'

And recoiled as Mickey turned on him. Faster than any man of his age had any right to move. Putting on the anger, just as he'd put on the studied nonchalance earlier. Held the other man's gaze for a hard-eyed moment. Then turned away and got on with the teas. Stirring the bags and then spooning them out, after a ritualistic squeeze with another teaspoon.

'Fucking right you can look nervous. Cut out the mind games, *Jason*. I said murder because there's a white tent been put up on the High Road. That being a bit of an overkill for the average Friday night punch-up.'

'You were on the High Road?'

Leaning back, raising an eyebrow in affected disgust.

'You *know* I was on the fucking High Road. You know because I was with Den, Steve and Deano for a beer. Your lads were probably talking to them a few minutes after I left. And you know because woodentop number one out there saw me walk past the scene. He was on my side of the road as the Teletubbies were getting ready to hoover the corpse. So don't play me for a cunt.'

Felgate watched in silence as he scooped out and squeezed the last teabag. Added the obligatory milk and two to the constables' cups and headed for the front door.

'No nicking Roz's spoons. She won't hold back like I did.'

He took two cups out to the waiting officers. Shared a quick joke with them, then went back in. Found the inspector drinking his tea and looking shifty.

'Come on then. I'm presuming it's Warren, or why would you be here? And cut the "I can neither confirm nor deny" bullshit, right?'

Felgate sighed. 'Off the record. Yes, it's Warren. Someone put a bullet between his eyes at close range. Close enough for powder burns.'

Mickey grimaced. 'They'll be scraping his brains off the wall then.' Another rehearsed line, which got him an appraising look. 'What?'

'The calibre used was small bore. A .22 most likely.'

He nodded slowly, wearing his "best absorbing new information" face.

'A .22? That's pro stuff. Either that or a very enthusiastic amateur.'

'Yes, well we're not ruling out any possibility. *Any* possibility.'

'Well you can rule my fucking Mickey right out, right now!'

He'd known Roz was listening, almost counted down to

her interjection. Jason looked nervous for the second time in five minutes. With, Mickey knew, fair justification.

'When his sister got killed by that bastard's dodgy pills, he never once showed any sign of being out for revenge. And we both know he could have. It's not like that bastard Margetson ever gave a shit. But he rode the punch like the man he is. And now, just as we're getting over it, you come here accusing him of—'

'Roz love?' She stopped in mid-flow, looking across the kitchen at him. 'Let me finish up with Jason so that we can get up to bed, eh?'

She nodded. Fired one last gigawatt glare at the inspector and stalked out.

'She's right though.' He leaned back and wiped a hand wearily across his face. 'I never went looking for payback, as well you know. Not even when he turned up at the funeral. Because that bastard's whole life was one long act of self-harm. It was only a matter of time before someone punched his ticket. Wasn't it?'

'When did you get to the pub?'

'What, and you've not already asked Deano?'

'He says he can't remember.'

'I bet he does. Not your biggest fan, our Deano. An old-fashioned copper, that's what he is.'

'An obstructive, obdurate, recalcitrant relic, *that's* what your Deano is.'

'Recalcitrant? You've done the senior officer's big words course then?'

The jibe fired in with a hard grin. Knowing the man's ambition, knowing it was frustrated. And because he was getting angry, despite the need to be cool and considered.

Although a shot of angry wouldn't hurt the act.

Jason's hackles rising in reply. Biting off his words.

'When. Did you get. To the pub… *Mister* Bale?'

Mickey shrugged. Thought for a moment.

'Just after eight fifteen. Went for a piss. Drank two pints. Had another piss. Drank two more pints. Came back here.'

'Which way did you go to the Carpenter's Arms?'

'The usual way. Down Nelson Road, so I don't have to look at the man who supplied the pills that killed my little sister. I've been doing it every week for months, ever since the funeral. Check the CCTV.'

A shake of the head.

'The CCTV's been out of commission for weeks. Every time it gets fixed some little bastards from the estate throw stones at it and smash it up again.'

Mickey laughed.

'That's ironic. A drug dealer's murder lacking evidence because he paid yobs to break the camera that might have recorded his killer.'

'But you didn't walk back down Nelson Road, did you?'

He shook his head.

'Nup. Because, Hercule Crapeau, I could see the tent being put up from the pub doorway. And white tents tend to mean something nasty these days. Plus that alley was always Warren's territory. So I guessed there was no need to go out of my way. Correctly.' He yawned ostentatiously. Knowing the stink of beer on his breath would wash over his former colleague. 'And now, unless you want to know where I was on the night of the fifteenth, I'm for my bed. Or is it down to the station?'

'No. That's all. For now, at least.'

He saw his former friend out of the door. Collected the mugs with a wink to the officers waiting outside and locked up. Upstairs Roz was already waiting for him in bed, her face disapproving.

'He's got no right.'

He shrugged, climbing out of his jeans.

'He's got every right. Someone put a bullet into that bastard Margetson's head, and I look like a suspect to him.'

'Plus he hates you.'

'Plus, to be fair, he does hate me just a bit.'

'He's stuck where he is until his thirty comes round. You escaped that shit and found something better.'

He climbed in beside her, snuggling in behind and taking a nipple-centred handful of breast in the way he knew turned her on. Pushing his crotch into her backside for good measure.

'Much, much better.'

'You dirty bastard.'

But she wasn't resisting the idea. Later, with Roz snoring softly and himself still wide awake, wired by the fact he had killed a man and got away with it, he pondered. Wondering if he was going to have nightmares about the moment he'd pulled the trigger. Wondering if the path he was taking was worth the risk of losing the woman lying next to him. Wondering if the Teletubbies had found his card yet.

3

Mickey was out of bed before dawn. Awake before the alarm, from long habit of 05.00 wake-ups for early turn. Looked in the mirror. His face not too haggard, for a man who'd lain awake half the night. And not looking bad for his early forties either. No more than a trace of grey in the hair. Pretty much wrinkle-free.

His mates were already starting to use the fact to wind him up. Yakking on about the supposed predilections of the women who were guarded by private security. *The lady of the house always likes a nice fresh-faced bodyguard, Mickey. They'll take you for a cherry boy, Mickey. Just wait until you're out in the private sector, Mickey.* He knew they were jealous that he'd started young. That he'd have his thirty in before he was clapped out. And that they all fantasised about getting a bit of posh Russian with her legs open.

Whereas Mickey had actually listened to his former Protection Command colleagues who'd made that change. And knew, thereby, that it didn't work like that. Security was there to be ignored. Nothing more, nothing less. Not unless you looked like Chris Hemsworth on a very good day, perhaps. And even then you weren't likely to be troubling the scorers on that particular strip.

'Are you going to admire yourself in the mirror all day?'

Roz, leaning on the bathroom doorframe. Her face a combination of pillow creases and sardonic grin.

'I was just wondering when the grey hairs are going to start showing.'

She gave him that pitying look she did so well. Practice, he guessed. Roz's hairdresser best friend did her roots twice a month. Making his relative lack of grey something of a provocation.

'They'll come soon enough. Then we'll see if you reach for the dye bottle.'

'Not me.' He wrapped her up in a kiss, tasting of spearmint. 'I'm growing old gracefully.'

'You'd fucking better, smart-arse. No younger model for you.'

'No, ma'am.'

'And you can cut that out too. Makes me sound like the Queen.'

He disengaged from her embrace and kissed her on the cheek. Headed downstairs. Wallet, warrant card, keys, Belstaff. A ten-minute walk to the station in the early morning gloom, the sun yet to make an appearance. Resisting the urge to whistle. Just in case Jason Felgate's hard-on for him had convinced the Murder Squad to get their long lenses and parabolic mikes out.

As the journey progressed south into the city he found himself reflecting on the last few months. His initial buzz abraded by the memories of what had driven him to the previous night's act.

Katie. Quite literally his sister from another mister. Mickey's dad having been killed in a traffic accident when

Mickey was ten. Riding his motorbike down the street and straight onto the lethal blade of a carelessly opened car door. Massive physical trauma, dead on arrival. His sudden death leaving his family just as brutalised, emotionally.

Mickey's mum had gone through the full gamut of mourning over the space of a couple of years. While trying, and failing, to save her son from coming to terms with death and grieving earlier than was fair. Mickey going through a phase of being the quiet one in class. Withdrawn from the usual cut and thrust of the playground, where most of the real learning was happening.

The arrival of Terry in his mum's life as Mickey turned twelve had been like sunrise through storm clouds. A gentle, older man, happy to take on a ready-made family. And, critically, to absorb Mickey's anger at an uncaring world. And give him back the closest thing to a father's love he could. To heal the open wound of his dad's sudden death. Terry introduced him to boxing. A sport where he had no choice but to participate to the maximum.

Gradually, without him realising it, Mickey's life came off hold. Normal service being resumed. And then rudely but joyously interrupted by the arrival of a baby sister.

Katie had been a revelation to Mickey. The realisation that it wasn't all about him, for one thing. The power she had to beguile him for another. Always his little sister, even when he was past forty and Katie was turning thirty. Not planning to settle down any time soon, like so many of her peers. Telling Mickey and Roz that they were leading the way in married bliss. Elbowing Mickey in the ribs after a few drinks and telling him to get on with giving her nephews and nieces. Remaining steadfastly devoted to her nights out and clubbing. No steady boyfriend to hold her back. Or, as it turned out, keep her safe.

One Saturday morning, out of the blue, a uniformed skipper had come knocking at Mickey and Roz's door. Doing the "serious face, can I come in please, sir?" routine. Instantly recognisable by Mickey from the times he'd had to do exactly the same. Treating him like a civilian, even though he knew Mickey was Job. Because, when it came to matters of family life and death, everyone was a civilian. Which put a shiver up Mickey's spine unlike anything he'd ever experienced. Knowing immediately, instinctively, what he was about to be told.

Sitting, numb, on his sofa, Roz's arms wrapped around him, he'd half-listened while the veteran copper gently broke the news to him. Katie, taken ill in a club at one in the morning; 999, ambulance to hospital, her condition deteriorating by the minute. Hallucinating and convulsing. Frothing at the mouth. Dead on arrival. Nothing anyone could have done for her, in the opinion of the medics. His sister had been a walking corpse from the minute she dropped the second pill.

Reading the medical report later, the cause of death was all too clear. Katie, out clubbing with new friends, had gone along with a group decision to experiment with some old-school entertainment. And taken what they had believed to be ecstasy, a blast from the past.

But what the dealer – now deceased Warren – had sold the group, by mistake, was something quite different. Ecstasy, MDMA, being a relatively harmless recreational drug, if made carefully. Not risk-free, not by a long chalk. But tame compared to PMA. Which was what Warren had fished out of his pocket by mistake. Para-Methoxyamphetamine. Street name: Doctor Death. An antidepressant, but with a psychedelic edge. And not a drug to take liberties with.

All the young women had taken one. Only Katie, finding it lacking the usual euphoric effect, had taken a second tablet. Having already snorted two lines of coke an hour before. Expecting it to put her on the ceiling for the rest of the night. Instead of which the stronger dose, lethally combined with the coke, had killed her in under an hour.

In the early days, coping with the arrangements for parents too torn up to manage, Mickey had avoided brooding. Encouraged by Roz to put it behind him and move on. Perhaps because she knew, deep inside, what he was capable of. That, and the funeral itself, obviously, had emotionally flattened him for the best part of a month. Doing his job professionally but seeing everything through a grey filter.

Until he'd met Martin for a drink a few weeks later. Martin, who, having practically lived at Mickey's during their teens, was equally bereft at her loss. And, in the course of spilling their guts, the idea of killing Warren had sprung to mind.

Whose idea had it been? Neither of them was very clear, once the hangovers had dispersed.

Was it feasible? Of that, there had never been any doubt.

Was Mickey really going to see it through? In spite of the professional and personal risks of losing everything?

That was never in doubt either. Especially once Nemesis took a hand.

4

Eddie liked his boss Joe's house. Sure, it was beyond ostentatious. But if Joe couldn't be a bit flash, then who the fuck could? Not that Eddie could have done flash without feeling like a right prick. Hench, if not tall, Eddie wore the suits that were expected in his "managerial" role without conviction. Pukka gear – Armani and Ralph Lauren. Church's shoes and Paul Smith ties chosen by his wife completed the image nicely, in theory. Problem was, every time Eddie caught sight of himself in the mirror he saw a gorilla in fancy dress. Having to shave his hair off to deal with male-pattern baldness didn't help much either. Looking like he belonged in a Guy Ritchie film. And not feeling all that comfortable with that on several levels.

A large part of him looked fondly back to when it had just been the two of them. Joe as the brains – and the necessary ruthlessness – Eddie as the unquestioning enforcer. But the years had brought then both unavoidable responsibilities to shoulder. For Joe, inheriting the family business with his dad's untimely death from lung cancer. For Eddie, having his previously simple role in Joe's firm abruptly expanded. Promotion, just without any choice. Taking control of what Joe liked to call his "black operations". Dealers, pimps, the supply of their product and the hard men needed to keep them in line. And to persuade other interested parties not to try butting in.

And to be fair to Eddie, he was good in the role. Hard as nails from long practice, and as fair as he could afford to be given who he worked for. And the hammer of the gods in dealing with would-be rivals. Smart with it. As proven by the fact that, able to choose any place to live he fancied, he'd wisely chosen not to rival Joe's epic residence. Made do instead with six bedrooms in a nice commuting suburb, a few miles from Joe's almost-rural idyll. Never compete with numero uno. He'd learned that one early. Made it his mantra.

Whereas Joe had taken over his dad's place in Cockfosters. Gutted and extended it. Paying off councillors for the outrageous amount of planning permission required. Made it into a palatial fortress, complete with a sheet-steel-lined panic room. Showing those Greek bastards what proper style looks like, as he'd been known to state while looking out over his infinity pool across leafy Hertfordshire.

The house was set back from the road behind high walls. With a well-designed garden, plenty of trees to absorb noise. And distant enough neighbours to guarantee privacy. Private enough that Joe still joked about the time that his bodyguard Lewis had shot Eddie's best mate Nigel on the terrace. Without his stunned audience ever hearing a siren. Admittedly the big man had used a suppressor on his black Smith & Wesson .45 automatic. Which lessened the validity of the boast somewhat. But the weapon's loud cough had still been enough to make Eddie shit himself, just a little bit. That and the shock of having a bloke he'd been at school with sprayed across his Hugo Boss cashmere.

Nigel having been a trusted member of Joe's inner circle, right up to the moment Lewis had put the gun to his head. His crime, it turned out, being seen talking to a rival gang leader's right-hand man. Thick as thieves, over coffee, in an out-of-the-way cafe. Very clandestine, and very disappointing, Joe said. And Joe, as everyone knew, didn't take that sort of disappointment well.

Turned out, when they unlocked his phone and read his texts, that they'd got the wrong end of the stick. As, it seemed, had Nigel, to be fair to the poor bastard. Nigel hadn't been ratting Joe out, he'd been seeing his lover. His only mistake, Joe had opined, had been not being honest about his sexuality. Everyone knew that he didn't have any problem with homosexuals. Sure, his *nonno* would have the poor bastard beaten to a pulp just for being queer. But then his granddad had had men beaten half to death for a lot less. That was just the Sicilian way.

No, Joe was cool with that whole gay thing. Just not with traitors. If Nigel had been clearer as to his preferences, as Eddie later attempted to post-rationalise, he wouldn't have been topped quite so dramatically. Just used to blackmail the other poor bastard. Who, heartbroken, had killed himself shortly after learning of his lover's violent demise. Or at least that was the way it had been made to look. More likely that Joe's rival wasn't in a forgiving mood either.

The two men, it transpired, had been planning to take their money and disappear. Had already bought a small house in Perth, of all places. The one in Australia, of course, which pretty much went without saying. Scotland, by common agreement, being full of nutters and miserable cunts. Joe had pronounced his retrospective sentence on the terrace, as his inner circle stood around the corpse and cast sidelong glances at Eddie's blood-spattered whistle.

'Nobody gets to leave without my permission. Nobody, right? If he'd been respectful, and they'd given me a nice going-away present, then that would have been different.' By which Joe had, of course, meant the betrayal of his rival by Nigel's boyfriend in some significant way. 'But just planning to fuck off and never be seen again? Totally disrespectful.'

And, it went without saying, Joe didn't take disrespect well either.

'Morning, Eddie.'

Joe was waiting for him in the kitchen. A quarter acre of Cotswold stone, gleaming chrome and white marble. Sipping a coffee and looking chilled in his zip-through Armani mohair.

'Morning, Joe.'

Joe was a relaxed sort of bloke with his men. Which went with the image that he'd cultivated, encouraged by the family lawyer. His granddad had been old-school. Always "Mr Castagna", unless he gave a man explicit permission to use his first name. And even then that man would have been well advised not to overdo the privilege. His dad had carried on that tradition. Big Giuseppe, like his old man, deeming respect to be all-important. So no guessing where Joe got that from.

But Joe tolerated informality, just as long as it was accompanied by instant, blind obedience. He'd turned to a blood, bone and brain-flecked Eddie on the terrace. The smoke still curling from the suppressor of Lewis's .45 automatic. While the big enforcer had stood contemplating Nigel's corpse with his usual weird, unreadable look. The psychopath incarnate, to Eddie's mind, having read enough Jon Ronson to know. His weapon ostentatiously not returned to its holster. And Joe had asked him one quietly stated but life-defining question.

"We got a problem here, Eddie?"

And Eddie, knowing in his gut that any hesitation would be the death of him, had answered in both the negative and a heartbeat. He knew that some of the crew had taken to calling him "Brains" behind his back. And not because they thought he was all that bright. And Eddie didn't give a fuck. Because Eddie was still breathing, and valued that fact beyond measure.

Joe looked at him questioningly across the spotless marble. Dark Italian eyes and skin tone to match. Always looking like he needed to shave, despite the fact he used a wet razor every morning. Jet-black hair kept that colour by something out of a bottle, Eddie suspected. Suspected, but never mentioned. Joe being proud of his youthful looks at forty-five years old. And a touchy bastard at the best of times.

'So what brings you here unexpected on a Saturday morning?'

Joe reached out and stroked the bronze horse's head sculpture that decorated one end of the kitchen counter. He loved that sculpture. Both because it was "proper art" – Joe holding no truck with "all that modernist shit" – and because it reminded him of his favourite film. No-one had ever done the old "who's the godfather?" joke in front of Joe to Eddie's certain knowledge. Because Joe thought the sun shone out of Don Vito Corleone's back passage. The first two films in the series were favourites in his cinema room. Which made an invitation to share vintage grappa, a cigar and Marlon of an evening one that wasn't refused lightly. Not if a bloke knew which side his bread was buttered. Eddie launched into his briefing, watching Joe's eyes intently.

'I got a call from Felgate. We've got a problem. One of the street dealers has been shot. Dead.'

Joe shrugged, eyes untouched by the news.

'So, get another one. Shit happens.'

'Not like this, Joe. He was tapped in the forehead with a .22. Felgate says it's a professional's weapon—'

Joe's eyes narrowed, and Eddie suddenly felt unaccountably warm.

'I don't need bent filth to tell me what a .22 is. When did this happen?'

'Last night, about eight, they reckon.'

Joe thought for a moment.

'OK, so someone offed one of my dealers. Which one?'

'Warren Margetson.'

'Margetson.' Joe shrugged, the name without any meaning to him. 'And no clues? Nothing to send Felgate's mates in the Murder Squad off after the killer?'

Here it came. The moment of maximum danger, to someone who knew Joe all too well.

'There was one clue. They only found it at four this morning when they got the clothes off him. This fell out of his coat collar.'

He held up his phone, and Joe reached out. Took it. Looked at the picture on screen. Gave it back.

'I see. That is interesting.' He went quiet, and Eddie knew better than to interrupt his thought process. 'Right, so you tell Inspector Bent that I want a daily update. Every day without fail, until they work out which cunt did it.'

Eddie nodded, respectfully, taking Joe's instruction as his cue to leave.

'I'm not finished yet, Eddie.'

Eddie turned back, working very hard to keep his face straight under his boss's ice-pick stare.

'Joe?'

'Double the guard on the house. And tool them up properly. Get the assault shotguns out of storage, and enough ammo to start a war with. Julie and the kids don't go anywhere without protection either. And get someone good, right? Someone *very* good. Because if any of my family catch any of this, the men guarding them better hope they die protecting them. You know what I've got when it comes to threats to my family, don't you, Eddie?'

Eddie knew the answer to that one. Both from frequent repetition and practical demonstration.

'An inexhaustible supply of meat hooks, Joe.'

'Exactly. Off you go. And send me a copy of that photo. I've got some asking around to do.'

5

Mickey got off the train at London Bridge and walked east. Enjoying the opportunity to stretch his legs. Even 109 Lambeth Road, LX to its inmates, as grim as ever, couldn't lower his mood. LX. Seventies brutalism in concrete and glass. All fur coat and no knickers, the Met. Which meant that Lambeth Road was a million miles from the shiny image of twenty-first-century policing on the other side of the Thames. Home to the Met's forensics department, the twenty-four-hour emergency response call centre and the special operations control room. The latter having probably seen more ruined careers in its time than White Hart Lane. And Protection Command. Prot to its members.

He carded in through a reluctant turnstile and went upstairs to the canteen. Walked through. Nodding to the inevitable huddles of masons, careerists and other assorted gatherings of the self-interested. Groups of Prot officers sorted by age, service and seniority. Coffee meetings, Prot's informal management structure. Mickey had heard it described by one participant as Prot's equivalent of Roman centurions running the legions. While their officers listened to poetry and eyed up the slave boys. Mickey, of course, never got invited to coffee meetings, Prot's equivalent of a power breakfast. Not anymore, at least. Because Mickey, from stubborn choice, wasn't any sort of joiner. Respect, for Mickey, was hard-earned. And down to more than who you shared firm handshakes, machine cappuccino and confirmation bias with of a morning.

Passing through into the changing room, he opened his locker. Casuals off, suit and boot up. A nice dark blue Ted Baker two-piece. Nothing fancy in Prot. Whose first commandment was to blend in. White shirt, sober tie, black shoes, polished before he'd gone off duty from his last tour. Blend in but look the part. Have recently cut hair, be clean-shaven and always smell nice. Or at least not offensive. A scruffy-looking protection officer was not the image the Met sought to portray. Not even one looking like Chris Hemsworth.

He checked his look in the mirror for the second time that morning. Acceptable. Pin-coded through the airlocks into the office. Half an acre of open-plan hot desks. Largely deserted in favour of machine coffee and professional machismo. Logged into the system. Waded through a dozen emails, reading them despite the urge to delete. Then checked that his duty allocation hadn't changed. Knowing it wouldn't have. Without the right people looking after your assignment, life in Prot could get very monotonous. Although Mickey had come to enjoy both the predictability of his work and the occasional frisson of excitement when he drew something different.

He shrugged. Printed off a firearms requisition and signed it. Logged out, got up, pin-coded into the armoury. Took arming booth four, as he always did when it was free. Slid his requisition and warrant card under the bulletproof glass. Vic, the slightly less morose of the two civilian armourers on duty, placed the firearm into the metal box beneath the screen. Grimacing at him through the glass.

'Your weapon, Sergeant Bale.'

The usual Glock 17 automatic pistol. Louder bangs and higher velocity were available, if needed. A full-on 5.56mm assault rifle, or a 9mm machine pistol. Not today though. The Glock was plenty enough punch where he was going. Plus he knew and trusted the Glock. Knew he could hit a target with it under any and all circumstances. That the hollow-point round wouldn't go straight through whatever he hit. Or, having done so, fly another half mile to kill an innocent.

Mickey waited until the spare mags and plastic ammunition tray were added to the box. Examined the pistol for any obvious damage. Then loaded the magazines with practised speed and a calloused thumb. Racked the slide and put the weapon into condition one. Round in the breech, ready to use. Standard Met firearms safety. Holstered the Glock on one hip, two spare mags on the other. Ready to go.

'The early bird gets the worm, eh, Michael?'

Once on duty he was Michael, never Mickey. There was no use of nicknames or abbreviations in Prot. He knew the voice and turned with a smile. Part genuine pleasure, part camouflage for sudden doubt. Wondering if Jason Felgate had been busy overnight. Wondering if he was about to be pulled from duty and sat at a desk for the day. Under suspicion.

Found himself face to face with Philip Green. Duty

inspector, and, as far as Mickey was concerned, all right bloke. Some inspectors were addressed by their rank, others less formally, depending on their ego needs. Philip, as it happened, very much dwelling in the latter camp. He reflexively glanced at his watch. The Tudor Black Bay with the official Royal Household crest on its face. A limited run of seventy-five for Prot a few years before, and the object of much jealousy for those outside the magic circle who had one. Mickey might not have been on the royal side of Prot at the time, but he'd been cute enough to know a good investment when he saw one.

'You know me, Guv. Creature of habit.'

Got a knowing grin for that.

'Plus if you get here early, you might get someone different, right?'

He shrugged.

'We all live in hope, sir. But a principal is a principal. I come to work, I do my job, I go home. Simple as that.'

Which got him a disbelieving, if sympathetic look. Inspector Phil, after all, knew the unwritten rules. And allowed himself to be guided through who should do what by the senior skippers on the team. Duty allocations and plum jobs already neatly stitched up between them over morning coffee.

Which was why Mickey never got to go anywhere exotic. Or do any of the more high-profile work. Just the usual, week in, week out. The same principal, the same locations. With only the occasional excitement of a head of state visit. All hands to the overtime pump, when a foreign leader came to visit. But the first rule of being Mickey Bale had long been never to be seen giving a shit. And besides, he had a new calling, coiled in the back of his mind like a sleeping cobra. The inspector nodded equably, clearly not giving too much of a shit either.

'Fair enough. It'd be a lot easier to roster you guys if you were all as easy-going about who you get to babysit. Have a quiet tour of duty, Michael. We'll see you in four days' time.'

He nodded, watching the inspector as he walked away towards the canteen. No sign of any interference by his former beat partner. Went through into the canteen and gathered his bag carrier up by eye. The man in question favouring the identikit Prot image too, his fair hair cut neatly, clean-shaven with the obligatory suit, tie and shiny shoes.

'You coming, Wade?'

Constable Harris rose from the table where he was chatting with several other junior officers. A collective antidote to the power of the cliques. And a clique in the making, obviously. Give them long enough and it'd be them stitching up the best assignments.

'Coming, Skip.'

Wade was already armed, and had collected their allocated car keys and log book. A switched-on guy, Wade. Could go far.

They headed downstairs to the underground car park. Gleaming under the fluorescent tubes, ranks of cars awaited. Jags, BMWs, Range Rovers of all persuasions. With a separate row for the armoured cars. Outwardly identical unless you knew what to look for. But two tonnes heavier. With supercharged engines to move that weight around.

Range Rover Sentinels, top-of-the-line protection.

Bulletproof, if a situation ended up going to the races, or so the theory went. Mickey, not so sure. Reckoning that a full magazine of 7.62mm at close range would open even a Sentinel up like a can of very expensive dog meat. He opened the boot of their car, a grey Range Rover Sport. Wade affected his usual Gary Oldman drawl to voice his approval.

'Range Rover. My favourite.'

Mickey grinned at the younger man.

'Mate, it's a car. And it belongs to the taxpayer.'

'Yeah, Skip, I know. But what a car, eh?'

'Is that your way of telling me you'd like to drive?' Got that enthusiastic grin that Wade wore much of the time. 'All right then, you can drive. And I won't even sit in the back. I'll just check the crash bag.'

Mickey checked that the medical kit was all present and correct. Then hung his jacket on the hook behind the passenger seat and climbed in. Waited while Wade programmed the satnav. Grimaced at the expected travel time to Beaconsfield, then looked soberly at himself in the extra-length rear-view mirror. He'd killed a man. Avenged his dead sister and got away with it. No shadow of a doubt, the right moment to step back into the shadows. Live his life and consign that revenge to the past. Limiting the damage to his own psyche to that one moment of catharsis.

Instead of which he was going to strike again.

Soon.

6

'Hello, Michael.'

'Tony.' The two skippers shook hands, Wade passing them as he carried his and Mickey's bags into the Hall. The minister's country house. Thirty-five rooms set in six hundred of the most expensive acres in the country. The spoils of his business career in Hong Kong and the UK. Sir Patrick having spent twenty years amassing a significant personal fortune before deciding to serve his country.

'Quiet tour?'

His fellow sergeant gave him a meaningful look.

'Let's do a quick handover. I've got a pot of coffee.'

Mickey followed him to the repurposed anteroom that was now the protection officers' office. Once inside the small room, the other man shut the door to give them some privacy. Picked up one of the coffee mugs and took a sip before speaking.

'Quiet as the bloody grave. The most exciting thing that's happened has been the new private secretary arriving this morning.'

Mickey raised an eyebrow.

'What happened to the old one?'

'No idea, officially. We were called over to Chequers

yesterday for a meeting with the PM. A meeting without biscuits, apparently, from the look on the minister's face when he came out. After which it was announced that a new private secretary would be joining his team.' The other sergeant sat back, sipping at his coffee with a look of contentment. 'Probably there to make sure he doesn't try to do anything stupid before the PM is ready to drop the axe on him. The press are chipping away at him like fucking woodpeckers. And who's to say he doesn't deserve it?'

'Not our concern.'

The other man shrugged.

'I hear that, Michael. But I've been reading around the subject. Everything from the *Times* to the *Clarion*. All of whom seem to think he's a dead man walking come the next reshuffle. And that if the rumours about him get any worse that'll be sooner rather than later.'

Mickey shook his head dismissively.

'Don't waste your time, Tony. Half of that shit's made up. And the other half is no better than speculation. We just guard him. So, what about this new private secretary? Another younger version of his wife?'

'Bloke.'

Mickey raised an eyebrow.

'Christ. The times, they really are a changing.'

'Yeah. What's more, he's an army major. Got time with the Regiment too, from what I gather.'

Mickey pursed his lips appreciatively.

'That'll make a change. He'll probably have more range time than both of us put together.'

'Yeah. He's asked for a meeting later on today.' Tony consulted his notes. 'At 17.00, in his office. And I got the impression that he wouldn't take lateness all that well. Right, we'd better be away, if we're going to get into London before rush hour.'

Mickey walked him out to his car. Watched the Jag pull out onto the road before speaking.

'Wade?'

'Skip.'

Wade was solid enough, in Mickey's opinion. Not quite as polished as he would be in another two or three years, inevitably. But trustworthy and keen was a good combination in Mickey's opinion.

'You can man the office, and get the kettle on.' He raised a pair of binoculars. 'I'm going eyeballs.'

Walking up the stairs to the first floor, he knew Wade would be grinning knowingly. One of Mickey's known foibles, the urge to scope out the environment around the principal. Wherever the principal happened to be. Like he took the job seriously or something. He walked down the landing to the window above the house's front door. Pulled up a chair and sat down. Raising the optics to begin a slow, methodical scan of the ground in front of the house. Nothing to be seen, although that didn't mean there weren't long lenses in play. Just as he was about to get up and go to another window, a voice spoke without warning close behind him.

'I've done much the same. There's nothing out there. Nothing visible from here, that is.'

Mickey restrained the urge to kick the chair backwards and go for the Glock at his waist. Just. Spoke without turning to look at the man behind him.

'Major...?'

'Cavendish. James Cavendish.'

The accent cultured, but the voice hard. Used to issuing orders. Probably under the sort of pressure that most of the coffee drinkers at LX could never imagine.

'Let me guess. Scots Guards?'

'Grenadiers, actually.'

Confident in himself too, no doubt about that. Probably not a man who'd be troubled if accused of his undoubted upper-class white male privilege. Secure in his social status.

Mickey sighed inwardly and stood up. Turned to find a man of roughly his own age, a hand extended in greeting. Immaculately turned out in army service dress, leather belt and shoulder strap gleaming. Clean-shaven face, brown eyes surrounded with the sort of lines that come from laughing. Either that, or possibly from squinting into brightly lit landscapes looking for targets. Hair cut short, tightly cropped at the sides. Even the facial scar that marked his chin a tidy line of white. Shoes with a shine he could see himself in, distantly. Not a big man, but with an aura of hard-won competence. Mickey shook the hand. Finding the other man's grip every bit as firm as expected.

'You'll be Michael Bale, I presume. Do you chaps do ranks? We can call each other Major and Sergeant if you like, but I doubt that's the way it usually works.'

'Michael will be fine, since you've asked. Rank obsession usually starts at inspector in my unit. Call me Sergeant when it suits you, but first names are usual in my branch of the Job.'

'In that case I'm James. Jimmy to a very precious few, none of whom reside within this poorly disguised open prison.' He laughed softly at the look on Mickey's face.

'What, you don't read the papers?'

'I make a point of avoiding them. It's none of my business.'

'Perhaps not. But a man's allowed opinions.'

Mickey shrugged.

'I don't need opinions. Just this…' He tapped the Glock at his waist. 'And the willingness to use it if I have to.'

Cavendish smiled politely.

'I can respect that. You asked for this role. And you're good at it, from what your file says. I, on the other hand, did not. The man we both serve, the "principal" as I believe you call him, is known to prefer female private secretaries. Now that it looks as if the sky is about to fall on him, however, that choice has been taken out of his hands. Which is how I come to be looking after him now. Despite my not really wanting the posting.'

'You'd rather just be crawling round in the mud?'

'With bullets flying past my ears? Oh God yes. But, as I'm sure you can imagine, the concept of doing one's duty is quite strong where I come from. So when the call to arms was issued, I wasn't really in any position to refuse. Anyway, I'll leave you to your survey of the grounds. Although I can pretty much guarantee you won't spot any lurking paparazzi.'

'Are you sure about that?'

Cavendish turned back with a smile.

'Some of those snappers can earn fifty k for a decent pic at the right moment. Which has a somewhat Darwinian effect on their competence. And this pile has ground-floor windows on the lounge you could fly a light aircraft through. So they're out there all right, camouflaged up and ready to get that money shot, in a manner of speaking. I could be

ANTHONY RICHES

fifty yards from here and you'd never see me, so what price
one of them at five hundred? I'll see you at 17.00, Michael,
and we can discuss Sir Patrick's engagements for the next
few days over a cup of tea. Shouldn't take long.'

7

'So, gentlemen, as you can see, the minister's calendar has been stripped clean, pretty much. Life around here just isn't going to be very interesting for the next few weeks.'

Mickey shrugged at James's somewhat doleful pronouncement.

'Boredom is an occupational risk around here. There hasn't been an attempt on a cabinet minister since the Brighton bombing. Half the trick of this job is finding ways to stay alert.'

Cavendish nodded knowingly.

'Sounds like my job. Ninety-nine per cent paperwork, bureaucratic idiocy and the toleration of fools. One per cent loud noises, shouting and terror. My previous job, that is.'

Mickey raised an eyebrow in return. Major Cavendish not looking like the sort of man who felt terror. More like the kind who inflicted it.

'Presumably you'll be able to go back to it, when this all blows over?'

The soldier shrugged again. 'As an army officer, especially in the infantry and past a certain age, it's either up or out, gentlemen. Fail to achieve promotion on schedule and you start coming under pressure to clear the pitch for the next chap. It was already being made pretty bloody clear to me that I'm not very likely to make it to Lieutenant Colonel. And then I was told that I was going to have to do a tour of duty in the MOD, without the option. I could either take some time to consider my options or just accept my bowler hat. Start a new life on Civvy Street.'

He grimaced at the prospect.

'And a new life out of uniform is something I don't consider myself ready for. Not just yet. Of course, when I got here I realised the real purpose of my being posted to the ministry.'

He looked at the two men for a moment. Shaking his head at their lack of reaction.

'Come on, you know what's going on here. Sir Patrick is on the skids. Too much gossip, way too much innuendo. Too many people queuing up to put the knife in. He'll be gone within the month. He's already being discreetly cut out of the loop when it comes to the most sensitive classified information. And in the meantime, I'm here to make sure he doesn't get up to any of what I suppose might be termed "his old tricks" to get out from under the falling piano.'

Mickey smiled quietly at the slightly drawling pronunciation of the last word. Pi-Ah-No.

'But, since I'm going to be here for a while longer than a month, I suppose you'd better brief me on how you chaps work. Be a shame if I were to do something unhelpful in the event that it all gets noisy, wouldn't it?'

Mickey nodded. 'There's not too much you need to know, really. It's usually mostly about letting us do our job when it comes to anything out of the ordinary. Although we do have a clear set of priority actions, in the event of an incident involving an immediate and serious threat.'

'Which are?'

'One, safeguard the principal first and foremost. Covering him from any attack by any means possible.'

Cavendish raised a finger to politely interject. 'Does that include taking a bullet?'

'In extremis, yes.' Mickey tapped the Glock on his hip. 'But I'd rather be on my feet and returning fire. 'Two, engage and neutralise the threat. By any means necessary. Shooting back usually being the best means. And three, relocate the principal to a place of safety. Which means that we do whatever we have to do to get him away safely. And if that means shunting other road users out of the way, that's what we're trained to do.'

Back in the Prot office he stretched wearily.

'All that talking has given me a thirst, so I'm calling a Code 99. You get the kettle on and get it brewing, while I go for a quick look around.'

Leaving Wade to get busy with the teabags, he walked out into the big house's silence. Stopped and listened for a moment. Reminding himself that he hadn't seen the minister all day. He walked down the corridor into the lounge, one hundred feet long by forty wide. Sofas and scatter cushions, side tables with family photographs and vases of flowers. Dimly lit, outside of the pools of light cast by table lamps. A fire lit and burning in the antique Adam fireplace. Just the way Sir Patrick liked it.

But of the man himself, as Mickey had expected, no sign at all. They hadn't seen him at all during the tour so far, a genuine novelty. All he wanted, it seemed, was to have his meals served in his private lounge and to be left alone. Not that Mickey viewed that as any sort of hardship, given his lounge was three times the size of the one he and Roz lived in, but all the same.

He crossed the room, staying outside of the lamps' light puddles, and touched the master control to switch them off. Leaving the room in late afternoon gloom with only the fire's flickering light. And stood in the near-dark, allowing his eyes to adjust. The immaculately maintained lawn was a dull grey, the trees beyond it so dark as to be more black than green. A moment of peace. Wade intruded in his earpiece, cheerful voice and clinking china.

'Code 99 is green, repeat code 99 green. Bags out milk in, opening the biscuit tin.'

He smiled. Ever the joker, Wade, when he knew he wouldn't be overheard by senior management.

'All received. I'll see if I can blag some cake from the kitch...'

And froze, staring hard through the picture window. Out into the near-monochrome world outside the house. There was someone moving through the trees. A presence made indistinct by the gloom, but unmistakable. Nature, Mickey knew, just didn't do straight lines. And the person in question was carrying something very straight. And very black. At the edge of visibility, dressed in some sort of camouflage. Not a gardener, finishing up for the day in the last of the daylight. For one thing the gardener and his apprentice would be in their shed, cleaning up their equipment. And for another, there was no urgency in the figure's movement. No hurry to get finished up and away. Instead, the cautious, wary advance of an intruder.

'Eyeball, repeat eyeball, west side. One person, in the

trees, carrying…' Was it a camera with a long lens, or something more dangerous? '…potential long rifle.'

Wade came back crisply, all levity abandoned. 'All received. Do you need reinforcement?'

He stared at the slowly advancing figure for another long moment. 'Negative. Just be ready with the external security lights.'

He eased down into the cover of the nearest sofa and drew the Glock. Watched as the intruder went down on one knee. And raised whatever it was that they were carrying.

'Well it's either a bloody long lens or a rocket launcher.'

Christ, he wished Cavendish would stop doing that. The major was standing in the doorway behind him, looking out at the kneeling figure.

'Lens.'

'And you're *sure* about that?'

'There's only one of them. It's not a man. And that's not big enough to fire a rocket. Plus she's just put it to her eye.'

Mickey stood up, crossing the room in half a dozen swift strides. 'Lights, Wade!'

The security lights blazed into life just as he swung the glass door open, raising the pistol in an unmistakable threat.

'Armed police! Stand still! Keep your hands where I can see them!'

The figure stood, making the urge to put a warning round into the turf almost overwhelming. But Mickey knew the way that would play in the papers. Not well, especially in the context of the principal's current news profile.

'Get down on your front!'

He kept advancing, within twenty yards of the intruder.

The price she was paying for the initial hesitation, more proof of amateur status. Close enough to see her fine-boned features. Close enough to double tap a man-sized target and have a reasonable expectation of hitting with both rounds. She raised her hands, allowing the camera to hang on its strap. Mickey slowed his pace. Keeping the weapon raised, finger on the trigger.

'There's no safety catch on this pistol. It's a design feature, apparently.' Walking towards her slowly now, pointing the weapon to one side. 'Which is why I'm not pointing it straight at you. Because I don't want to put a round through a freelance snapper. Even one unwise enough to get this close to the house. The man behind me...' he could tell that Cavendish was at his shoulder from the sound of his breathing '...is an army officer, and probably even fitter than I am. So running would be a bit silly, even if I didn't decide to shoot you. Wouldn't it?'

And shut up, waiting for her to respond.

'Yes.'

A strong voice, even if she was probably shitting herself.

'Exactly. So, slowly, no sudden movements, put the camera down. Lie down on the ground, face down. I'll put the gun away and pop on some cuffs. Then we can all go inside for a cup of tea, while we wait for the local Plod to come and get you. Right?'

Back in the Prot office, Tamara, as she turned out to be called, proved to be a resilient young woman.

'You're right. My mistake was getting too close. That and not staying in cover when the lights went out.' She looked at Mickey appraisingly. 'I could make you and your oppo famous. All you'd have to do is—'

'Take off the cuffs and give you the camera? You'd make us famous ex-Protection Officers, is what you'd make us.'

'Fair enough. So how big a book will "the local Plod" throw at me?'

Mickey affected to think for a moment. 'Trespass, for starters. Plus you were on land that belongs to a government minister. Which probably puts you in breach of more than one Act of Parliament you've never heard of. They can hold you for a while, if they choose to.'

'And? There is an "and", isn't there?'

He shrugged. 'They'll probably confiscate your memory cards. The one in the camera and the one you've hidden in your knickers. Or wherever. Then let you go, with a warning.'

'Is that all?'

Mickey raised an eyebrow. 'There was a time when a warning from the police was something real. But times change, I suppose.' He gestured to the camera. 'Get caught again, and that rather expensive piece of tech will be confiscated. Permanently.'

She smiled knowingly. 'Wouldn't be the first time. The *Clarion* will just give me another.'

'The *Clarion*? I thought you were freelance.'

'The problem with freelancers is that their pics cost a fortune. It's cheaper for the paper to hire people like me for the skills we developed in other walks of life, and—'

'I knew it! Using the word oppo was a dead giveaway!' Cavendish suddenly indignant from his place in the doorway. 'You're bloody well ex-army, aren't you?' He glowered into her smile. 'I knew there was something more to you!'

'Well spotted, Major Cavendish. I got some cracking

stills of you earlier, by the way. The way you were standing at your office window looking pensive, I almost felt sorry for you.' She tipped her head in salute. 'I was in the Royal Signals. I found it all a bit…'

'Hard work?'

She smiled again. 'There's that bias I got *so* bored of having to deal with. I found it tedious, Major. Hidebound, and with more than its fair share of brain-dead men. So I got out. And don't worry, I don't plan on telling anyone about my previous career. I wouldn't dream of upsetting *that* apple cart. Plus my dad would never live it down.'

At which point the local police made an appearance. Mickey released her from his cuffs, watching her smirk as she was formally arrested by the uniformed inspector who'd come to get her.

'This is just a rite of passage for you, isn't it?'

She shrugged at him. 'Every pap worth their salt has been arrested at some point. Perhaps now I'll get some respect.'

He shook his head at her in admonishment, which was, he was forced to admit to himself, somewhat forced. 'Yeah. Perhaps you will. Have fun at the local nick then. See you around!'

'Not if I see you first!'

Waited until the front door was shut behind them.

'Youth of today, eh James?'

Cavendish raised a jaundiced eyebrow. 'Not funny, Michael. So not funny as to be verging on a "Sergeant Bale" moment.'

Mickey shrugged. 'Sometimes only humour will do the job, Major Cavendish. So I'll fall back on a joke so old it probably originated in Caesar's legions.'

'Don't bother. And don't forget that I suffered under more than one vicious bastard of a senior NCO at Sandhurst. Which means I probably understand that old joke better than you do. I'll bid you both goodnight.'

He turned away, clearly still irritated. Whether with Mickey or Tamara the *Clarion* snapper, Mickey wasn't sure. Then turned back.

'Oh, but I meant to ask you. How did you know she was a woman? All I saw was camo and a suspicious length of black metal.'

Mickey nodded. 'Yeah. And your professional expectations meant that the target had to be male. And the long black thing had to be a rifle. Whereas we're trained to observe from a wider perspective, with all due respect to the army. It was in her gait and bearing.'

'Well I'm bloody impressed, Sergeant Bale, although it pains me to admit it. Good work.'

And left the two men staring after him.

'Not a complete stiff-neck then.'

Wade nodded. 'What was the joke he told you not to use?'

'Oh, that? It's that timeless classic. If you can't take a joke then you shouldn't have joined. Speaking of which, get the kettle back on. Like I said, all that talking has left me parched.'

8

'**Y**ou're serious? I mean *really* serious? You actually want to go after the most dangerous gangster this side of the river?'

Mickey nodded. Staring levelly back at his friend. He'd dropped in to see Martin with five minutes' notice. On his way back from LX, four-day tour of duty at the Hall completed. Knowing just how big an ask he was making of his closest friend.

'I'm deadly serious, Martin. I have to do this. For Katie.'

Martin stared at him in silence for a moment. 'You bastard. I mean I love you and all that. And you know I'd give my own life to bring her back in a heartbeat. But fuck *me*, Mickey, Joe Castagna?'

He shook his head in genuine disbelief. His face creasing into an incredulous frown. Stick-thin, no matter how much he ate, Martin did disappointed well. Like a pro, in fact. Mickey put it down to his having been blessed and cursed with a ready-made living. One that paid well, but made him constantly cautious. To the detriment of every serious relationship he'd ever had. Besides which, Martin's line of business wasn't exactly female-friendly.

Mickey had known Martin since they were both four.

Taller than Mickey, always looking under-nourished despite his healthy appetite. Two snotty-nosed kids in the same pre-school, all the way to Year Eleven. United against the bullies, sometimes bloodied, never beaten. Neither of them cool enough for girls to come between them. And then, one fateful evening in the late Eighties, that friendship had changed.

There was a party on the estate, three doors down from Martin's Auntie Steph's flat. Everyone invited. A welcome home for a well-known armed robber. Mickey wisely tried to resist his friend's suggestion they both go. Told Martin it wouldn't do for a would-be copper to go to a coming-out party. Martin had retaliated with the assertion that there'd be free beer. And girls. Which was how Mickey had found himself in a flat wreathed in bunting, fag smoke and the smell of cheap booze. Sipping a can of Red Stripe and wondering where the girls were. Auntie Steph and her two septuagenarian mates not really qualifying as such.

Something, of course, had been bound to kick off. And given that the returning hero's wife had been over the side with his best mate while he'd been away, the scene was set. A firearm had been procured, and violent revenge was planned. The would-be victim, however, wisely declined to attend his own execution. Forewarned by the errant spouse. Unlike the Met, who were more than happy to take his place. Someone had tipped the Feds off, and it wasn't hard to guess who.

And so the boys in blue attended in force. Mob-handed and tooled up for any eventuality. Word quickly got around that there were carriers full of battle-hardened Territorial Support Group coppers queued in the streets around the estate. Ready and willing for a replay of Broadwater Farm. Only this time it'd be the blue army on the offensive. Boiler-suited, shield- and baton-equipped squads were seen converging on the block from all sides. Armed officers at their head.

And so it was, as panic ensued, that Mickey handled his first ever firearm. The pistol, a battered, tired old Browning Hi-Power. Thrust upon him by the woman of the house. Having confiscated it from her hapless husband, she had momentarily blinded the closest young lad – Mickey – with the magnificence of her sizable chest. And then took advantage of his teenage bewilderment to issue the instruction: 'Get rid of this, there's a love.'

Disaster beckoned, especially for a boy with uniformed career plans. All hope seemed lost. With Mickey cast as "last man seen holding a shooter" even if he dumped it. The local hard boys had fallen about laughing. Telling him that even if he dumped the piece it still had his prints all over it. And then, with police entry squads only seconds from piling through the open front door, help had come from an unexpected source. And of all people, it was Auntie Steph who came to the rescue.

A woman well into her seventies at the time, Steph was what her neighbours called "redoubtable" when she was listening. And "that fucking old cow" when they believed she couldn't hear them. Glowering on the sofa between two equally life-hardened harridans, she had beckoned Mickey over.

'Give me that shooter. No good a young idiot like you being caught with it.'

She'd tucked the offending firearm deep into her capacious

handbag. Grinned at Mickey in a rather disturbing way. And then set her face hard against the invading army. In another time and place she might well have been searched, along with the flat and every able-bodied man in it. As it was, well over a dozen armed officers went about their futile investigation without ever thinking to demand she open the bag.

And so, in the end, all was well. At least in Mickey's world. Although not in the case of the robber's former best mate. Who mysteriously fell to his death from the top-floor landing a week later. And that, it had seemed, was that. A tight corner escaped, thanks to the brass neck of his best friend's auntie.

Martin and Mickey's friendship deepened at about that time, as most of their previous schoolmates fell away. Martin started work for the council. Mickey went to college to do three A levels. Pretty much de rigueur for coppers by then. Not being much of a joiner even back then, he had ignored the blandishments of college social life and remained true to his roots. And to Martin. Beer and girls being their main interests.

Three years later, with Mickey a probationer taking his first tentative steps in policing, Auntie Steph died. The inevitable result of too many fags and too much vodka. Mickey went to the funeral to pay his respects to his one-time saviour. Exchanged nods of mutual recognition with some small-time local criminals. Drank a few beers at the wake, turned a blind eye to a couple of minor possession charges. Generally chilled with his mate. And then, at the end of the evening, the metaphorical roof fell in. On both his perceptions and potentially his career itself.

'Here, come and have a look at this.'

The two of them were alone in Steph's flat, soon to be repossessed by the council. The last of the mourners having left five minutes before. Martin had locked the door and lowered the blinds, then led Mickey to the smaller of the two bedrooms. Mickey fearing that his mate was about to come out of the closet. Then lost for words when he'd opened it instead. And stepped back to let him see its contents.

'No *fucking* way!'

Martin had grinned at him. 'Way.'

'Auntie Steph? This lot?'

'Yeah. Auntie *fucking* Steph.'

The longer he had stared at the collection of firearms in the wardrobe, the larger it seemed to get. Martin's Auntie Steph had been the proud owner of enough guns, vintage and modern, to equip a rifle section. All with enough ammunition to put up a decent few minutes of carefully aimed shots. Pride of place going to the ancient Bren gun and its five curved magazines. Serious firepower.

'This is…'

Martin had grinned. Enjoying his mate being lost for words.

'Illegal? Totally.'

'Fuck! I'm…'

'Relax, mate. You were never here.'

Mickey had nodded gratefully. 'You'll have to get rid of… hang on.' He'd reached down, picking up a battered automatic pistol. 'This is the Browning that she hid in her bag that night. At Billy Wright's coming-out party…' He'd fallen silent, seeing the look on Martin's face. 'You *knew*.'

'Not at the time. But later, yeah. She brought me into the business. How else do you think I can afford to eat and dress proper on what I earn.'

'Jesus, Martin! You'd get twenty years for this lot! Or life, if they could prove they'd been used to kill. This flat could be under surveillance right now!'

His friend had shaken his head dismissively. Sparking up a Dunhill. A brand that Mickey had always thought a bit posh for the estate.

'No chance.' He'd blown a plume of smoke across the room. Master of the situation. 'Steph only ever dealt off-manor. No-one round here has the first fucking clue about this lot. She was what you'd call select in her choice of clientele. And she kept her prices sensible. After all, she wasn't exactly splashing it around, was she?'

Mickey had been forced to concede his point. A couple of hundred pounds here and there could make a huge difference to a modest lifestyle. And such a gentle cash flow, in arms-dealing terms, would have made for a nicely low profile. Auntie Steph had quite possibly been running so deep and silent that she had completely evaded the law's detection. He'd reached out and taken one of Martin's posh fags. Lit it with his mate's Zippo.

'You'll definitely have to get rid though.'

And he'd trusted his friend to see the sense in that. Not his finest piece of intuition, it had to be said. Martin had affected to drop the whole collection into the Thames. Had even invited Mickey to witness one such disposal. Just to prove he was doing as he'd been bidden. But, as Mickey had discovered much later, he had in fact dumped only the worn-out dross and more infamous murder weapons. Steph having kept notes, possibly with blackmail in mind.

Having retained the more useful and less infamous pieces, he'd rented a lockup. Filled it with junk, then hidden his shooters in the chaos. Half a dozen carefully selected firearms lived in a lock box, their exact location known only to him. Or so he thought. Twenty years of running his guns for hire business, following Steph's careful example, had made him, if not rich, at least comfortable.

His offering had been as simple as Steph's, if a little more up to date. Functional product at a reasonable price. Contactable only via the dark web. And all conducted with a high regard for safety and security. Both his own and that of his clients. Buying his replacement ammunition in small quantities from legal firearms holders.

As a result, he had flourished, quietly and without ever raising suspicion. Kept his council job, and never, ever, flashed the cash. No Audi, no Rolex, no drinks all round. Nothing to excite attention or jealousy. While Mickey's career had pretty much plateaued at the dizzy height of skipper. Nothing wrong with being a sergeant, of course. It was still the rank that made the service work. But Mickey wasn't ever likely to be an inspector. Too good at the nitty gritty of policing for one thing. And not impressed by the role management were forced to play. Stats, political correctness and the right "optics". Neither, if he was honest with himself, could he be bothered with the study required.

Martin wasn't about to give in on the subject without one last try. 'You *said* wanted to do Warren. So we did Warren. And now...'

Mickey shrugged. 'I'm sorry, mate. Warren just isn't enough.'

The two men stared at each other for a moment before Martin sighed.

'If you go after him, for Katie, then I'm in. You know I am. I've been in since we were thirteen and you spanked that arsehole who was nicking my sandwiches. But this is a whole different ballgame from putting a .22 into a dumb bastard like Warren Margetson. And there's no way I can get that shooter again. The bloke who supplied it isn't stupid enough to let the same weapon get used by the same punter twice.'

Mickey shrugged.

'Obviously. Murder Squad would be all over it. Some twat would come up with a nickname. The .22 Terror. Before you know it there'd be half a dozen detectives on it, and it'd be a thing.'

Martin laughed darkly, shaking his head.

'A thing? Fuck me, Mickey, it'll be a fucking *thing* all right. We start trying to kill our way up this particular tree, it might be the last thing we ever do! And what about Roz? What about your mum and dad? What do you think happens to them if you get caught?'

'I know. Trust me, I know. But...'

Martin got up and walked away down the length of his kitchen, leaning against the doorframe before speaking again.

'You know he's a psycho, right? I mean, Joe's old man was a decent enough sort of bloke, for a gangster. His granddad brought the old values with him from Sicily. And Joe's dad stuck with them. All right, it was all a bit heavy on the omertà, but you always knew where you were with the Castagnas. You always got a warning, if they thought you was out of order, and providing the crime was forgivable. You could even plead your case, if you felt brave enough. That all went out of the window when Joe took over.'

He walked back down the room's length. Absent-mindedly flicking a speck of dried coffee from the Gaggia as he passed.

'He's got no restraint. And neither do the blokes whose collars he holds. We do this, we could end up hanging from a hook in someone's cold store. And not just us. So think carefully, buddy. Think really carefully. You're absolutely sure there's no way for Warren to be the end of it?'

Mickey shrugged. Willing to let his mate off the hook. 'You don't have to be part of it, not if—'

'You can stick that right up your arse. It ain't *me* I'm worried about. And are you sure you can kill again?'

Mickey nodded slowly. 'It's not like I've got a taste for it.' He shrugged at his friend. 'You have to kill a man to know how it affects you. Some people enjoy the way it makes them feel. Psychopaths, mostly. And some people are destroyed by it. But me...' He paused, as if searching for the right words. 'I'm just... indifferent. I don't *want* to do it again. But I will.'

Martin stared at him for a moment. 'Yeah. But there's something you're not telling me. Isn't there? Something that makes you think you can get away with this. You going to share it with me, or just leave me in the dark?'

Mickey stared back at him. 'You sure you want to know?'

His friend nodded slowly. 'I get it. You're trying to protect me from whatever it is. Because I can't unknow whatever it is you might be about to tell me. But I don't care what the risks are. I'm going to be with you in this, I need to know everything you do.'

Mickey nodded. And told his friend about Nemesis.

9

Mickey knew how the money side of the drugs trade worked. He knew this because he had information not available to the public. Privileged information as to the how, where and when of Joe's operation. Which is how he came to be sitting in the passenger seat of a prehistorically old Vauxhall Astra. Apparently abandoned in the underground parking area of a block of council flats in North-East London.

The car had been parked in the same spot for weeks, one tyre slowly deflating. Windows illegally tinted to the point of opacity. A fading black respray, battered steel wheels brush-painted matt black. Someone's attempt to make their Astra look street, back in the long-distant day. Now just an embarrassment. A car nobody would ever buy at auction. Or steal. Or, most importantly, even notice. Perfect.

He'd purchased it for cash. Generous cash, no V5, no questions asked. Taken it to an out-of-the-way piece of waste ground. Drilled out the vehicle identification number and changed the plates. Left it there until four the next morning, then driven it to its final resting place. A five-minute journey. Mickey wearing a baseball cap to hide his face from cameras. Driven it straight onto the estate. Gambling that any sentries would either be half-asleep or just ignore such a piece of shit. Parked it and walked quietly away. And then ignored it for so long that it had become part of the underground landscape. Long enough for any CCTV of his short drive to have been overwritten.

And now, two days after Warren's death, he was ready to follow up. Ready to show Joe Castagna that he was serious. Deadly serious. Ready to start the clock.

He'd rehearsed the whole thing, pretty much, except for the noisy part. Talked it through with Martin. Whose considered opinion had been that Mickey was taking a proper risk this time.

'This ain't the same as popping Warren, right? You could get shot. No way round that.'

Mickey had shrugged. Supremely confident in his abilities when it came to a gunfight. Especially with the weapon now resting on his lap.

'What else?'

'They might see you in the car as they arrive to make the pickup.'

Mickey nodded. That was obvious enough.

'Or they might already be on brown alert, given the way you offed Warren. Have the car park scouted before they arrive.'

Mickey had considered that possibility too. Gang kids, perhaps, employed to check out the routes in and out of the block for threats. Which was why he'd bought a car with blacked-out glass all round. Illegal, but perfect.

'They do that; I'll have the scouts instead. Still sends a message.'

Martin stared at him disapprovingly. 'They'll be kids, Mickey. You sure you want to kill kids?'

Mickey shook his head. 'Have you listened to any drill music? These aren't kids, they're just not fully grown yet. But they're adult where it counts.' He tapped his head. 'In here they're all psychopaths.'

'You do know we'll be getting called the same thing, if we get caught in the act?'

He sat in the Astra, seat as low as it would go. Black balaclava already in place, cheap supermarket sunglasses over his eyes to render him invisible behind the smoked glass. Looked at his watch, raising the sunglasses momentarily: 16.01.

It was time, if they stuck to their routine. Joe's empire being not much more than one big cash collection scheme. Drugs and prostitutes, both trafficked, bought cheap, then sold as expensively as possible. For cash. And only for cash. Until such time as the government decided to take cash away from the citizenry, Joe would take full advantage of its ubiquity.

Pocketfuls of cash, flowing to collection points around the borough. Subject to spot audits by Joe's enforcers. And any discrepancy left unexplained – which meant any discrepancy, in practice – got the miscreant a warning. And in Joe's empire, warnings weren't meant to be forgotten. They left marks. Scars. And there was never, ever, a second warning. Only examples. Which made for a squeaky-clean system of accounting, at the street end of the pipeline.

Pocketfuls of cash became bags of cash, shipped to the flat on the top floor of the block above him for processing. Tens of thousands of pounds a day. Machine-counted, bundled, re-bagged and collected. Driven away to a secure location, which changed every few weeks at random intervals. Recounted, vacuum-sealed and shipped across the Channel. Converted into gold and then shipped to the Middle East. Becoming clean money. A lot of clean money even at fifty cents on the dollar. A month later half of it would be in one of Joe's offshore accounts as euros, or dollars, or Swiss francs. But not today. Today Mickey was going to blow the doors right off Joe's money machine.

It was Steve who'd first told him about the collection routine a couple of months earlier. Having discovered the detail from a snout. And, having reported it to his DI, been told to quietly forget it. His DI being Jason Felgate. He'd recounted the story to Mickey over a quiet pint one afternoon. Still fuming.

'It's already known to SCD7, apparently. Which means that it's over my pay grade. And if any of my dirty footprints get found by Serious and Organised, that's me doing my last two years in uniform.'

Mickey had noted the information. Confident that Jason was pulling Steve's pisser. That Serious and Organised Crime were nowhere near to getting on top of the Castagna gang. And wondering why Jason was warning his own detectives off such an obvious opportunity. Coming to the only possible conclusion. His old mate Jase no longer being someone he could trust.

He'd bribed an Amazon delivery van driver to let him ride onto the estate in the back with the parcels. A hundred quid in cash, and no questions asked. Mickey had slipped from the van and into a stairwell whose exit was only a few yards from the Astra. Taken up position with Martin's MP5SD loaded, the first round chambered. Ready to go.

The machine pistol was familiar to the hand, from his years of practice on Job ranges. Still tight. Well maintained. Barrel clean and magazine springs taut. Two mags, although he only expected to need one. Thirty rounds of 9mm parabellum in each. Selector set to burst. One squeeze, three rounds. A laser projector clipped to its top rail. Put the red dot on the target, squeeze the trigger. And the piece de resistance, the fat, oversized barrel that housed an integral silencer. In the car park's confines it still would be loud enough. But inaudible to anyone on the floors above.

A pair of gang youngers slouched out of the same stairwell he'd used moments before. Roadman vibe, black Stone Island and Nikes. Both with the obligatory front-worn bumbags. The older of the two close to adulthood. Seventeen, perhaps eighteen. Tall, and angular with the look of muscle to come. Bearded too, probably eager to look old enough for full membership of Joe's firm. Every move loaded with the need to portray street cool. He performed a desultory eyeball of the car park. One sweeping glance, not even trying to get a look into the Astra through its blackened windows. Just part of the landscape.

He made a call, spoke briefly. Then walked over to the stairs leading up into the flats, practising his hard look. Waited by the door, leaning on the wall and ignoring the younger kid. Twelve, from the look of him, or an immature fourteen. Looking around him like this was all new and exciting. A younger brother, most likely.

The collectors arrived. Their BMW 5 series estate a shining contrast to the car park's other occupants. A nice shade of blue, Mickey mused. Cool rims too. Who said drug dealers don't have taste? Four up. Two guards and two to carry the cash. Sharp threads, compared to the gang kids. Hair styled, footballer 'dos and razored facial hair. Chains and diamond studs. They stopped by doors to the main stairwell. Got out and generally posed their way past the scouts. Bad boys, carrying. Heavy with attitude. All doubtless wearing the mandatory Rolex Subs that were the first thing any member of Joe's gang bought on admission. Mickey had left the Black Bay at home and was wearing a cheap Casio instead.

He glanced at the watch: 16.09. Figured five minutes to make the journey up to the top floor. The time needed to pass through the heavy iron gates that blocked access to both floor and flat. Expected to be locked at all times. And failure to do so just as punishable as embezzlement. Two minutes for minimal small talk, and signing for the bags of cash. With street titles, of course, not their real names, but still accepting responsibility for Joe's cash. And another five to get back down through the relocked gates.

He breathed deeply, rhythmically. Waited patiently. Watched the scouts. When they straightened up he knew the cash was close. Dumped the shades and put one hand on the car door's release. Ready to go. Instinctively glancing down to check that the weapon was in battery. Ejection port filled with bolt carrier, tight on the chambered round. His lips twitched in a momentary smile at the force of habit from hundreds of range sessions.

The first man came through the doors. Shoulders tensed against the weight of the bags he was carrying. Then the second. Sub-optimal. Preferable to have had the gunmen out front as priority targets. Nothing he could do anything about though, except adapt.

He popped the car door open and stepped out. Brought the weapon up to his shoulder as the third man came through the doors. The guard unsuspecting, turning to look at the scouts with a lordly smirk. Evidently confused as the younger of the two kids reacted to Mickey's unexpected appearance.

Mickey leaned into the weapon. Put the red dot on the gunman's chest and took a swift, shallow breath in. Then squeezed the last tenth of an inch of trigger. A three-round burst, the first impacting in the middle of his chest. The second a few inches higher. The third blowing a gout of blood out through the back of his neck. Hopefully into the eyes of the man behind him.

The bag carriers froze. Helpless under the gun's basilisk one-eyed stare. Mickey dropped them both with two more swift bursts. Both men going down before they had time to realise what was happening. He went down on one knee as a precaution against return fire, given one gun unaccounted for. He needn't have bothered. The last of the four came through the door with his pistol raised. Blinking furiously, face covered in blood. The wrong choice. Turning and running back up the stairs would have saved his life.

Mickey put three rounds into him, centre mass. Their impact smashing him back through the door and onto the stairs behind it. He let the breath out and started walking forwards. Keeping the weapon's barrel pointed at the scouts.

'Run.'

They goggled at him. Ignoring the instruction, or simply paralysed by the speed of his ambush. The younger of the two had pissed himself. The older kid was looking down at a pistol lying at his feet. Mickey knew to make the Authorised Firearms Officer's three assumptions. Assume the weapon is loaded. Assume the weapon is cocked. Assume the safety is off. And added one of his own. Assumed that the man-child staring back at him would pull the trigger.

'*Run!*'

He saw it in the adolescent's eyes before he moved. The chance to be a hero, like in the drill tracks. Splash man down. Be instantly feted among his peers.

'Don't make me—'

Mickey waited until the young guy's hand was on the weapon's butt. Allowed him enough time to straighten up halfway before firing. Resisted the urge to close his eyes, maintaining awareness even as he pulled the trigger. Saw every minute detail as his bullets smacked the teenager contemptuously back into the concrete wall. Put the dot on the younger boy and repeated the instruction. Almost pleading with him.

'Run.'

The kid stared back, sudden irrational anger in his eyes. The discomfort of his incontinence forgotten. And why wouldn't he be angry, Mickey wondered, as the knife came out of the boy's waistband. He stamped forward, the decision not to shoot both unconscious and unwise. Just shooting the idiot would have been quicker and less risky. Reversed the machine pistol in a close-quarters combat drill. Drove the weapon's butt into the kid's midriff. Hard enough to double him over, puking.

'You even get up before I'm gone, I'll shoot you dead.'

He left the boy there, struggling just to breathe. All four of the gang members were dead. Or so close as to make no difference. Searched the man he'd shot last, finding the car keys in his pocket. Left his fallen pistol beside him. Turned back to the bags, opening all four to reveal their tightly packed contents. Then looked up to see the kid glaring at him, breathing easier now.

'See this money?' Mickey pushed the bags together, far enough from the Beemer for safety. 'Looks good, doesn't it? Buys nice trainers and clothes, like you're wearing. Except it's blood money. Made from suffering and death.'

Knowing he ought to shut up and get on with it. He picked up the pistol that had been the death of the older boy. Dropped the mag and racked the slide, a bullet tinkling on the dirty concrete floor. Threw it away across the car park. Did the same with the boy's knife. Wasting time, safeguarding himself against a threat he could have removed with a single bullet. Knowing it was the right thing to do, even as he took the risk.

He collected up his spent ammunition casings. Walked quickly to the Astra and opened the boot. Picked up the MP5's carry bag and the petrol can. Went back to the money. Soaked the bags, pouring it carefully to avoid splashes onto his feet. Stepped back and took a box of matches from his pocket. Snapped one to life against the striking surface. Dropped it into the first bag and stepped back as the petrol ignited. Then repeated the act with the other bags. Walked back to the Astra, pouring more petrol into the car's thinly carpeted boot and throwing a match in after it. Nodding in satisfaction. *Have that, Joe Castagna. And know that you're under threat.*

He bagged the machine pistol, then made his way back to the Beemer. Watched all the way by the younger kid. A brooding look on the boy's face. Fired up the engine and put the gear selector into drive. Cranking the wheel hard over, a U-turn back to face the ramp up to ground level. Shot a last glance over at the kid. Who was no longer there. Twisted his neck to look back at the stairwell door. Which was just closing. *Shit*. His careful plan was about to go right off the rails.

'Little bastard!'

He floored the throttle. Instinctively knowing what the boy had gone looking for. Darted a glance in the mirror as the car rocketed forward. Seeing the diminutive figure coming back through the door, the last gunman's pistol in his hand. Knowing that the kid didn't have to be any good to put a round through his spine. Just lucky. A spark of light flickered in the mirror, distant bang of the gun firing an instant later. A thud from the rear bodywork. Beginner's luck? Flash, bang, thud. Not just luck then. The car hit the ramp already doing fifty, springs bottoming out. Another bang. Mickey tensed. Waiting for the rear window to craze. For that final shot to be the one. No thud. A miss.

He powered the car up the ramp and into the daylight. Slowed to make the turn onto the estate's perimeter road. Looked up to see heads craning over balconies and walkways. The kid's shooting all too audible then. There'd be fingers hitting keypads. Calling Joe's boys. Calling the police. And him driving a car with two bullet holes in the back.

He pulled out onto the road. Ripped off the balaclava and donned a baseball cap. Busy with traffic but mercifully between school run and rush hour. Drove quickly but carefully. Cringed as the first police car screamed past in the other direction. Area car, uniformed cops, likely not armed. They'd wait for SCO19 firearms officers before going onto the estate. SOP with shots fired and the perpetrator quite possibly still on scene. Every minute ramped up the risk of the car's description and index being reported. And Mickey in possession of a machine pistol that had just been used to kill five men.

He reached the turn off into his planned rat run just as a silver and dayglo yellow X5 blue-lighted past. Trojan. An SCO19 armed response vehicle. Proof the Met was taking the 999 calls seriously. Looked down again to avoid being caught by the on-board cameras. And took to the back roads with an inward sigh of relief. Telling himself not to fall into the classic trap of relaxing too soon. Two more minutes of driving took him to the Beemer's final resting place. A featureless space between two brick-built warehouses. Off a back street, with no cameras, or housing.

Mickey poured the rest of the petrol into the car, threw the can in and tossed the cheap sunglasses after it. Took off the boiler-suit and threw it in as well. Added the balaclava, the baseball cap and the black latex gloves. Peeled the black overshoes off his boots, image totally changed. Tossed in a lighted match and waited until the car was burning nicely. Picked up the gun bag and walked quickly to the car Martin had rented for him. Got in, covered the weapon with a blanket, then drove carefully away. Job jobbed.

10

Joe took the news with his usual apparent lack of reaction. Ice cold. An Antarctic ice cap concealing a simmering volcano, as Eddie knew only too well. Shrugged on his Gucci leather jacket and turned his dead eyes on Eddie. Heading for the door.

'I've got men in bodybags down on that estate. So the rest of them need to see me giving a shit.' A pause, as he thought some more. 'And I want to talk to your man in charge.'

The latter spat over his shoulder as he climbed into the Rhino. The blacked-out Mercedes AMG G-Wagon he used for everyday business. Armoured, needing the 577 horses under the bonnet to move all that weight. But once it was moving, it *moved*. Like a charging fucking rhino, Joe had whooped, the first time he gave it the beans. A rare demonstration of enjoyment. The name had instantly stuck.

Big Lewis was driving, wearing a suit tailored to accommodate his shoulder-holster. Lewis Dearlove. An impeccably groomed beast of a man, blessed with the most ill-fitting surname Eddie had ever heard on a man. The biggest and nastiest of Joe's inner circle. Not a leader, like Eddie. Not legally minded, like Richard. Not a strategist, like Nigel had been. Just a warrior, plain and simple. No need to carry a weapon when you were with Lewis. Because Lewis *was* a weapon. And totally devoted to Joe. Had been ever since Joe made sure his mum's last months were peaceful.

The evening traffic was approaching its peak, but Lewis knew all the back doubles. Got them from leafy suburbia to the estate in less than forty-five minutes. Eddie following up in the second car, a nondescript 5-series saloon. Four up with a driver and two of the house bodyguards, both tooled. Busy on his phone, warning his people to be ready for the boss.

They parked the cars close by, in spaces kept empty by low-level gang members. Walked onto the estate through the low-rise, staying clear of the known police presence. Over a dozen or so detectives and forensics officers. Working inside a protective ring of blue-clad SCO19 officers openly carrying assault rifles. SIG MCX. Firing a military spec 5.56mm round. Met standard issue big boys' toys. When it chose to flex its muscles, the Met could bring that sort of juice to the party by the gallon.

Which meant, for the time being, that this part of the manor was locked in their iron grasp. Five gang members dead enough to get the commissioner breathing down necks. And the mayor breathing down hers. Enough to make everyone nervous. And Joe knew better than to antagonise a nervous police force.

He walked into the block by a side entrance, outside the cordon of blue-clad stormtroopers. Made his way up to the slightly risibly named "control room". A flat on the third floor with a bedroom full of CCTV monitors. Screens showed scenes from around the block. The counting room, the gates, the car park. Eddie might have laughed at the fact that the police had completely missed the camera relaying their underground investigation, but for Joe's stone-like expression.

'Show me.'

The clip was lined up and ready.

'They drive in...' Joe, delivering the running commentary. Something that got right on Eddie's tits whenever he was invited to watch a flick chez Castagna. Not the right moment to object though, he judged. Not that there ever really was a right moment with Joe. 'They park up... they go upstairs. Anything worth seeing before they get back down there? No? Let's see the attack then.'

The scene jumped, sudden movement as the bagmen came out of the stairwell. And walked into something out of a Tarantino flick. A black-clad figure, head to toe darkness. Hard to make out in the slightly grainy image, like a vengeful ghost. Climbed out of the piece-of-shit car that nobody watching had made for his hiding place. Carrying an instantly recognisable machine pistol. No muzzle flash as he opened fire. Joe nodded knowingly.

'Silenced. Nobody would have known a thing upstairs, if the kid hadn't grabbed that shooter and given him some back. Fuck he's quick! Roll back ten.'

Ten seconds back. The gunman just clear of the car, weapon coming up.

'Stop. Look at the clock. OK, start it again.'

Eddie nodded, standing behind his boss. Had to respect the man's intellect. Cutting straight to the facts. The swift slaughter played through. Ending with the last of the bagmen being punched back into the stairwell.

'Stop. See? That took him seven seconds. And three of them were him waiting for the last man to show himself. That, Eddie, is a professional. A gunfighter. Like that geezer on Netflix.'

'Raylan Givens.'

One of the ironies of being Joe's right-hand man. Expected to share his taste in box sets, however counter-intuitively. When Joe said he'd started watching something, Eddie made a point of getting through it first. Missing a cultural reference probably wouldn't put him on the skids. Probably. But why take the risk?

Joe nodded expressionlessly.

'Yeah, that's it. OK, roll it on.'

They watched the black-clad figure pace forwards, weapon still raised. Watched the older of the two gang members go for the fallen pistol. Watched him die.

'He didn't want to do that, did he? This was a gang hit, he'd have done them all without thinking twice. Just not so fast. Probably got himself tagged in the process. And it wouldn't have been one man. That was a pro, I'd say. A pro who didn't want a kid on his conscience. We had any other hits that look like they were done by pros recently? Eh?'

Eddie knew where this was going. Joe might be a scary bastard, but he was nobody's fool. And he was right.

'Warren Margetson.'

'Yeah, Warren Margetson. Shot in the head with a .22.'

Joe nodded as the gunman methodically sent a hundred grand up in flames. Then burned out the car he'd waited in with equal calmness.

'See? No hurry, no worry. That's a pro, knows exactly what he's doing.'

They watched as the black-clad figure got into the Beemer and made his exit. Joe nodding as the boy came out of the stairwell shooting.

'Kid's got some balls, got to give him that. Get Richard down to the nick, double quick. Make sure the filth behave themselves with him.' He stared at the screen, shaking his head at the scattered bodies of his men. 'That bloke, he was something else. He was stone fucking cold. In, do the job, out. No drama, just business. That, my son, is an assassin.'

Eddie would have rolled his eyes at the repressed excitement in Joe's voice. Except Joe had turned to look at him, so he just nodded.

'Someone's coming after me, Eddie. Someone nasty. And they're using hit men. Which means that we need to get our shit in a pile, before this gets any worse. I want to talk to Felgate, and I want to talk to that kid.'

He rolled his head on his neck. Like a boxer loosening up for a fight.

'Go back through the recordings. See if you can find him dropping the car off. And now you can bring out the prick who was supposed to be running this operation for you. I think a few well-chosen words are in order. Not to mention a tickle or two from Lewis. Success is its own reward, but failure needs a more results-based approach. Don't you think?'

11

Mickey strolled up the road from the railway station, feeling exhausted. He'd driven the rental back to Martin's lockup. Returned the weapon and drunk a cup of tea with his friend. Recounting the events of the last hour with a feeling of detachment. As if someone else had wreaked all that havoc. Martin had listened to him talk. Expressionless. Giving no clue as to his thoughts on the matter. Which was just as well, because all Mickey had wanted was to unload.

He stopped to look in a charity shop window. Wondering why, even as he listlessly examined the items on offer. Insight came with an unbidden memory. Of talking to a uniformed skipper a few years before. A decent bloke, with a solid reputation. Chatting, as they shared a cigarette break before a royal event. Exchanged backgrounds, Job ritual along with "when's your thirty up then?". And the sergeant in question had proved to be an interesting case. An ex-RAF non-commissioned officer, he'd flown drones over the Middle East for three years. Before deciding to take his leave of the Air Force and do something less stressful instead. He'd laughed at Mickey's look of incomprehension.

'Less stressful than sitting in a portacabin in Lincolnshire, playing with model planes, you're thinking. The thing about being a drone pilot is the sense of unreality. You look at the world below through a camera and a satellite feed. And you follow instructions from the spooks. Fly *there*. Film *that*. Drop a Hellfire on *them*.'

'Hellfire?'

'Anti-tank missile. Sounds nice and precise, doesn't it. Except it isn't.' He saw Mickey's lack of comprehension. 'Fifty-metre lethal blast radius. Means you get collateral damage. That's innocents dead and maimed, if we're not doing the official language. They started using Brimstones after I punched out. Same missile, smaller warhead. Less risk of collateral. Made the Yanks ever so jealous. But in my day it was the Hellfire. With collateral unavoidable. A necessary evil.'

'Ah.'

'It affected everyone differently, of course. I knew people who walked away after their first kill. The RAF let them go, of course; they were no use behind a stick from that moment. But there was at least one guy who was completely unaffected. Nice enough bloke too. Just not bothered by the implications of what he was doing. He's probably still doing it now.'

'Essential work though.'

'Yeah, I told myself that. Kept me going for another year. Wasn't me who made the decision to leave in the end.' Mickey looked at him questioningly. 'The wife. She was supportive for as long as she could be. Problem was, every time I punched off a missile and took out a target, it hollowed me out just a little bit more. I could still function, but with every shot I took she said there was a bit less of me left. The real me, the man she married. So she gave me the ultimatum.'

'And you walked.'

'Fuck yes I walked. I worship the ground that woman walks on. And the thing is, I knew she was right. All the special duty pay in the world wasn't any use when I came home like a zombie. Silent through dinner, asleep by twenty-one hundred. Ignoring the kids. Ignoring her. It took me a year to properly start getting over it.'

He'd taken another drag. Pinched the butt out and dropped it in the steel bin provided.

'I talked to a few of the guys who'd fought on the ground in Helmand. Helped me to understand what my problem was. Turns out, killing in the field is one thing. Because you've got mates to share it with. Help you talk it through. And of course the first one of your mates gets his leg blown off, it makes it personal. Makes shooting to kill a whole lot easier. But killing a man, from a portacabin in Lincolnshire? Not knowing who else might have been caught in the blast? And then just going home for dinner? Too corrosive for me.'

Standing in the street, looking at a window full of other people's cast-offs, Mickey finally, completely, understood the point he'd been making. About the price of vengeance being the loss of the revenger's humanity. Took a deep breath and wondered whether to burst into tears. Decided not to, even if it would have been therapeutic. Started walking again, composing himself. Walked in to find Roz busy baking. Some coffee morning for cancer or other. Kissed her and went upstairs to change.

Diverted to the bathroom, realising he needed to use the toilet. Hands shaking, explosive diarrhoea. His body telling him it wasn't happy at being flushed with adrenaline like that. He showered. Dried himself off. And took a long, hard look in the mirror. Looking a bit tired. But OK, overall.

Through the physiological reaction to combat, perhaps. But without any hint of the quiet elation he'd felt with Warren's death. Was that strange, given he'd just taken four evil bastards off the board? Plus an adolescent gang fantasist who was undoubtedly going to turn out bad, if he'd lived. And fired a body blow into Joe Castagna's operation.

'You going to be all night up there?'

Called up the stairs in that mock-gruff way she had of showing affection. And momentarily, Mickey wondered just what the hell he thought he was doing. Taking so many risks. Risking prison. And losing Roz. And that was before the danger that Joe Castagna posed. Then flashed on the image of the last of them going backwards through the doors. Brought to justice. Mickey's justice, without the right of appeal. No obfuscation by smart lawyers. No threatening of defenceless jurors. And he nodded slowly at the face in the mirror.

Worth it. Almost. Because at the back of his mind a quiet, relentless voice was muttering the same words, over and over. So quietly as to be almost transparent, mentally. And yet so insistently that he knew it was the first thing he was going to think about when he woke up the next day.

And now the clock's ticking.

12

'Come on in, little man. We're all friends here.'
Eddie shepherded the boy into Joe's office. Noted, and was unsurprised by, the child's awed reaction. If the kitchen was a masterpiece of shining metal and marble, Joe's inner sanctum was something else. As far from the stereotypical man cave as you could get without reaching orbit. A screen the size of a five-a-side goal dominated one wall. Flanked by a pair of B&O speakers the height of a tall man. On the other side of the room, a single-paned panoramic window looked out onto the terrace where Nigel had met his grisly end. On the other sat a desk the size of a decent dining table, pristinely empty. Joe was sitting on one of three large leather chesterfield sofas arranged around the TV, beckoning the boy to join him. Eddie tapped the kid on the shoulder.

'Go on, he don't bite.'

He does have legs broken though. And he's definitely been known to make people disappear, he thought. But decided not to add. The boy walked across the room slowly, as if balancing on a high wire. His gaze locked disbelievingly on Joe. He perched on the other end of the sofa. His expression stuck somewhere between simple awe and just completely losing his shit.

'You're Samuel, right?' Got a nod in reply. 'All right, Samuel, we're gonna call you Sammy. Because we like you. We like you a lot. Some of my own men wouldn't have shown the guts you did.'

Samuel's mother, grieving the loss of her older son, had reluctantly returned to her cleaning job that morning. Leaving her son to be unexpectedly picked up from their door an hour later. Samuel not really having been given much choice in the matter, but in a kindly enough way. A pair of hard-looking men in suits had walked him to a large black Mercedes SUV. Watched by his disbelieving peers, who knew the car was Joe's just as well as he did. And, when they got there, Cockfosters was a revelation. Green. Well kept. And with big houses that had proper gardens. Joe's house another step up again. Like a royal palace, to a boy used to a two-bed flat.

'Your mum should be proud of you. I know I am. Four of my men killed right in front of you. And your big brother. And still you had the balls to pick up a gun and come out shooting.'

'How did you know that?'

Joe grinned at the forthright nature of the question. Looked round at his assembled lieutenants.

'Kid's fearless. None of you pussies would ask me a question that way, would you? I tell you, this little man is going to be in my crew when he's grown.' He winked at the boy. 'Thing is, Sammy, I know a lot more things than I'm supposed to. I know the car that the shooter left the estate in had two bullet holes in the boot. I know that because the filth found it a mile away, burned out. And I know that not one of the muppets he ambushed managed to get a shot off. The only gun fired was the one that put those holes in the back of my Beemer. And the only man left standing when he drove off was you. You, Sammy, were the only man to stand up and fight. And for doing that, I'm going to employ you. A hundred quid a week to start with, paid into your own account. And all I want from you in the short term is one thing.'

'What's that?'

'That, Sammy boy, is your ears. Not literally. I ain't had anyone's ears off for years.'

Eddie made a mental note to always make sure he had a nice sharp blade from now on. Joe would order some miscreant or other to have an earlobe carved off inside the month, now that he'd reminded himself of the idea. And it didn't pay not to be ready for Joe's orders.

'You see, you're the only person to have spoken to him. He was wearing a mask, right?'

'Black bally.'

'Yeah. Disguised his face, which was wise of him. But he didn't disguise his voice. And I know he spoke to you, because you told the filth he did. So when I catch him, or even just think I've caught him, I'll need your ears. You can listen to whoever I find talk, tell me if it's him. Bet that's one voice you'll never forget. What did he say to you?'

'Told us to run. Three times. And then a load of yak about how you make money from death.'

'Enough you'd know him again.' Samuel nodded confidently. 'Good lad. Right, off you go. Eddie's boys will drop you back off at home. Bet you're a clever one, right?'

The boy nodded. 'Top set in maths and science.'

'I bet you are. And we'll make good use of those skills, when you're older. Give you some new ones too. In the meantime, keep thinking what he said to you. Because the time will come when a bloke's life hangs off it.'

13

Saturday morning. Mickey and Wade back on duty at the Hall. Mickey surprised to find Major Cavendish waiting for him.

'Morning, James. Don't they give you weekends off?'

The soldier tipped his head in recognition of the point. Smiled thinly.

'Good morning, Michael. Weekends don't really count for much in this job. Not when the shit and the fan collide with such force. The minister needs to go into London for a meeting with the PM. This morning.'

Mickey, whose second rule was that Mickey Bale was never to be seen to be surprised, nodded equably. While diary planning was usually impeccable, short-notice meetings between the big man and his cabinet were not unknown.

'No problem, James. When would he like to be driven...'

He fell silent, taking in the look on Cavendish's face.

'I'm going to assume from your insouciance that you haven't seen the papers yet.'

Mickey shook his head. He had, of course, a sneaky peek on the train into London. Curious to see what the press had made of what he'd done the previous evening. So when the major raised a broadsheet, he was ready with the deadpan face. The *Clarion*, as it happened, and Mickey thought momentarily about Tamara. Hoping she'd seen sense and gone to harass some other public figure. The bastion of red-top journalism having excelled itself. The half-page headline announcing: 'Gang War Slaughter!' With the last word printed twice the size beneath the first two.

'It's good to see that the art of good old-fashioned tabloid emphasis hasn't been completely lost.'

James raised an eyebrow at Mickey.

'Not the drugs massacre. The criminal underclass can kill each other all they like. This.'

He pointed to a secondary headline. Mickey read it. Shrugged.

'"Defence Minister Scandal Deepens?" I'd imagine that's one article that'll be shot through with *allegedly* and *informed sources*.'

'Quite so. And not a shred of hard proof. But the prime minister isn't best pleased, it seems. And so Sir Patrick will be attending what I can only imagine will be a meeting without biscuits in…' Cavendish consulted a Patek Philippe worth roughly the equivalent of Mickey's annual salary. 'One hour and forty-eight minutes. We'll have the car ready to leave in twenty, shall we?'

Mickey checked the Jaguar they'd booked out that morning. Made sure it was squeaky clean inside, wiped away a few flecks of road dirt from the paint. And then waited, Wade ready in the driving seat. Engine running, ready to go. Cavendish escorted the minister out of the front door right on time. Sir Patrick's face just about as grim as Mickey had expected. He opened the car door, greeting the minister in the expected manner.

'Good morning, sir.'

Expecting no response. And got none. Perhaps a vestige of the usual curt nod. Hardly a people person, the minister. Not that Mickey gave a shit. This, as he repeated to himself routinely, was just a job. He closed the passenger door. Waited until Major Cavendish had taken his seat alongside Sir Patrick. Made one last careful scan of their surrounds. Satisfied that all was well, he boarded last, shooting Wade a meaningful glance. The meaning being that today, of all days, required a smooth drive. And his fellow officer, being astute enough to know the score, delivered.

Up the long drive, tall hedges on either side. Out through the gate, past the scattered photographers. The snappers caught off-guard by the small convoy's unexpected exit. Through country lanes for a mile, then onto the M40. Accelerating smoothly up to the legal limit and holding it there. The car's occupants obeying the unwritten etiquette of ministerial travel. Prot officers not speaking unless necessary, and not to the principal unless addressed or for operational reasons. Who in this case busied himself with his smartphone. Rallying allies, perhaps. Or just trying to nail a difficult crossword.

Mickey had broken one of his own cardinal rules during his time off. Driven by curiosity to read up on the man he was guarding. And found himself both impressed and disquieted. Sir Patrick Sutherland, age fifty-seven. Born in the Sixties to unremarkable parents. His childhood spent in an unfashionable Midlands railway town. A decent education had led to a place at Cambridge. Earned, fair and square. A bright boy, young Patrick.

Fresh out of university, he'd opted for five years in the

army. Grenadier Guards, perhaps not the instinctive choice for a middle-class boy lacking a private income. Evidence that he was determined if nothing else. And the Guards, working hard to meet a changing social landscape, had done right by him. But what came next was to impact his life for decades. Proof that it's not what you know, but who.

Leaving the regiment, he'd gone straight into merchant banking. The City being a traditional route into lucrative employment for a chap from a good regiment. And then found himself just as quickly back out again. Not "one of us", the overall sense from the unauthorised biographies. And, perhaps predictably, the making of him. Mickey smiling to himself that they shared a derogatory title. Although in Sutherland's case it stood for "Failed In London Try Hong Kong".

He'd been a multi-millionaire inside five years. Ten times as rich inside ten. His business empire growing steadily despite the end of British rule. A billionaire by the time he was forty-five. Profiting from the rise of China's dragon through astute investments. He'd learned to speak Mandarin, rather than Cantonese. And mastered the knack of cultivating close relationships with the right people.

Relationships based, it seemed, on carefully concealed bribery. The evidence thin to non-existent, of course. A rare picture of his being helped to leave a banquet all that Mickey could find on the internet. Clearly heavily intoxicated, plum wine copiously spilled down his Jermyn Street shirt. But nothing more salacious proven, despite the rumours. Expensive escorts, luxurious gifts, outright bribery. All behind closed doors. All deniable. And boys will be boys. With no wife to spill the beans, on finding herself scorned.

He'd been knighted in 2004 for his prodigious and carefully targeted UK charitable giving. Not to mention a significant backhander to the ruling party. And then, counter-intuitively, he'd decided to try his hand at politics. Perhaps reasoning that what had made him rich could also make him powerful. Put his business empire into a blind trust and joined the Tories. Handily, just in time to participate in their predictable resurgence at the fag end of Labour rule. Had served as a backbencher for a few years. A test of the Johnny-come-lately's stickability. Proving himself loyal. And, critically, always on message when called on to defend a difficult policy. More than capable of putting a hostile interviewer on the back foot. Adroit, even. Which had resulted in him starting his ascent of the slippery pole of power. Displaying all the skills of a veteran.

First step: junior minister. Department of Business, Innovation and Skills, naturally enough. His innate understanding of deal-making and relationships with China making him a stellar performer. Promotion to Under-Secretary had followed. Sutherland working hard to champion the cause of globalisation in general. And China in particular. Both in his day job and after hours. Hosting dinner parties with powerful attendees from the Middle Kingdom. Who let it be known that they were looking for influential people to join their think tanks and lobbying efforts. Quickly gathering a roll call of recently retired senior UK politicians and academics to their cause. Their other main choice for lucrative sinecures being to break bread with the unspeakable lizard men who controlled social media. No choice at all, it seemed.

Sutherland was by that point no longer any sort of

outsider. Welcome in all the right places and by all the right people. And eased back into the old boy's association fold by his former regiment with suspiciously astute timing. A new PM leading to a new challenge. One suited to a man with military experience. Catapulted into the cabinet, he'd taken the helm at the MOD. A move some observers found interesting, given his close links to the biggest long-term threat to the UK. Their sniping from the pages of the broadsheet press ignored by the establishment. And beneath his dignity as a patriotic citizen to even comment on.

A series of carefully staged photoshoots had cemented his reputation as a hard man, ready to defend the realm. Pictured with the SAS: "Britain's stealth warriors". On the bridge of a brand-new aircraft carrier: "Britain's big stick". On the flight deck of a Globemaster transport plane: "Britain's global reach". By the close of the decade, Sir Patrick Sutherland was very much looking like tomorrow's man. Well positioned for a major cabinet role. Rumours mentioned the Home Office. The current incumbent being viewed as lightweight and with numbered days. And after that, well, who knew?

And then, in the space of a few months, the bottom had dropped out of his world. China, abruptly no longer anyone's idea of an acceptable regime, given the mounting evidence of a Uighur genocide to rival Nazi Germany. Forced life-ending organ donations from live prisoners. Compulsory re-marriage of Uighur women whose husbands were interned to Han Chinese men. And, of course, its role in the biggest catastrophe to hit the UK since 1945. A hardening public mood had politicians of all shades running for the moral high ground. Which meant that Sutherland been looking increasingly isolated even before the latest rumours.

They drove into the other end of Downing Street, off Horse Guards, ten minutes before the appointed meeting time. Leaving the gate guards to mind the vehicle, Mickey and Wade escorted Sir Patrick and the major down the steps and into the basement level of Number 10. Where stone-faced members of the Met's Parliamentary and Diplomatic Protection unit waited to check them in.

Mickey, like most coppers in the know, still thought of PaDP as what they used to be called. The Diplomatic Protection Group. Or Doors, Porches and Gates, in one moderately polite alternative. The term 'Post Monkeys' having been forbidden on pain of the disciplinary process being applied. Although that hadn't stopped a previous deputy assistant commissioner dubbing them, along with their Royalty Residential and Aviation Policing Command colleagues, the "Triangle of Laziness". To universal and poorly concealed merriment.

The skipper in charge of the entrance checkpoint gestured to the empty Prot office.

'You can wait here, lads, or get a coffee in the canteen.'

Mickey and Wade chose the lesser of two evils, if only by a nose. Sloping off to the basement canteen. Plastic chairs, vending machines, wet trays and the smell of microwaved bacon. All the charm of a chain hotel breakfast buffet. Two cups of machine tea, the caffeine alternative being, from both men's recent experience, unpalatable.

'That was fun. Times like these, I'm happy that you're the skipper. Good thing we weren't taking him to Glasgow, eh?'

They sat, blowing on their scalding tea, enjoying the momentary change of pace from constant readiness for anything. Mickey exchanged greetings with Roz via WhatsApp, sending her a heart-eyed face emoji and getting 'I love you too, you muppet' back.

'So what are your plans, Skip? For when your thirty's up, I mean.'

Mickey turned to his colleague with a resigned look.

'You too, eh? I thought you were better than that, Wade.' He raised a hand to forestall the protest. 'I know, you're just making conversation.' He grinned. 'And it's not like that's the only thing coppers ever talk about, is it?' Thought for a minute. 'Truth is, it isn't something I've given much thought to. Private bodyguarding, I suppose, while I'm still young enough.'

'Private sector, Skip? You? I doubt you'd last a year.'

'It's not like there's much alternative. Not for decent money, anyway. Not that I delude myself I'll like it any more than anyone else who's done it.'

Wade nodded agreement. 'I bet you wouldn't miss the boredom though. I mean take this. Here we are, waiting around with jack shit to do.' He sighed. 'I once tried to work out how much of my life I've spent hanging around doing fuck all. Just waiting for something to happen.'

'But you ran out of fingers and couldn't get your shoes off?'

The other man ignored the jibe.

'That photographer was the first bit of excitement I've had since the last royal wedding. And even then it was you who made the collar.'

Mickey raised an eyebrow at him.

'Yeah, but you'd miss the buzz. Not to mention the authority over lesser mortals. Wouldn't you?'

Wade nodded slowly. The two men sharing a knowing smile.

'Yeah, wouldn't I just. The first time I had a uniformed inspector take instruction from me on how to deploy his serial down a parade route was just...'

'Unreal. And addictive. Not many roles like it in the Job.'

'And you think you could go from that to carrying Mrs Oligarch's shopping? It'd be one great big let-down.'

The PaDP skipper put his head round the corner.

'Heads up, boys, your principal's going to be on the move in two minutes.'

The two men looked at each other, Mickey making a show of looking at the Black Bay with a raised eyebrow before getting to his feet. Leaving his tea half drunk.

'Ten minutes, soup to nuts? Ye gods. If he was chilly on the way here, I dread to think what he's going to be like on the way back.'

The minister emerged a minute after they got back to the door. Walking fast, his gaze fixed on the floor. White-faced, either from shock or anger. Steadfastly refusing eye contact. He climbed into the car and pulled the door shut, not waiting for Mickey to close it. Cavendish shot Mickey a look as he walked around the vehicle's rear. Back at the Hall the minister was out of the car the moment it was stationary. Not waiting for Mickey to get out, much less open his door for him. He vanished into the house, leaving Cavendish and the Prot officers staring after him.

'You know I can't say a word about what I heard. And I'd suggest that you forget you saw his reaction to it.'

Mickey nodded at Cavendish, a faint smile on his face.

'Prot officers aren't big on that sort of detail in any case. The way I see it, the less I know, the better. That way I can't ever find myself in a closed misconduct hearing for letting something slip. Although I'll take one bet with you.'

The major raised an eyebrow, reluctantly drawn in by Mickey's grin.

'Go on then. I can't wait to see what you think might be funny about this.'

'You mentioned a meeting without biscuits.' He paused for a moment. Every copper knowing the secret of comedy to be timing. 'The speed you were in and out, I'd give decent odds there wasn't any coffee either.'

14

Joe hadn't ever been in the press before. Not properly, anyway. Sure, there was the occasional rumble about London crime families. Mainly focusing on his grandfather's wilder exploits in the Fifties and Sixties. The stuff of legend, alongside the Krays and Mad Frankie. But Joe had a considerable legitimate business. Built by his old man, the second Giuseppe. His name usually abbreviated to Big G by his men, on account of him having been taller than his old man. Castagna Property having become a serious player in the Seventies and Eighties. In the days before the authorities got properly wise to money laundering. Property, building, development. Originally built on dirty money, but now as clean as driven snow. Managed by professionals, employing thousands of people. All of which made Joe a legitimate businessman.

The dirty money his clandestine empire spewed out didn't come back onshore, once it was clean. It went to buy more product. More women. More drugs. With no traceability back to Joe. That, and property in far-off places. Lots of it. One of these days Joe was going to abandon the UK, Eddie reckoned. Go and live in the sun like the properly rich man he was. While he was young enough to enjoy it. A day, Eddie reckoned, which would be a profound relief for more than a few people. Including, it had to be said, Eddie himself.

And so it had come as something of a surprise to Joe when a crowd of press reporters had appeared at the front gate. Held at bay by hastily drafted uniformed security. Fifteen of them, all print media from the look of it. No news cameras yet. 'Give it time though,' he'd muttered through clenched teeth.

Richard counselled him to ignore them. Calm as you like. Urbane, even. But then it wasn't his name on the front pages.

'Once it rains they'll soon get bored. Give them time, there'll be another story for them to chase. Look at this royal thing, for example. There's plenty of juice in that. All it takes is for that idiot to take another piss on the family reputation and you're tomorrow's chip wrapper.'

Eddie had been inclined to agree with Richard, when considering the day in his bathtub that evening. Joe's response to his innocent enough remark had indeed been a little unkind.

'Yesterday's chip wrapper, Richard? In case you hadn't noticed, I'm today's fucking headline news.'

He'd crossed the room, putting his face six inches from his lawyer's. Removing the need to raise his voice. Joe having long known that speaking quietly was way more threatening. Close enough that Richard looked properly unnerved. His employer explaining the error of his ways at knife-fighting range. Social distancing clearly not on his list of priorities. His demeanour that deceptive uber-calm that was when he was at his most dangerous.

'This, Richard, could put me out of business. All it takes is for another crew to decide I'm ripe for taking and they'll all be on me. Like something out of an Attenborough show. Hyenas on a wounded lion. And I'm forced to reflect that this is pretty much all down to you. Isn't it?'

He waited for a moment while Richard's brow had creased. The smooth-suited lawyer momentarily lost for words. Trying to work out how he was at the root of the attack.

'You don't get it, do you?' Joe turned away. Shaking his head in evident frustration. 'When you suggested I tone down the punishments, I did. When you advised me not to draw attention to my activities, I followed your advice. And when you said I might be better off finding different ways to communicate my displeasure to those of my people who failed me, I tried to do so.'

Eddie wasn't sure he'd done any of those things. But Eddie wasn't about to interject with Joe quite so white with anger.

He walked away to the kitchen window, staring through the blinds at the cluster of people gathered at his front gate.

'And now it seems as if listening to you was a mistake. Because now those people out there are ready to put the boot in. And all because we failed to keep the right level of fear out on the street, I'd say.'

He stared through the window for a moment. Still shaking his head in disgust.

'Get a lawyer. Get a *proper* lawyer. One of those big firms with the fancy names.'

Richard nodded, the implied slur as to his abilities ignored in his relief at no longer being the potential target of Joe's ire. Joe's patronage – ownership, he'd have admitted in a reflective moment – brought him many good things. Nice house. Tick. School fees. Tick. The ability to keep his wife in the style to which she had become accustomed. Tick. Holidays in exotic places. Tick. Porsche, 911 obviously. Tick. But it also brought those occasional moments of fear – terror – when Joe's inner demon rose to show its teeth. Big, sharp teeth.

'You want me to put an injunction on the papers?'

Joe stared at him for a moment, with that patient look. The one that told you he was trying to work out just how big a cunt you were.

'I want you to put the frighteners on them. I want them to know that I've got deep pockets. And a very short fuse. I want them to cease, *Dick*. And indeed I want them to desist as well. And I want it fucking *now*.'

Richard took his cue, and his opportunity, and left. Sharpish. Drove past the hacks and snappers, ineffectually shielding his face with one hand.

'Right, now that idiot's gone to play with himself, you and I need to talk.' Eddie, aware that Joe's temper was still bubbling volcanically beneath the calm veneer, simply nodded. 'I've been thinking. We need to up security on the cash. Move the counting houses more often. Double the number of guards, and make sure they're properly tooled. And tell them the next crew to get ripped off gets buried by me. Personally, dead or alive. So there'd better be someone other than a twelve-year-old shooting back next time. It stops, Eddie. Here and now. So I suggest you go and sort it?'

The last two words spat out with the sort of rare

vehemence that told him Joe was on the edge of a melt-up. Time to go.

'Oh, and Eddie?' Eddie paused at the door, knowing that Joe had timed it perfectly. Let him get nine-tenths of the way out, then reeled him back. 'Felgate. I want to meet him.'

'He won't like it.'

Shrug from Joe. Who knew that he was the only one with any choice in the matter.

'I couldn't give a fuck. I pay that bent bastard enough every year that he'll never have to worry who's going to wipe his arse when he's old.'

Eddie nodded. It was true enough: Jason Felgate was properly on the payroll. Generously so.

'You just tell him something from me, eh Eddie? Tell him that if I don't start seeing some results, getting old won't be a problem he ever has to deal with. And tell him I want a face-to-face. Tomorrow.'

15

Mickey was sharing a coffee and a chat with James Cavendish in the private secretary's office when the papers arrived the next morning. The major spread them across the floor at their feet, grimacing at the front pages.

'Ah, here's this morning's daily dosage of unhappiness for Sir Patrick. What they'd be printing if they weren't keeping the gloves on, I shudder to think.'

'This is restrained?'

Mickey waved a hand at the slew of headlines. Most of which seemed to centre on the minister's visit to Number 10. Which, given they'd managed to get in and out without being papped, could only mean that the press had been briefed. Off the record, of course.

A formal announcement from Number 10 had been provided. Stating that the minister's business dealings of the last two decades were a well-known matter of record. As were his close relationships with certain members of "the Beijing regime". And that the prime minister was well aware of both and keeping an open mind. Not prepared to be rushed to judgement. Doubtless when the issue was inevitably raised in a press conference, he'd make some mention of Solomon in his wisdom. And about right too, given the king's ability to go through concubines.

So pretty much "no comment" for the most part. But the very fact of the announcement being made at all had hit the press and social media like a low-yield media nuke. With all the expected fallout in every possible direction.

'Restrained? Yes, I suspect it is.' James pursing his lips, looking around before continuing. 'You only have to scratch the internet on the subject to see where the story might be going.'

'Which is?'

'It's not pretty, Michael. Not pretty at all. The best case is that he's been in China's pocket for the last twenty years. And tempted a fair few people who probably should have known better to get in there with him. Important people. Possibly unethical, but hardly illegal. But the worst case… is much, much worse. Treason, basically. Now that the rules of the game have changed so dramatically.'

'Treason? So why aren't the press going with that? I'd have thought they'd be all over it like flies on fresh shit?'

The major paused again. 'I can tell you why I think they're holding back. But you'll have to promise not to repeat it to anyone. Not even your man Wade.'

Mickey resisted the temptation to fall back on Job humour in the pause that followed. While James waited for his answer, wearing a serious face. Mickey knowing that a cheap joke probably wouldn't land well. Actually wanting to hear the other man's view. But there was something deeper too. A colleague was reaching out, offering an insight.

'I can keep it to myself.'

'I'm sure you can.' James thought for a moment.

'Thing you have to bear in mind, Michael, is that I'm a Grenadier, first and foremost. I probably wouldn't be in this godforsaken job if I weren't. I know exactly the call that went out, when Sir Patrick's tumble from grace started.'

'To find someone they could trust?'

James smiled wanly. 'More than that. They went looking for an insider. Someone so close to the whole ethos of the regiment that they could be trusted *implicitly*. Someone who would instinctively put the regiment and therefore the army first every time. And they found me.'

'And you're perfect for it?'

'Yes, sad to say, I am. Active service as a young subaltern, without any major mistakes. Two more tours after that. A medium-weight gallantry decoration, to buff the image. For an act of overconfident stupidity under fire that I managed to get away with. And having achieved the ideal rank for this sort of role.'

Mickey frowned. 'Ideal?'

James waved a dismissive hand. 'I'm a major, Michael. Significant, but disposable.' He smiled bleakly at Mickey. 'I'm the perfect man for this benighted role. Utterly, totally, unimpeachably trustworthy. And, in the event that matters get too hot to handle, I can be dropped over the side with Sir Patrick. I'm the spy in his camp, and he knows it, of course. Doubtless he's busy telling everyone he knows what a shit I am. Which means I'm going to find getting any sort of decent job a bit of a stretch, when this is all done with.'

'It all sounds a bit piss-poor for you, put that way.'

'Quite so.' Cavendish shook his head in bemusement. 'Certainly not quite the glorious end to my career I'd envisaged. Mind you, it could be worse.'

He pulled a paper from the collection. With a rare headline, not focused on allegations of ill-considered mendacity and depravity on the part of the man they both served.

'See? "Faces of evil!" I wouldn't want to be any of those gentlemen this morning, would you?'

Mickey looked at the paper. The *Clarion*, of course. Known for ploughing its own furrow. Refusing to run with the press hounds. Alone in not having chosen to go with the Sutherland story. And froze, momentarily. Staring back at him, one of three men pictured, was Joe Castagna. Recovered his equilibrium, hoping that the momentary shock had gone unnoticed. Scanned the page for the picture credit. *Clarion Newspaper Group/Tamara Egerton. Shit.*

16

'Clarion Group.'

'I'd like to speak to the picture desk please.'

Mickey waited while his call was directed, looking at the *Clarion*'s front page. The three men whose faces had been letterboxed to fit next to the headline were all familiar, from his research of the past few months.

Joe Castagna caught staring out through his kitchen window at dusk. His face an exercise in light and dark. Looking like the truly evil bastard he was. Brilliant photography. Even if the camera had done all the technical heavy lifting. Tamara Egerton clearly had a talent.

His right-hand man Eddie Hickey. Shaved head, hard eyes. Reputedly Joe's right-hand man from day one. One of the few people able to unblinkingly match his brutal sadism. Looking out through an open doorway, his stare icy.

His lawyer, Richard Holmes. Nominally his brief. In reality little better than a procurer of the best legal minds going. The kind of lawyers who'd sell their soul. And their genius. Caught climbing into his car in the same half-light. His expression deliberately blank.

Three faces. Their expressions differing, but the subtext the same for all three. These were the men who trafficked helpless women. Who smuggled drugs into the country. And sold both commodities, regardless of the harm they did to product or buyer. Not to mention all the other routine gang crimes. Protection. Fraud. Extortion. The usual litany of the strong preying on the weak. The way it had been since the dawn of humanity.

'Picture desk, Mark speaking.'

'Good morning Mark. I'm the policeman who arrested Ms Egerton in Beaconsfield last week.'

'Constable.'

The first syllable predictably pitched to be an insult.

'Yes, well the old ones are, unfortunately, the old ones.' He paused to allow the disparaging reply to sink in. 'Given your hostility perhaps I should hang up? I'll just nick your photographer friend, shall I? Rather than give her a chance to avoid being banged up? Let her sit in a cell for forty-eight hours and tell her it's down to your infantile sense of humour?'

'Wait, what? What grounds could you—'

'Possibly have for that? The fact that she was arrested inside the security perimeter of a secretary of state's private residence. But please, do keep arguing.'

'So... what is it that you want?'

'A swift conversation with Ms Egerton.'

'Well I'm not giving you her number.'

Mickey laughed softly.

'I don't need you to, Mark. I could call her now, if I wanted to. But I don't know where she might be. Always a bit of a problem if you're camped out in a gang leader's hedge and the phone goes off just as his goons walk past. Isn't it?'

'Er... yeah.'

Perhaps a hint more sympathy in the voice at the other end.

'So ask her to call me please. You can see the number on your caller display, I'd imagine.'

'OK... give me a minute.' Mickey waited while Mark wrote the number down. 'Got it. So, what's your n—'

He cut the call off. The probability was that she'd either call within the next five minutes or not at all. If it was the latter, then the matter was out of his hands. He waited, flicking through the newspaper. The same crusading tone as ever. "Your *Clarion*". "A challenging newspaper for challenging times". "We sound the alarm on uncontrolled immigration/top boss's pay rises/Islamist extremist infiltration of society". Populist pick 'n' mix. Taking undoubtedly uncomfortable truth and adding an unsubtle political twist.

His phone rang.

'Mickey Bale.'

'I thought this was Thames Valley Police?'

There's that self-assurance, he thought.

'Ah, well I didn't say I was Thames Valley Police. Just that I was a policeman who arrested you in Beaconsfield.'

'You're the man with the gun, right? The all-right-looking one.'

'You're too kind.'

'Well you did me a huge favour. Being arrested at gunpoint is the sort of thing the grumpy old bastards with cameras like to boast about. So now I can tell them to stop whingeing and get away with it!'

He laughed softly. Flashing on the image of her defiant expression after arrest.

'I'm glad being thrown off the premises was so good for you.'

'My dad always tells me to take the positives, Mister Bale. So tell me, what can I do for you?'

He paused for a moment. Knowing how unlikely his answer was going to sound.

'I saw your pics in the paper. On the front page. Faces of evil. Great work, by the way.'

'Thank you. And…?'

'I'm guessing you got those shots from somewhere quite close by. Longish lens, to get in nice and close, but not from a mile away. Right? More like two hundred metres.'

'Keep talking.'

He laughed softly. 'You've been hiding in the bushes again, haven't you?'

'It's not exactly illegal, Sergeant.'

'No.' He allowed the silence to drag out a little. 'It isn't. But I'll tell you what it *is*. If you want to know?'

Make her ask the question. And, therefore, listen to the answer.

'You're going to tell me that taking photographs is dangerous?'

She'd seen where he was going with it. And sounded unimpressed.

'More than you'll ever know. Unless they catch you at it. But if that happens, you'll get far too intimate an understanding of the risk I'm trying to point out.'

'Really? What, you think they might *rough me up*?'

The last three words in that mock-terrified "ooh I'm scared" tone used by people who weren't scared.

'*Rough you up?*' Gave her that acid tone back, with a good squeeze of sarcasm. 'No. I don't.'

A hint of perplexity crept into her voice. 'So…'

'Why the call?' Mickey allowed some of the irritation he was genuinely feeling to show. 'Let me put it this way. Do you know how many people disappear in Greater London every year? I don't mean wander off, stay lost for a while, tearful reunion, all ends well. I mean never seen again. Hundreds. One or two a day. Lost among the thousand or so calls a day regarding missing persons. And if you were one of them, the excitement over your loss would last for a week or two. Unless someone came across your body.'

'You're not trying to say th—'

'Trust me, if Joe Castagna makes you disappear, you're not going to be found. Not unless he wants you to be. And the time between you being taken and going into the cement wouldn't be the happiest days of your life.'

'He'd be arrested! The *Clarion* would know what I was doing, and where I was.'

He gave it a moment's silence. A telephonic shrug.

'Joe would just no comment the whole thing. He employs the best lawyers that money can buy. And there'd be no evidence. No trace of you. And, as the press would soon enough reveal, you wouldn't be the first. Just the best known. Until the next one.'

The tone of her voice was different now. Less bullish. 'So what are you telling me?'

Christ, how clear did he have to make it? 'To stop covertly papping Joe Castagna. Sure, stand at his gate with the mob and take your pics. But for the love of God stop doing the undercover thing.'

'I'll think about it.'

'You'll think about it? Think hard, Ms Egerton, and think fast. Because this is the best warning you'll get.'

'And this warning. It's from you, right? Not from anyone else? Not because he's paying you? Not because you're investigating him?'

He laughed. Not having considered that she'd suspect self-interest.

'No. I'm not on Joe's payroll. Although he will have cops in his pocket. I guarantee you that. And no, I'm not part of an investigation team. You know what I do for a living. Although I can't guarantee there isn't such an investigation in place.'

And then shut his mouth, pretty sure he'd said enough.

'All right, I'll do it. Stop doing it, I mean.'

Mickey opened his mouth to say *good*, but it was his turn to get chopped off before he could speak.

'But there's a price.'

'A *what*? You want something from me for potentially saving your skin?'

'An exclusive. Talk to me about what it's like in there with the minister.'

'Abso-fucking-lutely not.'

Her voice softened. 'Off the record. Unattributable. Just colour, no operation detail.'

'Give you that break into photojournalism you're craving? Not a chance. I'd have my nuts in the mangle for the rest of my life. Now you're going to tell me that sources are always protected. What would you do, when Special Branch pulled you in? And threatened you with jail, unless you cough up the name of your source?'

'Ah.'

'Yeah. Ah. Plus you were stupid enough to ask me over an open line. So all they'd have to do is examine your phone records in any case.'

A sigh. Concession of defeat?

'OK, tell you what, my best offer. I stop stalking Mr Murderous. You have a drink with me.'

He stared at the phone for a moment. 'Why?'

'Because you sound like a decent guy. And a girl needs all the friends she can get, in this game. Will you?'

17

'Detective Inspector Felgate.'
         'Mr Castagna.'

With most of his associates, Joe would have been happy to use first names. The fact that he didn't do so with his tame policeman spoke volumes as to their relationship. Something Felgate knew only too well. In days gone by Joe would have met a bent copper on the car park's top deck. Appreciating the lack of potential watchers, seven floors up. These days, who knew what might be overhead. Or, for that matter, overheard. So the two men were sitting in the back of the Rhino. Parked on an intermediate floor, with solid concrete above them. Felgate having been patted down and scanned for bugs first. Lewis and Lewis's deputy Rocco on guard. Rocco at street level to provide warning of any unexpected arrival. While Lewis was leaning against a concrete pillar close to the car. His jacket open to display the butt of his pistol. Giving precisely no shits whatsoever.

'What have you got for me then?'

Straight to business, Joe. No time to waste on small talk. Especially with a man he despised.

'Not very much, it has to be admitted.'

Joe fixed the shark eyes on his employee, wordlessly

communicating his disappointment. Following up with a terse instruction.

'So tell me what you do have.'

'The first murder was carried out with a small-calibre weapon. A pistol, most likely, a rifle being too difficult to—'

'I already know all that. And that you lot don't have any sort of any handle on it.'

Felgate shrugged. 'It was a professional job. At least from the look of it. All the killer left behind was the bullet. No shell case, no DNA, no footprints. Nothing. He was either a pro or bloody well coached.'

'And there are no suspects?'

'I did go for a word with one of our sergeants. Bloke I used to serve with, when we were both constables. His younger sister died after taking a contaminated pill he bought from Margetson.'

'You fancied him for it?'

A shake of the head. 'Not really. More like a box that I had to be seen to tick. He's a protection officer, for one thing, so he wouldn't want to risk—'

'Protection? So he's got access to guns?'

'Not really. He has to sign them in and out. And besides, the Met doesn't use .22s.'

Joe grunted, disappointed. 'What about the card?'

'Nothing useful forensically. And it could just be a smokescreen to cover up for an act of personal revenge.' Felgate knowing the card would have been on Joe's mind. A lot. One word, one symbol. His name, above a skull and crossbones. A threat. Direct and unmistakable.

'So the investigation into the Margetson shooting revealed nothing. What about the car park?'

'That got our attention, good and proper. Daily progress reports to ACC Frontline Crime. An entire MIT… sorry, Major Investigation Team. Twelve detectives led by a DCI. With his superintendent breathing down his neck.'

Joe skewered him with an exasperated look. 'And? I didn't ask you for the *Heat* magazine version. I couldn't give a shit who's trying to build their career on my blokes getting killed. All I want is a name. After which you can leave the rest to me.'

'It's early days. You can't—'

'Yes I *can*. You're not seriously trying to tell me you lot don't have anything?'

'Close to it.' Jason raised a hand to forestall another outburst. 'The car he used came up a blank. No VIN, no traceability. Probably bought from a back-street dealer. And nobody's going to put their hand up for that. Especially not with you involved.'

Joe nodded. His face telling Felgate that he liked the power implied by that fear, even as it frustrated him.

'And your car was no better. Two bullet holes, both made by the same 9mm pistol. Fired by a twelve-year-old who picked up one of the dead men's weapons. And that was all we got from the vehicle. Serious and Organised have been trying to trace the car's ownership, by the way. Without any luck.'

A grunt. Joe expecting nothing less from Eddie. And disinclined to tell Jason how that one worked.

'What else?'

'CCTV footage from the first responders who passed it on the road gave us nothing either. He was wearing a cap, brim low. No facial pic. No DNA, no footprints. Whoever it was wore gloves and overshoes. Which the MIT suspect was the case in the Margetson killing too.'

Joe jumped on that point. 'So there is a link?'

'They think it's possible. They're working on the basis that this is someone with a serious grudge against you. That, or a rival moving in.'

Joe thought for a minute. 'The list of men with a grudge against me probably isn't all that short. There was no card this time?'

'No. Which means the two may not be linked.'

'They're linked. I can feel it in my water, as my old granddad used to say. So, what do we know?'

'We know that our armed response vehicle on-board camera footage indicates that the driver of your BMW was white. And ballistics reckon that the weapon was probably the same MP5 that was used in a drive-by in Hackney last year. Which means it was probably a rental.'

Joe nodded. Eddie having already put the frighteners on every known weapons dealer. Without any result. The guns were coming from further afield. Or from an unknown source.

'And when it comes to rentals, we've got nothing. They're either already banged up or we don't know them. Doubtless you've had a quiet word with all the usual suppliers. But you might want to investigate a little more clandestinely.'

'Clandestinely?' Joe held up a hand to forestall any attempt at either explanation or humour. 'I know what the word means. What I don't know is what *you* mean.'

Jason's turn to shrug.

'Might be nothing.'

Joe snorted mirthlessly. 'You already gave me a bargain

bucket of fuck all. Try telling me something I might find valuable. Go on, just this once, surprise me. And while you're at it, why not try to justify the ten grand that goes into your pocket every month without the taxman ever getting a sniff?'

Jason nodded, apparently unruffled. Which might have impressed Joe, if he'd felt it was genuine. Truth was, he suspected that Jason reckoned he had Joe by the nuts. His knowledge of the Castagna family's operation. And his funds tucked away offshore. If push came to shove, and he had to turn Queen's on Joe, he wouldn't need to think twice. Whereas Joe knew that a swift application of Lewis could solve that problem easily enough. Wash whiter than white. The policeman pulled a serious face. Like he was about to impart something valuable.

'You might want to invest in someone with a working knowledge of the dark web. The Onion Ring router.'

'The *what*?'

'My words exactly, when a bright young DC brought me the idea. Google it. We reckon there's at least one dealer operating exclusively on the dark version of the internet. Hard to contact. Harder to buy from. Never deals on his own manor. Always does business somewhere wide open, with multiple entrances and exits. And never for big money, so it's not worth stiffing him on the deal. Low risk, reasonable income. And we reckon he's foreign, given the name he uses. Steph. Short for Stephane, my boys reckoned.'

'Jesus, really?'

Jason smiled, gratified to have Joe's full attention. 'We even tried to do business with him. And collar him, obviously. The first time round he must have smelt a rat.

Perhaps even traced our IP back to the nick. We never even got an answer. So the second time we covered our tracks. Managed to get hold of him. Arranged a rental. He gave us a location. Somewhere nice and open. But he never showed. Probably had us for police before we even reached the meet. So whoever it is, he's so low profile as to be almost invisible. You find him, you might just have the man who provided the shooters.'

Joe nodded slowly. 'I will. In the meantime you keep the information coming, right? I find you're holding anything back…'

'You won't. I know which side the butter goes.'

Joe turned the dead eyes on him one last time. 'Yeah. Just make sure you don't land butter side down.'

Felgate got out of the car and walked away. Leaving Joe wondering if his bent copper ever felt that itch between the shoulder blades. The one that came with the fear that he'd dined with the devil using too short a spoon. Eddie walked past him and climbed into the car in his place.

'You got anyone who knows the dark web?'

Eddie, not stupid, but no sort of expert on the internet, shook his head. 'I thought that was all just drugs. The Silk Road and that.'

Joe shook his head. 'Well apparently they've moved into renting out guns. So we need a hacker to help us track down whoever it was rented the gun that shot my guys. I suggest you get one.'

18

The WhatsApp message had arrived on Mickey's phone three months before. Unexpected and jaw-droppingly straight to the point.

'I know about your sister. I know what killed her. I know who dealt it.'

He'd frowned at the screen. Wondering if this was some sort of trolling. But kept reading.

'I know you want the people who killed her to pay. So do I.'

Do you now? he thought. And why would that be? Did you know Katie? Why else would you give a shit?

'I can give you that revenge. Proper, biblical revenge. Old Testament.'

Biblical? As in an eye for an eye?

'I can tell you where to strike. Where the man who was ultimately responsible for Katie's death can be hurt the most. I can give you enough on Joe Castagna's organisation that you'll be able to kick the legs out from under him. Time and time and time again. Enough to finish him.'

Finish him? Bloody hell. Mickey went from yeah so what to near incredulity in the blink of an eye.

'All you have to bring to the party are the weapons and the ability to use them. And the anger. You must be angry.'

Had the writer meant that he'd have to be angry to do whatever it was he had in mind? Or that Katie's death must have left him raging inside? He'd supposed that both were true.

'What I need you to do now is think. Quickly. If you join me in doing this, the clock will start to count down from the second you pull the trigger the first time. Joe's no fool. Given enough time he will find you. And kill you. And everyone you love. You will have to get ahead of the clock. Which will mean doing a lot of violence in a very short time. And there will be no space for second thoughts. If you're in, you're all in. There will be no way back.

'All I need from you now is a single word. Yes or no. If you're ready to consider revenge on the man whose product killed your sister, you need to tell me. Now. You don't need the time to think. This decision will come from your guts, not your head. Take a few minutes to consider it. But if you've not given me the signal in 15 minutes after I see you've read this I'll destroy this SIM card. And your chance of ever getting that revenge will be in the wind with me.

'If you want to work with me, just say yes.

'Make your mind up.

'Do it now.'

There was a name at the bottom of the message.

'Nemesis.'

Jesus Herbert Christ. Mickey sat and thought for a few minutes. Pros and cons.

The pros: revenge for his little sister. And the chance to put his very particular skill set to use in a way he could never have imagined.

The cons: possible death. Possible capture by the gang involved, meaning torture and death. Possible capture by the Met, meaning imprisonment, and probably death in prison. And the consequences for Roz and his parents in any of those events.

It had been a no-brainer, really. He'd replied with a single word.

'Yes.'

On several occasions thereafter he'd received a

WhatsApp message written in the same manner. The first communication had been a long one. A detailed plan. Some initial tasks to perform. And an instruction that he needed to prove himself ready for war. By killing Warren Margetson. Not the clock starter, just proof of willingness and ability. After which he'd get the detailed information he'd need to start taking vengeance in earnest. Along with a suggested modus operandi for Warren's death. One that Mickey had followed to the letter, pretty much.

'Perhaps your need to take blood for your sister will be satisfied by one death. Let's find out, shall we?'

The next message, with Warren dead, had been a detailed briefing as to his second target. The date, time and place. Which explained the car he'd been instructed to pre-position.

'You'll have to kill low-level gang members to do this one. Decide if you have the stomach to kill so-called innocents. But remember, once you've done this, the clock will start counting down to a death. Either Joe's or yours.'

The result: the Car Park Massacre. As the press had dubbed it.

And now he found himself looking at a third set of instructions. Reading the first line and wondering what lay behind it.

'37 Walcott Road.'

19

'So did you take my advice?'

Mickey sipping on a beer, Tamara watching as the barman finished putting her margarita together. They'd agreed to meet in a bar on the Strand, handy for Mickey's commute home. Service commendably swift, driven by the continued lack of the sort of debit-card-waving crush at the bar that had typified a happier time. She waited to answer until her drink had been poured. Smiling her thanks and raising it in salute.

'Sort of.'

'Sort of?'

She grinned at the disgust in his voice.

'I'm a covert snapper. All that pushing cameras into people's faces is just so…'

'Boring?'

'That, and… well… common.'

'Common.'

'It has all the flair of a microwave meal. And besides, when the subject knows it's coming they tend to be ready. Which makes for a picture that's about as illuminating of their interior life as a Mickey Mouse mask.'

'Illuminating of their interior life?'

She took another sip. 'Good margarita.' And waited ten seconds before speaking again. 'I just thought I'd see if you were going to repeat that as well.'

Mickey was unable to avoid a smile. Despite his intense irritation at her lackadaisical attitude to her own safety.

'I gave you an excellent piece of professional advice. Whether you choose to use it is up to you.'

'You warned me off the best story there is right now. Not what I'd call "excellent advice". More like "here's how not to have a career". My editor has a raging hard-on for this Castagna thing. And she's not going to thank me for bottling it just as it's getting real.'

'So you're still sneaking around with a 400mm zoom and hoping not to get caught.'

'No.' A shake of her head, long hair accentuating the gesture. 'I've upgraded to better glass. Nikon 1000mm. If I'd had the kit I've got now back in Beaconsfield you'd never have seen me.'

Mickey drank from the bottle.

'Same risk though. What if he thinks to have the ground around his house searched?'

'I'll see them coming. And exfiltrate like a pro.'

Mickey sat back for a moment, thinking. 'So why is your editor so keen on Joe?'

That one got him a raised eyebrow. 'Joe, is it? Like you know him or something. Which you pretty much denied on the phone.' Mickey's turn to remain silent, until she continued. 'She reckons "Joe" is responsible for pretty much half the serious crime in North London. Sources in the police, it seems. Between you and me, I think she goes to dinner parties with some pretty senior officers.'

Mickey snorted a laugh. 'Must be a hazard of the trade.'

'I'm not joking. We had that assistant commissioner in the office last week. The oriental-looking woman who keeps popping up on the television.'

'Jasmine Chen?'

'Mmm. That's the one. Comes across as a bit of a politician.'

Jasmine Chen, Assistant Commissioner Specialist Operations. Ferocious intellect and furious ambition in a tiger-mother-inspired package of talent and the need to achieve. And, somewhere in the Met's stratosphere, Mickey's uber-boss.

'That's because she's a total politician. Pretty tough to get to AC rank if you're not. And you think she's feeding your editor just enough information to have the *Clarion* go after him?'

'Looks like it. With an added side order of "all girls together" for encouragement.'

Mickey nodded slowly. 'Our Jasmine's a player all right. And she loves the game. Job gossip says she's a decent pick for deputy commissioner, if she keeps her nose clean. And pulling something spectacular out of the hat wouldn't hurt either.'

'Something like Joe Castagna.'

'Yeah.' He took another pull at the beer. 'Although how setting the *Clarion* on him changes anything, I can't imagine.'

'It's not just the *Clarion* that's after him though, is it?'

He raised an eyebrow at her, the well-practised innocent look. 'I haven't seen it in any other papers.'

'You know what I mean.' A penetrating stare left Mickey

wondering if she'd have made a good detective. 'A dead drug dealer. Dirty money set on fire in a ring of corpses.'

'Yeah, but that's not the Met. That's just turf wars.'

'That's not what "Your Jasmine" told my editor. Off the record, of course.'

'Really?' Doing his best not to betray his very personal interest in what AC Chen had had to say. 'What did she have to say then?'

'That the recent shooting of a drug dealer in North London bore all the hallmarks of a professional killing. Gun for hire stuff. Wouldn't tell us what they were, obviously, but off the record she was pretty bloody clear about it.'

Mickey shrugged, affecting to be unconvinced.

'One contract killing does not a vendetta make. Lots of drug dealers make enemies.'

'Yeah, but...'

She drained her cocktail and put the empty glass on the bar. Gestured for another one. Mickey raising a hand to decline a second beer.

'The Car Park Massacre though, that was something else, right? Four men, all armed, taken down by a masked gunman who left no trace. No DNA, no footprints. Even collected up his spent brass before setting fire to God alone knows how much money. A pro job, no doubt about it.'

'AC Chen told you that?'

'She didn't have to. Most of it's common knowledge, if you ask the right people. But she did hint pretty strongly that whoever did it has to be pretty highly trained. Ex-military, perhaps. Which could make the two shooters one and the same person. Somebody with a grudge, perhaps.'

'And your editor wants to do what with this, precisely?'

'Nothing, for the time being. There's nothing to go on, as the policeman said when his toilet was stolen.'

Mickey grinned, despite himself. Wondering if this was an opportunity he hadn't seen coming. Or just a chance to fuck up very royally indeed.

'So…'

Mickey paused, not sure if he was going to take the next step. Tamara accepted her second cocktail from the barman in the gap. Shot Mickey the "ready to rebuff tonight's proposition" look.

'What if I could get you an exclusive on Joe Castagna?'

The cocktail glass stopped halfway to her lips. Not the proposition she'd been expecting.

'What sort of exclusive?'

Careful, Mickey, he told himself.

'I've been a copper for over twenty years. Which means I know a lot of people in the Job. Some of whom, you might be surprised to hear, also have a raging hard-on for Joe. They'll know things about his empire that would make for front-page material any day of the week, if your editor's serious about it.'

'Yeah, but what sort—'

'Not yet. If I give you anything – *anything* – you have to keep my name out of it. Nothing in writing, nothing recorded. Agreed?'

'Of course.'

Her tone deadly serious. Margarita forgotten. Mickey thought quickly.

'You want to make the jump into photojournalism, be more than just a snapper, I might be able to make that happen. But if I get the chance to put you in the right place at the right time, you can't fuck about. You have to promise to be where I tell you, when I tell you to be there. And to do exactly what I tell you, when I tell you. Miss the chance, it won't be along again. Fuck it up through ignoring the instructions, same goes.'

She nodded, suddenly quiet, clearly trying to work out what it was he was offering her.

'And in return?' Her look knowing.

'Nothing. I'm happily married, and I have all the money I want.'

Which was true. Prot paid well enough, and his and Roz's lifestyle had never been lavish. And Mickey knew better than to go over the side. Both ethically and with regard to his personal safety.

'So you'd be getting what from this potential arrangement, exactly?'

Which, he had to admit was one hell of a question. Which had a one-word answer. One he couldn't voice. But which was the only possible reason for what was otherwise an act of insanity.

Escalation.

20

'So, the question is, who is it?'

Mickey looked sideways at Deano across the scarred pub table. Frowned at the terse nature of his friend's question as he took a sip of Guinness. Friday night, three pints in. The point where the conversational threads started to get tangled.

'Who's what?'

The big man shrugged.

'Thought you'd know what I was talking about. After all, nobody's talking about much else round here. We talked about it all last Friday night.'

'While I wasn't here.'

Deano shrugged. 'Doesn't take a genius to guess, does it? The Car Park Killer. No-one's talking about anything else, not with Joe Castagna getting his arse handed to him so publicly. There's even a book running on my relief as to who's got the minerals to go after him.'

Mickey nodded vehement agreement.

'I'll bet there is. And dollars to donuts you're the one running it. Don't let the bosses find out, or you'll be in front of AC-12 with your federation rep before you know it.'

Deano rolled his eyes at the popular culture reference

Mickey had deliberately dropped in. Being of the highly vocal opinion that *Line of Duty* was one giant bag of shark-jumping shite.

'Professional Standards can suck my dick. And as it happens, since you mentioned donuts, we're playing by cakes for stakes rules. Let's see them make something out of that, eh. Since there's no *dough* involved?'

Mickey sniggered and nodded. Challenge accepted.

'Cakes for stakes? In that case I'm definitely not up for it. I'm not looking for a *turnover* like that.'

'Are you sure, Mickey? I think you need to be a little more *eclair* about that.'

The usual rules: whoever couldn't continue the thread would be the man to get the next round in. Mickey knew that Deano would have laid the bait carefully, luring him onto prepared ground.

'I'm not sure I like the *panettone* of your voice, mate.'

Deano grinned widely, deploying what he expected to be the killer blow.

'You do not want to *croissant* me, my son. Or I'll have you over before the *bun* goes down.'

Groans of pain and appreciative nods. A double shot demanded a double shot in return just to stay in the game. Or a triple for the win. Mickey bared his teeth in a hard grin.

'Double shot, eh Deano? I'd offer you outside for that, except you don't look well enough... you look pale... a bit...'

'For the love of God, no.'

He ignored Steve's plea for mercy.

'...*pastry*-faced!'

Silence, Deano shaking his head.

'That's only one, my son. And right from the bottom of the barrel.'

'Yeah, I'll have to get them in.'

Deano spread his hands in triumph. But his celebration faltered as Mickey raised a finger. With a grin that told him the game wasn't over.

'I had one a minute ago… but it's *scone*.' Mickey looked around gleefully as he delivered the coup de grâce. 'Seriously, Deano mate. I've got *muffin. Muffin* at all. Now do you want some more *sponge*, Victoria, or have you had enough?'

Beers in, hysteria subsided, Deano tried again.

'Seriously though, someone's after Joe Castagna. Big style. And they're literally not taking prisoners.'

'And you're trying to work out who?' Mickey shook his head. 'It could be anyone.'

'Yeah, but you miss my point. The bloke doing the shooting could be anyone. Although there aren't many people with the cojones, right? But who's telling them *where* to shoot? And *when*? And *why*? Eh? I'm not going to lie, we even wondered if it was you. Because you, my son, are a dark fucking horse.' He looked at Mickey expectantly, clearly waiting for a response. Got nothing more than an amused eyebrow raise in response. 'Nah. You've got the stones all right, even if you hide it most of the time. But you don't have anything like the information needed, do you?'

'Me?' Mickey pushed his expression up from amusement to incredulity. 'No. I'm not exactly plugged into the gangland underground.'

'Yeah. We thought that too. Because whoever's going

after Joe knows their shit.' Mickey tried very hard not to look offended. Given that not knowing his shit was central to his not coming under suspicion. 'Whoever's going after Joe knew where he needed to be, and when, and what would be happening at that moment. And that has to mean he's got inside knowledge.'

Mickey nodded, darting a glance at Steve. Whose frustration, at that very table, with Jason Felgate's cease and desist order on going after Joe's money-laundering operation had been the genesis of his going after it, in his own way. But if Steve even remembered the discussion, he wasn't showing it.

Den frowned, making a rare interjection. 'Inside knowledge? Couldn't the shooter just have been a proper copper?' He shot a glance at Mickey, half-apologetic. 'No disrespect, Mickey son, but you're a long way from the sharp end.'

All three of them marvelled at Den, usually the quietest of them. Happy for the most part to listen and make the occasional gnomic intervention.

'Yeah...' Steve the first to answer. 'But the sort of copper who'd have that information wouldn't have the time to do the prep. Given that being a detective is a day job, and not nine to five neither. Whereas the blokes with the time tend to be woodentops on shift. And, given the .22 was probably a rental, you show me a woodentop with those sorts of contacts.'

'Unless he was some sort of arms dealer on the side.'

Mickey's glance flicked to Den. An unusually perceptive Den, if only he'd known it.

Deano voiced what they were all thinking. 'A beat copper

who's a gun dealer? Fuck me Den, *you* could write for *Line of Duty*, you mad bastard!'

The cue for all-round amusement. Even Den grinned at the thought. And Mickey took care to ensure he looked as amused as his mates. While feeling cold fingers brush his spine.

'Anyway, doesn't really matter who he is, not unless it's fucking Batman. Because when Joe catches up with him…' Deano looked around the table for confirmation '…and we know he's going to catch up with the prick, right? When that happens, he'll have the poor bastard skinned and dipped in brine, just for starters. It'll take days for that mug to go to meet his maker, with Joe recording the whole thing for an edited highlights package.'

'Why's he going to bother with that?'

Deano gave Den a slight sad smile.

'Den. Mate. Just when I thought you were right on the money, buddy. He has to make an example of the geezer, doesn't he? Has to show everyone who's got an interest in his falling off his perch that he's still the big dog. And what better way than to torture the bloke who's been chopping away at his empire to death on camera? All set for a few private screenings to prove to the competition that he's still the same lovable psychopath. Trust me, whoever it is that's been stupid enough to start this vendetta is going to wish they'd never been born. And so will anyone they care about.'

21

'So this is your hacker, right?'

Joe stared at the kid before him with poorly disguised disbelief. Although, to be fair, the outward signs weren't all that auspicious. A skinny, nerdy-looking teenager wearing ripped jeans and a death metal tee. Nondescript trainers and a baseball cap. The sort of look that'd get him a good kicking if he strayed onto gang turf. Except, Eddie suspected, anyone giving this kid a shooing would pay for it. Big style. Their credit rating in the toilet for the next ten years. Their mobile devices infested with all sorts of nasty shit. Or worse, planted child pornography. With the police called. Now that he'd seen what the kid could do, he had no illusions on that subject.

He'd gone recruiting the only way he knew. Lacking any better means of searching than putting the word out. Offering a small fortune for a hacker with the required skills, without specifying what the job was. What had washed up to his door had been a depressingly large number of wannabees. Some of whom hadn't even been able to hack the Castagna Property website, Eddie's ordained starter test. But the moment the kid had sat down at the table he'd sensed something more. Perhaps it had been the laptop the size of an aircraft carrier. Or the complete lack of any concern as to whether he was "the one". Castagna Property had been a pushover. The local nick's web page had taken a few minutes longer. Which Eddie had left undefaced, despite the obvious temptation. It was when the kid had offered to change his credit rating that he'd really started paying attention.

'This is Acid.' The kid's handle was actually Acɪd, but Eddie being keen not to blow Joe's mind too quickly. 'And he's good. Not only can he do all that hacker shit, he already has a lead on our gun trader. This Steph bloke.'

Which made Joe pay attention. 'What, already?'

'Kid's golden. Wait 'til you see. C'mon, Acid, use the boss's desk to set up.' Shooting a reassuring glance at Joe as the boy slouched over and slumped into Joe's chair. Fired up the machine and plugged in a USB drive.

'The thumb drive does all the dirty work.' Eddie explained to Joe, who was watching with a neutral expression. 'Leaves the laptop totally clean. So Acid here can access the dark web without any trace being left, if his laptop gets scanned.'

'So you could just chuck the stick away and be squeaky clean?' Joe nodded his belated, if limited, understanding. His mood lightening. 'Sweet as. Go on then, what you've got?'

Acɪd opened a new window, some sort of internet forum. Just without the smooth graphics.

'This is Dread. Which is like a chat room for people who want illegal stuff, right? Like an uncensored Reddit.'

Eddie jumped in to translate. The last four hours having been a near vertical learning curve. Joe nodded his head. Purporting to show understanding. And reading some of the thread titles.

'That's some weird shit right there. You sure this is safe? I don't want the filth round saying I'm a paedo.'

Acıd shook his head. Game face on.

'Nah. This machine is totally invisible, fam.'

Eddie jumped in quickly, inwardly cursing the kid's inability to understand the command "show some respect".

'You're right, Joe, there's some right nasty shit. But there's also some very helpful shit too. Show Mr Castagna what we did earlier.'

Kid opened another window. Looking like a standard email program. Revealing a dialogue between himself, albeit using a different name, and the aforementioned Steph.

'You just emailed him? I thought we had to be super careful?' Joe was a little incredulous. The kid unable to hide a smirk.

Eddie, realising that his tech guy was close to engaging Joe's ever-present ire, intervened again. 'Not email. The two magic words are Tails and PGP. Tails is the USB stick. PGP is Pretty Good Privacy. Seems all these programs have clever names like that. Means Acid here can email this Steph without any way the geezer can trace him back.'

Joe nodded again, like this was all making sense to him. Read the chat between Acıd, posing as a random called Neutralise, and Steph.

'So he's offering you a choice of guns. Including an MP5 and two clips of ammo. No .22 though.'

Eddie shook his head. 'No. And we didn't ask for one either. Way too obvious.'

'You haven't answered yet.'

'No.' Eddie, knowing from long experience the limits of

his autonomy, had gone so far and no further. 'I thought you'd want to be part of this.'

Being Eddiespeak, for Joe taking complete control. A wise judgement.

'Too right I do. Good work, Ed. And you too, er, Acid.'

'So, what do you want me to reply, Mr Castagna?'

'Let's see…' Joe, thinking hard. 'Tell them that you're making the enquiry on behalf of a client. Some gang banger who doesn't understand all this dark web stuff. Ask how much he wants to rent us the MP5 for a day. And how much the ammo is per round fired.'

Kid nodded and started typing. Fast. 'Done.'

'Excellent.' Joe, beneficent in the face of apparent success, said, 'Good work, Eddie, and you, son. Eddie, sort the kid out with a suitable cash payment. Make it generous too. You, Acid, are on the payroll.'

22

Two in the morning. Mickey supposedly away, on overtime. Which was what he'd told Roz. Except Mickey wasn't anywhere near a government residence. Mickey was sitting in a car in the north London suburbs. Checking his gear. Keeping an eye on the mirrors while he did it. In case someone should wander past and clock the arsenal on his lap. Although the car was calculated to avoid any interest. Another dead-end dealer, another dead-end motor. A late Nineties Nissan Micra in light blue – or at least mostly. The rest over-sprayed with primer. A car bought to be ignored. Parked within two streets of what was about to become a media firestorm.

He was dressed for the job to hand. Black cargo pants, slim fit, bloused into high top combat boots. A tight-fitting black Under Armour training top beneath the webbing patrol harness carrying his equipment. In the shoulder holster, a Beretta 9mm. No suppressor. The weapon of last resort. For when the need to go loud was no longer in doubt. Neighbours three doors down from Number 37 would hear its unmistakable bark. And nobody would be mistaking it for fireworks, not at two in the morning. If he pulled that trigger it'd be 999 time for at least a dozen rudely awakened sleepers. A military fighting knife strapped to the left front harness strap. Hilt downwards. And a set of stainless-steel knuckles on a magnetised pad on the right strap. Mickey was loaded for bear.

None of those his first choice of weapons for this job though. Getting into knife-fighting range would risk getting into a brawl. With the danger of leaving DNA on an opponent. Skin or blood from under a fingernail could identify him in hours, courtesy of the Met's elimination database. Worse still, a close-in fight risked incurring a wound, in the random violence of a struggle. Better to stay at a distance, even if it meant waking the whole street.

With that in mind, the carry pouch on his left hip contained two cylindrical grenades. One with a thick metal case that was mostly holes. Allowing free rein to seven million candelas of instant sunshine. And 170 decibels of sonic rage. Powerful enough to leave a strong man prone, deaf and blind for crucial seconds. Disorientated for minutes after that. Nobody in the house would be in any fit state to return fire if he threw that little monster at them. But that would quite possibly include Mickey as well. And have everyone in Walcott Road calling 999. Exit strategy only.

The other grenade had solid walls, a red band around its cylindrical green body. Chemical smoke, strong enough to reduce anyone lacking protection to weeping, choking helplessness. Nasty shit, especially inside a dwelling. Also capable of igniting furniture and burning down the house. Pretty much last resort too.

His go-to weapon nestled in a holster on his right hip. A big, boxy pistol. Its carbon-fibre body black and yellow, flaring to a square at the business end. Pure science fiction vibe. He had non-violent equipment too. Ten double-cuff zip ties in a trouser pocket. Five six-inch strips of Gorilla tape stuck to his leg by an inch of adhesive. The rest of each strip still covered with backing paper. The ability to silence and immobilise.

He got out of the car and closed the door quietly. Walked, medium pace, along the street and round the corner into Walcott Road. A street lined with big, century-old houses. Long since converted into multiple apartments. All except for number 37, which was owned in its entirety by Joe Castagna. The house put to a different use. No indication that Number 37 was anything out of the ordinary, of course. Not unless you knew the purpose to which the house had been put. And what was delivered, and collected, always at the dead of night. Product, to be worked on. Made ready for consumption.

Mickey walked silently towards the target, in the dark post-midnight gloom. Looked up and down the street. Nothing moving. And from the outside, Number 37 appeared equally lifeless. He climbed over the low garden wall, giving the front door's video bell a wide berth. Stopped in the house's deeper shadow, fishing patrol gloves and overshoes out of a pocket. Adding the usual balaclava. Then eased up the hasp of the side gate, ghosting into the back garden. Ducked beneath the darkened side window.

He flitted past the French windows at the rear of the house. Stopped to listen at the kitchen door. Nothing. Still as quiet as the grave. Drew a long, slow breath. It would probably have been easier on his nerves to shoot his way in. Indeed Martin had exactly that comment, when he'd told him what he'd need for this one. Especially one piece of kit.

'What do you want that for? I mean, shooter, yeah, obviously. The knife, the knuckles, yeah, I would too. The grenades...' He'd shaken his head in some kind of admiration. 'I mean, fucking hell, Mickey, but yeah. A good idea, if you need to blast your way out. But that? I thought the whole idea was to kill as many of them as possible? Your mate Nemesis going soft?'

He opened a pouch, taking out his lock pick and setting to work on the door. The mechanism clicked, and he froze again, listening. Still nothing. He put the lock pick away, then drew the boxy weapon from his waist holster. Opened the door and stepped inside, listening intently for any sign of movement. Nothing. Took another slow, deep breath and paced forward into the hallway, looking at the doors on either side intently. Both secured by locks, the keys inserted. He turned the key in the lock on the left, feeling it click over. Unlocked. And therefore empty. Probably. He turned the key back and opened the door carefully. Slipped into the room with the black and yellow gun ready. Empty. He closed the door behind him. Holstered the weapon and pulled a Mini Maglite from his pocket.

The room was austere. Bare even. Walls, looking like plasterboard but, Mickey was sure, with solid brickwork behind them. No window. Carpet covered the floor, spotted with food stains. The only furniture a double bed. A cell.

He opened the door and moved back into the hall. Listening carefully, hearing only silence. The door opposite was locked. Occupied. Mickey didn't bother opening it. He knew that the occupant wasn't likely to be rational. He contemplated the stairs. Knowing the odds that they would creak were high. Put a foot on the first step, right next to the wall. No sound. Took another step up, the other foot against the banisters. Still nothing. The theory was good then. Advanced slowly upwards, wincing at every tiny creak. Hearing snoring coming from one of the rooms at the top.

Doors on the right and left. Mickey took another long, slow, tidal breath, then opened the door on the right. Went in as swiftly as he could while retaining some semblance of stealth. But he needn't have bothered. The occupant was fast asleep, a half-drunk glass of dark spirit on the stand beside him. Snoring loudly, dead to the world. Mickey crossed the room in rubber-soled silence. Closed to within touching distance of the sleeper. Eased a strip of black tape from his trouser leg and peeled off the backing strip. Eyed up his victim for a moment, then struck. Slapped the tape over his mouth. Almost simultaneously thumbing the Taser's contact discharge button. Pushing its boxy snout onto his bare skin with a staccato crackle of current.

The effect was instant, the gang member's body convulsing. Writhing under the pulsing charge, exhaling violently through his nose. What would have been a scream of pain muffled to a low moan through his nostrils. Mickey gave him a two-second shock. Released the button but kept the stun gun ready to use again. Simultaneously pinching off his nostrils with his other hand, preventing him from inhaling. Then holstered the Taser and punched the trembling man in the head. Hard. No half-measures. Hard enough to add a new layer of pain and disorientation.

He released his grip on the other man's nose and smiled grimly at the frantic inhalation that resulted. Took out a set of zip tie cuffs and secured the bastard's wrists while he was momentarily stunned. Punched him again, keeping him reeling. Tied his legs at the ankles and knees. Pulled the zip ties as tight as he could. Then flipped him over to lie face down, hearing his breathing against the mattress.

Mickey bent to speak quietly in the trussed man's ear. Pulled the Beretta from its holster and ground the muzzle against his temple.

'I know you can hear me. You need to be very quiet now. If I hear any noise from you, the next thing I shoot you with won't be electric.'

He holstered the pistol. Retrieved the Taser and turned to face the door. Ready for anyone who might have heard any of the brief struggle. And waited.

Ten seconds convinced him that the brief, one-sided fight had gone unheard. Perfect. He opened the door to find himself face-to-face with the biggest man he thought he'd ever seen. Timing, the secret of comedy. The door opposite was open, player two in the act of coming through it. Almost having to duck under the frame. An empty glass in his hand, he was bare-chested, wearing pyjama bottoms. Eyes half open, stinking of alcohol. The two men so close they could have reached out and touched each other. Mickey reflexively shot him in the chest.

The effect was instant. Instant, but not ideal. Big Man too close for the darts to get the right separation. He staggered backwards with a loud grunt and pissed himself. A dark stain flooded down his pyjamas. Momentary loss of all bodily control from the massive jolt of current running through his body. His eyes clenched against the pain, and he groaned loudly as the current flailed his body. And, just for a moment, Mickey thought that was that. Until the stun gun stopped discharging.

The other man's eyes snapped open, and he fixed them on his assailant. Put a hand to his chest and tore out the barbed darts. Fuck. One shot left in the Taser. After which he would have to choose whether to go loud or hand to hand. Big Man drew breath, getting ready to shout a warning, Mickey guessed. Time to go Lafone on his ass.

A decade before, Mickey had been a serious fighter. And not just of a Friday night. Talent-spotted on the High Street, by a sergeant with an eye for a well-thrown punch. Impressed by his application of swift footwork, a quick left jab and a jackhammer right hook. And Mickey, who'd been boxing since he was twelve, had initially been flattered by his praise.

Pride that had only lasted until the suggestion that he enter the Lafone Cup. The Lafone, the Met's boxing trophy, coveted by uniformed psychopaths across the Greater London area. Mickey's choice in the matter being a Hobson's. And besides, the winners at all weights would score an all-expenses-paid trip to the United States. To represent the Met in competition with the NY Fire Department. No choice at all, really.

And so Mickey had trained. Lost weight and gained muscle. Boxed clever in the heats and actually reached the finals evening. Come home from the O2 looking like he'd gone twelve with Floyd. Although, as he still liked to tell it, the other guy had been some punchbag. Soaked up a pasting and then decked Mickey in the third.

So Mickey could box. And the big man still had the look of a bleary-eyed half-awake pisshead. Who'd just been tasered, for all his hulking menace. So Mickey holstered the boxy black stun gun. Ripped the knuckle duster from its mag pad. And went for him, all guns blazing. Or at least as fast as he could, loaded with kit and wearing a shoulder holster.

Two lightning-fast left jabs to put Big Man back on his heels. And shut his mouth. Loving the moment, Mickey doubted that his opponent was used to being on the receiving end. Probably more used to having to chase down his prey. Having got the chump where he wanted him, he unloaded with his iron-shod right fist. Time to nuke the bastard from orbit.

The right hook landed perfectly, ganglion style. Every ounce of power in his body behind it. Staggered the bastard, blinking, back across the room to his bed. Which he sat on involuntarily, as the backs of his knees encountered the mattress.

Which gave Mickey a moment to contemplate him. To watch tensed arms bulging with muscle starting to push him back onto his feet. After which, Mickey glumly predicted, he would storm across the room. And take his ire out on Mickey in the form of non-Queensbury-approved fighting moves. Probably involving kicking, biting, strangulation and death. Back to plan A it was.

Drawing the Taser, he stepped back and shot Big Man again. The stun gun spitting its load across the space between them with a percussive bang. Putting another two darts into his already bleeding chest. Proper dart separation this time. The result immediate. Big Man slumped to his knees with a groan. Looked up at Mickey with hate-filled eyes, momentarily helpless. And this time Mickey didn't wait for him to get over the shock. He stepped forward and kicked out. Nothing fancy, just a steel toecap driven into the big man's groin. Hard. His victim grunted, unable to stop himself hunching over his abused genitals. Mickey holstered the Taser and went back to the knuckles. Wrapped them up in his right hand, rust-flecked steel with undoubted history. Punched down into Big Man's temple as his head sank forwards. Dropped him like the proverbial sack of shit.

Game. Over.

'What the fuck is going on?'

Mickey snatched the Taser from his waist, lightning fast on a wave of adrenaline-fuelled muscle memory. Turned to face the doorway. Pulled the trigger on the woman as she came through it. Her mistake shouting before knowing what she was dealing with. His, unforgivably, not counting his shots. Two charges, both fired. They stared at each other for an instant. She in disbelief, Mickey in self-disgust. He dropped the Taser and started forwards. Stopped by an angry grunt from behind him. Telling him that Big Man wasn't out of the fight yet.

His seemingly indestructible opponent was rising from the floor. Bloody-faced from a cut on his scalp, a mark left by the knuckle duster. Still in pain, but still intent on doing harm to Mickey. Who put twenty years of endless repetition into his response. Trained power and muscle memory. Spinning to his right in a tight half circle, his arm whipping around in a brutal haymaker. The punch to be used when an opponent lacks the coordination to duck.

His iron-clad fist caught the rising jailer squarely beneath his ear. He followed the punch through, hammering Big Man to the floor with the blow's ferocious power. And as his seemingly indestructible victim teetered on the edge of consciousness, Mickey reset his body. Leaving nothing to chance. Lunged forwards with a straight thrust kick to the reeling gangster's head that snapped it back. Big Man went down, permanently out of the fight. Unconscious or dead. Either acceptable.

He staggered as the woman hit him from behind. Untrained, but incensed, her fingers scrabbling for his eyes. Her nails slipping on the balaclava's smooth silk. Mickey grabbed her wrists and twisted hard. Put her over his shoulder before her plastic talons found flesh. Her body hit the bedroom wall hard, then fell onto the bed. She scrambled off the mattress with an inchoate cry of fury. Full respect, Mickey stepped forward to meet her. Using his forward momentum to snap a full-on palm strike into her chest. The blow catapulting her back against the wall headfirst. She crumpled, lifeless.

Mickey, breathing hard, stood and waited. Panting from the sudden burst of exertion. And drew the Beretta. Anyone else appeared, he decided, he was just going to shoot them. No sound disturbed the quiet. After a moment more he holstered the pistol, then gagged and zip-tied both of his victims. Alive, albeit stunned.

Walking out onto the landing, he found two more doors. Both locked. He ascended the next flight of stairs to the top floor. Two more. Either side of the unconscious woman's empty bedroom. Both locked. Five cell doors locked. No sound from their occupants. "Trained" to remain silent under all circumstances. He made his way back down the stairs and went back to his first captive. Dragged the wild-eyed man through into the same room as his fellow-abusers by the hair, provoking a loud squeal through his nose.

'Hurts, does it?' Mickey stared down into furious eyes.

'Excellent. But I'll tell you what's going to hurt a lot more.' He gestured to the two comatose bodies. 'I'll tell you, you can tell them later. Because I want you all thinking hard about it. What's going to hurt you a lot more than that? Not the police, obvs. They're required by law to treat you carefully. You'll get a doctor. Then a lawyer. Joe'll send someone down to make sure you keep your mouths shut. Which you all will. Because you all know what Joe does to anyone he even suspects of grassing. You've heard the stories. We all have. So you'll keep it shut. Won't you?'

Fury instantly became fear. The trussed man nodded frantically. Mickey laughed.

'Oh, don't worry, you don't need to convince me. For a start, I couldn't give a shit what you do. And for another thing, it doesn't even matter to me whether you talk or not. I've already done the damage I wanted. No, I only ask just to find out how stupid you are. And the answer's clearly really fucking stupid. Stupid enough to keep Joe's secrets until it's too late.'

He paused, looking closely at his captive's face. There it was. Confusion.

'You mugs. You think all you have to do is keep quiet, do whatever time you're handed. Keep your head down. Which you will. Sure that when you get out, Joe'll have you collected. Which he will. And then... and you can trust me on this... you'll vanish. Never to be seen again. You'll end up in the cement.'

The captive shook his head in disbelief. Mickey shrugged.

'Yeah. He's an evil bastard when he's crossed. And he's already promised to make an example of the next members of his "family" to slip up.' Mickey extended a hand to indicate his two fellow abusers, still both comatose. 'I'd call this a slip-up, wouldn't you? Think about that, while you're waiting for the police.'

He took a moment to inventory his kit. Pocketed the Taser wires. Made sure he had everything he'd come with. Leaving no clues. Then stood and made his way downstairs and out the back door. Looked at his watch: 02.36. Took out the pay-as-you-go phone he'd purchased for cash earlier in the day. Made the call, number withheld. Tamara answered after a single ring.

'Hello?'

'Where are you?'

His voice distorted by a downloaded app. Understandable, but not recognisable.

'Where we were told to wait, in the all-night caff on Washington Street.'

'Good. So here's how it works. In a minute I'm going to tell you where to go. Don't wait to finish your hot chocolate, smoke another fag, or generally fuck about in any way. Get in your car, now. Drive to within a hundred yards of the address. Not right outside, you'll just get in the way and probably get nicked as a precautionary measure. Wait for the police to arrive. Let them batter their way into the house before you make your move. Once they're in, get out of the car and walk… *walk*… to the house. Have your camera ready. And don't run, it'll make any firearms officers who've attended nervous. They'll start bringing people out. Probably the bastards I've immobilised first. Take pictures, get faces. Two men in their thirties and a middle-aged woman. Once they have them away, they'll start bringing the girls out.'

'Girls?'

'Girls. Teenagers, usually. Promised a good life in the west, with a job, working to pay off the people smugglers. Except that isn't how it works. Ask the police, they'll probably tell you. Get pictures. Tell them you're photojournalists, and that you intend to follow the case.'

Mickey waited for a reaction.

'The case…?'

'It's a training house. They bring the women there first. Before putting them to work. Teach them obedience. Show them what they're expected to do. With all sorts of practical demonstrations. Do I need to spell it out?'

'No.'

Her voice was suddenly quiet.

'You wanted a scoop. You're getting one. Remember the conditions.'

'Never mention the name of the man who put us in touch with you.'

Mickey having told Tamara he'd get his mate to get in contact. Not knowing whether she was taken in by the ruse. And not caring much either.

'And?'

'Use pseudonyms to credit the story and the pics.'

'Make sure you do. Make very sure. Because the man I'm hunting will be very interested in you. And you won't enjoy the sort of attention he'll pay you. Either you or your mate Mark. Got that?'

'Yes.'

'OK, 37 Walcott Road. Say it back to me so I know you've got it right.'

'37 Walcott Road. Wait for the police to go in first, then

approach calmly, camera ready. Stay calm, get pictures, tell them we're journalists. Don't credit actual names on the article or the pics.'

'Good. Move.'

He cut the call and fished in his pocket for the micro-recorder. The one he'd had Martin speak into earlier. Dialled 999 and waited for the answer.

'999, which service do you require?'

'Police.'

Using the voice distortion app even for that single word.

'Police, state your emergency.'

Mickey put the recorder to the phone. Triggered the recording and started walking back to the car.

23

'What next? What's he going to do next? Eh?'

Joe's usual calm was badly frayed. His knuckles white from being clenched so hard. His eyes, the usual clue as to his mental state, beyond rage. Lost somewhere in that hinterland where repressed anger slides effortlessly sideways into murderous fury. Richard, sitting on the other side of the table from them, looked as if he was about to swallow his own tongue from sheer terror.

Funny the tricks memory plays on you, Eddie might have mused. If every fibre of his intellect hadn't been working flat out to keep the fear off his face. Joe's murderous expression playing havoc with his pulse rate and blood pressure. Because whenever Eddie saw that look, he couldn't help but reflexively recall the 23rd of November 1999.

Late evening on a cold Tuesday. Rain beating against the roof of Joe's lockup like constant machine gun fire. More than a lockup, really. More like a spacious workshop turned to Joe's nefarious purposes. Nicknamed, inevitably, the Batcave. With Joe's matt black 911 parked in the middle as the Batmobile. Eddie's equally blacked-out Rangie as backup, and for load carrying. A stout dog guard bolted in for live human transport.

The lockup used for storage, for the most part. Stolen goods in the main. Before Joe had inherited his dad's empire and specialised in drugs and trafficked women. The years when he had cut his teeth by playing gangster games. Sheltered from grown-up competition under the protective umbrella of his dad's reputation. Big G having put it about that anyone who messed with his son messed with him.

But the Batcave hadn't just been intended for use as storage. In one corner of the large space, Joe had built what he called the games room. Twenty feet square, and heavily soundproofed. As proven by Joe bringing in a boombox and playing a Motorhead CD at maximum volume inside the room. The Ace of Spades very distantly audible in the lockup. On the street, nada. A games room that might as well have been on the moon. Lacking any drainage, which, they realised soon enough, was a bit of an oversight. One corrected on the next iteration, in the improved premises they moved into after Big G lost his fight with lung cancer.

So not really just a lockup. And the two men Joe and Eddie had entertained that night not really guests either. Middle-aged chancers. The sort of easily biddable mugs found in boozers and bookies around the world. Desperation leaking from every pore, need driving them to acts of foolishness. One of which had ended up with their being brought back to the Batcave. Tied to chairs, bound but not gagged, to emphasise their helplessness.

Joe had even encouraged them to shout their heads off. He'd smoked a cafe creme while Eddie made a brew. Applauded their efforts to summon help. And by the time the tea was made, they were silent. All shouted out, but to no effect. Very much aware that they were very much alone. And in the hands of a man whose reputation was already starting to precede him. Both self-evidently terrified. Expecting serious punishment. One of them bold enough to straight out ask for it.

'Do what you have to do. Make us an example. Then kick us out, and we'll spread the word you ain't to be fucked with. Right?'

Eddie later decided that just a bit more respect might have worked. "Do what you have to do, Mr Castagna, and please accept our apologies" might just have defused Joe's anger. He'd seen it happen. But in the absence of grovelling respect, all Joe saw was the opposite. And so he had nodded slowly. With that dead expression in his eyes that Eddie had already learned to recognise.

Counter-intuitively, some of the tension had seeped from the situation. The mugs mistaking a lack of immediate violence for the possibility of clemency. There was still a beating in their near future, obviously. But survivable. A story to be told in a late-night lock-in. *See that? Joe Castagna done that, back in '99. Fuck I've sailed close to the wind, ain't I?*

And then Joe spoke. 'Did your granddad ever tell you stories, when you were kids?'

They had stared back at him, confusion evident. But Joe had ignored that uncertainty. Getting into his story-telling groove like he was something out of a Tarantino movie. And Eddie knew, Tarantino being another firm favourite, that Joe liked to imagine himself in that world. Preaching, like Samuel L. Jackson, to the unrighteous.

'My nonno did. All sorts of stories. He was an old man by then, of course. And he spent a lot of time round ours, of course.' Smiled at them knowingly. 'That's Italian families for you. So I saw a lot of him when I was growing up. At what you might call an impressionable age. These days they'd probably call it child abuse, the stuff he used to tell me. How he was captured at Salerno in 1943. His mates ripped to dog meat by British artillery, the infantry doing the rest of them with rifles and bayonets. Scotsmen, he said. He always liked employing Jocks in the firm, reckoned they were the hardest bastards going. He survived by getting shot and then playing dead. And he ended up in the Lea Valley, as a prisoner of war. Met a girl, stayed after the war. Made a name for himself, a man to respect. Which for an Italian, in those days, meant he had to be a right hard bastard. And trust me, he was. You should have heard the stories he told me. Some of it would have your arses doing the old five-pence fifty-pence tremble.'

He'd grinned, staring off into space, eyes still dead. And then he'd turned that stare on the two mugs. And Eddie had reckoned he could hear the pennies dropping. And the creak of contracting sphincters, as they realised what they were in for. And in that moment Eddie had known for a fact that in Joe's mind both men were already dead. Which was why that stare still had such a power to chill him. A power of which he was pretty sure Joe was all too well aware. He looked up to find Joe waiting for him in silence. As if knowing exactly where Eddie's mind had been.

'Play that recording again.'

A 999 call made at 02.39 that morning. From a burner, of course. No clues there. A copy of the recording had been provided to the Major Investigation Team hunting the Car Park Killer. And quietly lifted from their database by Jason

Felgate. Who knew their DCI's habitual password from years gone by. A calculated risk, Eddie guessed. Probably calculated by Jason as less risky than continued non-delivery of any results. He pushed the play button.

'Police, please state your emergency.'

'This ain't my voice, so don't bother trying to analyse it. The geezer doing the talking ain't on any databases.'

The first few words confirming that whoever had hit number 37 had their shit in a tidy pile. Either a proper local or working hard to sound like one. Bother pronounced "bovver", Catherine Tate style. G's omitted, h's likely to be dropped. The word "geezer" trying a little too hard though, to Eddie's mind. And the voice not quite natural. Put through some sort of filter to deepen and distort it just enough to be unrecognisable. Eddie pressed stop.

'He's got a mate to pre-record the 999 call for him. Cute bastard. I ain't so sure about the Guy Ritchie impression though. Sounds a bit Mockney to me.'

Joe grunted agreement. Gestured for him to press play again.

'I'm reporting the presence of several trafficked women at 37 Walcott Road. There are a number of incapacitated traffickers too. They will need medical attention.'

That was true enough. Whoever had hit Number 37 had left all three with a mix of concussion and heavy bruising. One poor bastard with a hairline fracture of the jaw and a ruptured testicle. And Taser wounds. Punctures and burns. Still seeing double the next day.

'The women will need medical attention too. They will all have suffered multiple rapes.'

Joe reached out and pressed the stop button.

'We're looking for a clever bloke with a not quite so clever friend. Did you hear how he stumbled over the word incapacitated?'

Eddie nodded, wondering what sort of starting point that was. But making a point of looking both thoughtful and purposeful. Braced himself for Joe's reaction when he heard the next sentence again. Not having been all that happy the first time.

'And when this message gets leaked by one of your bent filth, here's a message for Joe. Joe mate, I know you're looking for me. But here's the thing…'

A pause. A new voice. Freighted with promise. Menace.

'I'm closer than you think.'

Click of the phone's disconnection. Joe looking unimpressed at the threat. Definitely preferable to the rage Eddie had been half-expecting.

'So, what do we know?'

Eddie glanced at his notes. 'There's no known voice match on any database Felgate can access. Too distorted. No traces left at the scene. Nothing at all. He even took the Taser wires with him. And the filth didn't even look for any forensics on him. Too busy gathering DNA to prosecute our people with.'

'Yeah. Our people.' A grimace from Joe. Somewhere between disappointment and anger. 'They solid, Richard?'

'Rock solid, Joe.'

Not entirely true, as it happened. Eddie having had to talk one of his men down from grassing. Terrified of what Joe would do to them when they were released. Doubts seemingly introduced by his assailant. Capitalising on Joe's threats to bury the next cash crew to allow themselves to be robbed. He'd pointed out in graphic detail how much worse it would be for a grass. Then soothed the man's fears with some reassuring lies. That nobody could have predicted the maniac would change his approach, for one. Joe a man to keep his promises, for another. Families would be looked after. Yadda yadda, as Eddie well knew. Because if Joe decided to make an example, that example would be biblical in its ferocity. Living by one of his favourite catchphrases: don't get mad, get medieval.

'What I don't understand is why he's doing this? First he's having a go at the drugs side of the business, now he's banging holes in the sex side.'

Sex. The euphemism that Joe's family had always used for their prostitution operation. Even before it had got quite so industrially non-consensual. But then "sex" made it sound as if the girls had a choice.

'I don't know. I'd assumed that he was drugs focused for some reason, but it seems like…'

He thought for a moment, weighing up the safest way to put it. But Joe wasn't interested in subtlety.

'Like he's got a hard-on for me? Yeah. Does, doesn't it? But that ain't what's boiling my piss.'

Eddie nodded, knowing what was on his boss's mind. 'I know. Where's he getting his information from?'

'Just what I was wondering. Could be the filth, of course. They must know a lot of what we get up to, one way or another.'

'Could be someone on the inside though.'

Joe's gaze lifting from the coffee mug on his desk to Eddie. Then flitting across to rest on Richard. His stare sharp and hard. 'Exactly. Someone who knew our cash collection routine. And where to ambush my boys.'

"My boys" when they were dead in defence of Joe's cash; "your useless bastards" whenever he thought about that loss for too long.

'Could be an insider. Could be the filth. Could even be the competition. Whoever it is, when we find them I'm having blood. All of it.'

Joe's expression was merciless. Wordlessly setting an expectation.

'So start yanking chains, Eddie. Start yanking them nice and hard. We heard anything back from Acid yet?'

'He's still waiting to hear back from this Steph.'

Joe nodded fractionally. Not satisfied, but knowing nothing the hacker could do would speed up any reply.

'I want to know the minute he does. I reckon that's the way we'll catch this prick. And in the meantime...'

Eddie acknowledged the unspoken dismissal with a raised hand. And went to yank chains. Nice and hard. Leaving Joe and Richard to talk about Joe's disappointment that the press weren't off his back yet. Not a conversation he envied the lawyer.

24

The *Clarion*'s front page that morning was testament to Tamara's photographic skills. Not to mention some last-minute editorial work. Mickey read the paper in a Costa, nursing an adrenaline hangover. Still smug from having got what he wanted without killing anyone. Top of the page, the faces of five women. Their eyes blacked out with masking tape sunglasses. As seen in special forces kiss-and-tell books. Protecting their anonymity. With the stark headline 'VICTIMS.' Below, three larger pictures. Two men and a woman. All visibly battered. Lips split, battered faces starting to puff up. Accorded the same privacy as their victims. A lawyers' decision Mickey's best guess. With the sub-headline 'VICTIMS?'

Inside, the first few lines were enough to make the *Clarion*'s answer to that question clear to even a casual reader. Rescued by an unknown benefactor, it seemed, the five women in question clearly trafficked for abuse. Illegal immigrants, they would be taken into the care of the state. Protective custody, to enable them to testify without fear. And would probably be returned to their own countries in due course. Whether that was fair, or even sensible, given their desire to work, the article questioned. But that they had been trafficked, raped, and were destined for prostitution before their rescue, beyond doubt.

Tamara had come up trumps. Proving that Mickey had judged correctly in handing her the scoop. She had, Mickey guessed, either bribed or sisterhooded her way into the house. Unless, of course, Jasmine Chen had been instrumental after a call from the *Clarion*'s editor. The resulting pictures both familiar and chilling.

The individual cells in which the women had been held. Their abusers' quarters, complete with a PlayStation and satellite TV. A cupboard full of spirits bottles. Whereas all the women had was bare walls, a mattress and a blanket. The racked packs of condoms used by the men in the "training" of their victims. An unnamed officer explaining to the reporter that this was for the avoidance of pregnancy. Or rather the loss of income that would entail.

Tamara's outrage shone through the paragraphs of terse, biting prose. Mickey nodded. Happy with what he'd achieved. And her ability to lay Joe's operation out for examination with pictures and words. Relieved to see that the article went under the by-line "*Clarion* Investigation Team", as instructed. Ensuring both her protection and his own.

Physically weary, but wired, he sipped his cappuccino and pondered. The main focus of his pondering being two words. What now?

As if to answer, his personal phone buzzed. Incoming message alert. Early, for Roz. But it wasn't Roz. It was Nemesis.

'Why did you involve the press?'

He wasn't going to try to deny it. Typed in his answer.

'Because I want to ramp up the pressure on that bastard. It was you that said the clock's ticking.'

A pause. He sipped his coffee. Considering the sheer incongruity of the conversation.

'The pressure is high enough already. This is a significant additional risk. For us both. Do not do it again, or I will cut you off.'

Fair enough. Once was enough for Mickey. And besides, his next action against Joe wasn't one he'd want Tamara to have any part of.

'Agreed.'

There was no reply. Two minutes later, his Job phone rang.

'Michael Bale.'

The voice at the other end crisp and efficient.

'Good morning, Michael. Is the early bird getting the worm today?'

There was a laugh in the other man's voice. Philip Green. Presumably Prot's duty inspector in LX for the day.

'Good morning, sir.' Sir, rather than Guv, when there was no guarantee the man at the other end was alone. 'Probably not, but I'm still a creature of habit.'

'Well I glad you're out of bed, and hoping you've got nothing planned for today. Or the rest of the week.'

Mickey was unfazed by the unexpected alteration of his routine. It being an article of Prot faith that the job came first. And everything else second.

'No, sir. Nothing planned.'

'Good man. In that case pack a bag, report here asap and get kitted up. Constable Harris is also being called in. The minister will be travelling to a destination I'd rather not discuss on an open line, and will be needing some HRE support. Since you and Constable Harris are both HRE qualified I thought you might be just the man to lead the protection team. And Major Cavendish concurred, when I mentioned it to him. It seems you've got a fan there, Michael. I told him that you're on down time, but he really was very keen.'

'That's not a problem, sir.' He put a smile into his voice. 'And it's nice to be wanted. How long will this be for?'

'It's a two-day trip, so you can tell your wife you'll be back for the weekend.'

'Yes, sir. I'll be there by...' Mickey consulted the Black Bay. 'Midday latest.'

'Excellent. Thank you, Michael, I knew you wouldn't let the side down.'

The inspector disconnected, and Mickey looked at the phone for a moment. Put it away and dug out his own phone. Called Roz. Explained the change of plan, to general unhappiness, given their restaurant booking that evening. Told her he loved her and clicked off the call. Drank the rest of his coffee. Then grabbed his bag, fully packed for several days' duty as usual. Including. As usual, a set of HRE kit. And hit the street.

HRE. High Risk Environment. A euphemistic acronym

for Prot officers trained to accompany UK VIPs to certain countries. Those nations where the potential threat to the principal was deemed too significant for Prot's usual modus operandi. Partly because of the threat level. Partly the result of deficient protection infrastructure on the part of the host government. It was a qualification that had to be earned, and one with a significant failure rate. HRE teams often contained former Counter Terrorist Specialist Firearms Officers, already partially trained in their previous roles. And up to the physical demands of the job.

Every HRE certified officer had been trained by real special forces instructors. They were expected to be fitter than the average Prot bodyguard. And qualified in a myriad of skills. Advanced marksmanship, navigation, counter-kidnap, interrogation, secure comms, use of specialised munitions and more. Accompanied on their travels by Peli cases full of mil-spec weaponry and equipment. Leading some to consider themselves as akin to special forces. Indulging themselves in expensive kit: North Face, Molle, Buffalo Systems and the like. Everything in khaki and with plenty of straps. Whereas Mickey harboured no such illusions.

Mickey had been certified for HRE ops for several years. And endured a series of annual refreshers at Credenhill Lines in Hereford. Short, intense courses intended partially to revisit and sharpen skills. And partially to remind the victims just how unfit they were. And he'd come back from each one more motivated than ever to stay fit and honed. Pushed himself with the weights and roadwork. Hit the canvas at his local boxing club two or three times a month. Knowing he'd never match the fitness or attitude of the average special forces soldier. But determined to try. Having had it hammered into him that the most Gucci equipment going would be wasted if it wasn't in the right place at the right time.

He made it across town to LX in under an hour. Reported to Inspector Philip for formal tasking. To be told nothing more than that the destination country was in Central America. Detailed briefing en route. And that the flight would be leaving from RAF Brize Norton in Oxfordshire late that afternoon. He changed and drew his radio and car keys, having beaten Wade in for once. Collected a pair of Peli cases containing his weapon and equipment. Then killed an hour over coffee with a shooting magazine, waiting for Wade.

'All right, Skip?' Wade, eventually. Looking a little the worse for wear. Properly dressed, of course. Clean-shaven and tidy enough to the casual inspection. Just very, very hungover.

'Good night, was it?'

'Is it that obvious?'

Mickey raised an eyebrow. Otherwise not replying. A copper didn't have to be CID to know that silence was the best interrogator.

'Fuck. Yeah, I got to bed about four this morning, and I wasn't alone.'

'Sounds good to me. The only problem now is that you look like shit. Here…'

Mickey reached into his bag and pulled out a steel travel mug. Screw top, spring-loaded cap. Almost idiot proof.

'Get this filled up with espresso. You're going to need to look a bloody sight better than you do now by the time we get to Brize. And take some painkillers.'

Cruising out on the M4, Wade was relegated to the passenger seat. Drank some coffee. Fell asleep. Leaving Mickey pondering the next step that Nemesis had mapped out for him. A return to lethal form, if it went to plan. Ideally to be carried out as soon as possible after the raid on Number 37. The anonymous messages very clear that Joe was already working on ways to find him.

The next task would result in a single kill, if successful. Someone close to Joe. Important to him. And delivering justice beyond anything he'd attempted to date. Whilst representing the most dangerous of his attacks on Joe Castagna's empire yet. He was still working through the plan in his mind when his airwave came to life.

'Romeo Four Six, Romeo Control.'

'Romeo Control, Four Six receiving.'

'Romeo Four Six, message from Major Cavendish.'

'Pass your message, Control.'

'Message is: Contact me when you arrive on site and before entering the terminal. Private briefing required. Message ends.'

'Control, Four Six, all received.'

'What's that all about, Skip?'

Wade, awakened by the radio. Mickey pursed his lips. Shaking his head in bemusement.

'Your guess is as good as mine. But I suspect it might just have something to do with this apparently sudden decision for the minister to go to Central America.'

Cavendish met them in the car park that served the air terminal. He walked over to the car, shooting a knowing glance at Wade through Mickey's open window.

'I presume you've had a good night, Constable Harris?'

Not waiting for the answer. 'I suggest you check in and join your colleagues? Reception will point you in the right direction. And when you get on the plane, be sure to sit behind Sir Patrick. I doubt he'll spare any attention for his protection team, but best to be sure, don't you think?'

Mickey nodded, tipping his head towards the terminal in an unspoken signal to Wade. Cavendish waited until the younger man was on his way into the building, then climbed into the car. Closing the door and turning to Mickey.

'I wasn't entirely open with you when we first met, Sergeant Bale. My appointment to the position of private secretary to the minister wasn't just a case of the defence establishment putting one of their own in place. Speaking very frankly, I was appointed to this role by the Royal and VIP Executive Committee.'

Mickey nodded. Thinking. RAVEC, the committee whose secretive deliberations determined protection policy for past and serving politicians. Chaired by a "former senior civil servant". A euphemism that fooled nobody with half an interest. And the major, with both a relevant regimental background and special forces experience.

'You're not just a private secretary, are you?'

'No, Michael, I'm somewhat more than that.' Cavendish nodded, stone-faced. 'Let's say that I'm in constant communication with the people dedicated to the security of this nation.'

Mickey was pretty sure that he knew exactly who the major was in communication with. And what information they were passing to him. Every phone call. Every email. And, he mused, a look inside Cavendish's personal file would probably make fascinating reading. If it wasn't redacted to the point of incomprehensibility.

RAVEC reported to the Home Secretary. The woman who also held the reins, however loosely, on MI5. And who, in the matter of a senior cabinet member, would put aside political rivalries and work closely with the Foreign Secretary. Who, in turn, controlled MI6. At least in theory.

'OK, so now I know who you really are. And that I mention that fact to anyone else at my personal risk.' Thanking his lucky stars that he'd been savvy enough to use a burner phone for the 999 call. 'So what is it that has you... and the people in the background... so bothered by this trip?'

Cavendish lowered his voice. Subconsciously recognising the significance of what he was about to reveal.

'What I am about to tell you is to go no further, Michael. I'm telling you because you won't be able to do your job if I don't. But you cannot tell your colleagues. Not unless the situation on the ground goes completely tits up. And you cannot tell your command structure. This is a matter of the utmost delicacy. And it carries significant security implications. National security. Either you can agree to that level of discretion, or—'

'I understand, Major.'

The other man looked at him levelly for a moment, then nodded. 'Very well. The minister has been tasked with making a very clear statement of intent to our rivals. By travelling to a country we have an interest in and making a speech to their national assembly. That country is Belize. You may be aware that it was the British armed forces that kept the country from being invaded by Guatemala in the

1970s and 80s. We pulled back from the country in 2010. Then went back in when Guatemala started getting uppity again a few years later. There's a permanent training unit based in Price Barracks, only a dozen soldiers, but we rotate infantry companies in routinely for jungle acclimatisation. Which is a polite fiction to camouflage what's effectively a rotating garrison arrangement.'

He pointed at the hulking airframe of an RAF Voyager transport plane squatting close to the terminal.

'That aircraft will be taking off in an hour or so with two companies from 40 Royal Marine Commando on board. Two hundred men with the same fitness, skills and mindset as some US special forces. Destined for a period of intensive jungle warfare training. It's a snap deployment apparently, designed to test our ability to put boots on the ground within twenty-four hours. But there's another agenda hidden behind that innocent explanation. And this, Michael, for the avoidance of doubt, is the sensitive part.'

'Go on. Nothing you say here is going any further.'

Cavendish looked at him. Nodded and continued. 'The Guatemalans have fallen on hard times. And so, as countries often do these days, they've turned to the Chinese to help them.'

'And Chinese assistance usually comes with strings.'

'Exactly. In this case, future access to a port facility on the Pacific coast for visiting PLA warships. In return for which the Guatemalans have enlisted their new allies to help push for the return of Belize. And, intelligence suggests, to provide them with the sort of equipment that might enable them to bulldoze the Belize self-defence force out of the way. Light armour, mobile artillery and some spotting drones would probably be enough. All in China's interests, of course. One in the eye for the UK, if their allies were to pull it off.'

'And HMG doesn't like the sound of that, I guess?'

Cavendish smiled humourlessly. 'Lost influence tends not to play well with Johnny and Joanna Public. Who've had enough of government incompetence in the last few years to last them a lifetime. And so Sir Patrick has been despatched along with the marines. To make it very clear to the people of Belize, and thereby Guatemala, and of course China, that HMG will not stand for any such thing. The marines' training area will be close enough to the border for them to react quickly to any incursion. And two more of those monsters...' he gestured to the Voyager '...will be on stand-by to drop in the rest of the battalion. Plus some Special Boat Service operators to take the fight back into the enemy rear area. Along with a Globemaster or two full of the sort of kit that we tend to call force multipliers. Gun drones, area denial systems and the like. The PM is determined to make sure that a hands-off message is taken seriously.'

'Hence Sir Patrick's short-notice mission.'

'Exactly.'

Mickey shook his head.

'But that can't be all there is to it. Or why are we having this cloak-and-dagger conversation in the car park?'

Cavendish nodded. 'The wild card here is obviously China. And sending their former best friend to give them the good news isn't without calculation on the PM's part. But neither is it without risk.'

'There's a chance the Chinese will try to take him out?'

The major shrugged. 'It's not out of the question. For one thing, such an action would send a very clear message back to HMG. Written in blood. And for another, Sir Patrick knows where plenty of bodies are buried when it comes to corruption high up in the Communist Party.'

'But even if they kill him, surely he'll have made records as to what they're afraid he might publicise?'

'Hardly the point, is it? Look at the way the Russians dealt with their dissenting oligarchs. Mysterious deaths that tended not to be quite such a mystery if you were in the same position. Publish and be damned seems to have been superseded by publish and be assassinated these days, don't you think?'

Mickey thought for a moment. 'But if it's that risky, why—'

'Why put the poor bastard in that unenviable position?' Cavendish's lips compressed in a grim smile. 'Because, Michael, this already *is* a war. Don't let the optics of it fool you. We've been at war with China since the turn of the century. Just by other means, and for most of that time not really facing up to the fact. Now it's getting hotter it's just somewhat more obvious. And clearly we have some catching up to do. Which is why the PM has made it very clear that Sir Patrick, having apparently chosen his side, needs to stand up to be counted. And accept the risk he helped to bring about.'

'And you know all this how, exactly?'

The major shook his head. 'That's for another time. For

now you'll just have to take my word for it. And make sure your colleagues are ready to deal with any attempt on the principal. We need to make sure that in this instance accidents do *not* happen.'

25

Mickey and the rest of his team kitted up for their HRE role once the Voyager was airborne. Their clothing appropriate, if a little individual. Varying shades of khaki, for the most part. Looking like a slightly motley version of an infantry fire team. Lacking only the Kevlar helmets, and only then for reasons of profile, rather than availability. The sniggers from the marines seated behind them drying up when Mickey took his long arm from its Peli case to clean and oil it. A Heckler & Koch G36C carbine; 5.56mm, high velocity stopping power. Standard HRE issue. Twelve rounds a second from thirty-round magazines that clipped together for fast reloads. Gucci kit, and proper heavy close-range firepower. The bootnecks casting the weapon envious glances.

Mickey had already given his colleagues as much of the good news as he could. Telling his team that this was, in part, an evaluation mission. With Cavendish, not only ex-SAS but looking crisp and efficient in his number 8 combat uniform, as the evaluator. Not true, but a very effective way to make sure all concerned got up on their toes. And stayed that way.

'We're going to assume that the other side are very much

after kidnapping or assassinating the principal. And we'll be managing his security in a way that befits that threat. In short, HRE doing exactly what it says on the tin.'

He'd noted the presence of four additional bodies on the flight. Three men and a woman. Fitting a certain profile, one that Mickey reckoned he knew from his days at Credenhill Lines. But on drawing the major's attention to them, the only response had been a dismissive shrug.

'BATSUB.'

'The what now?'

Cavendish had rolled his eyes. 'Sorry, I forget we don't all talk Green. British Army Training Support Unit Belize. BATSUB. They tend to be experienced soldiers who've done the training course and fancy living out here for a while. It's a pretty cool posting, if you don't mind the heat. And the spiders. Black widows for show, brown recluses for go. With a bite that'll rot a finger clean off. Snakes, of course. The fer-de-lance being bloody horrible. It's got venom that can pre-digest an entire limb if not treated promptly. And the Mayan coral snake's bite can kill a man in minutes. So watch where you tread. Mosquitos, of course. Poison frogs. Bullet ants...'

'Bullet ants?'

'They have a bite like a bullet wound, from a pain perspective. Lasts for a whole day too. At least one of those poor bootneck bastards is going to find that out the hard way.'

'So those four have volunteered to train soldiers in an environment that is basically trying to either kill them immediately or digest them from the outside in?'

Cavendish had smiled, wry amusement shining through the fatigue.

'I do believe he's got it. Don't tell me, you thought they were some sort of elite commando unit.'

He'd wandered off down to the galley to get a coffee, volunteering to fetch one for Mickey. Who took another look at the quartet. Forced to agree that they didn't look all that alert. Three of them fast asleep in their seats, the fourth reading a book.

The Voyager touched down smoothly just after midnight. Taxiing into a protective circle of local defence force soldiers. Platoon strength: thirty very alert and determined-looking men. While the two companies of marines deplaned via the rear and middle steps, the minister and his protection team were directed forward. Coming down the stairway, Mickey directed his colleagues to spread out in a loose box formation around the waiting vehicles. Their loaded carbines, mags double stacked, drawing knowing glances and muttered comments from the soldiers.

'One minute.' Sir Patrick called Cavendish over and gestured to the marines. 'I'd like to talk to these guys. Can you ask their CO to get them to listen in?'

The major nodded his understanding and walked over to the marines' commanding officer. Who nodded in turn, calling his men into a tight half-circle. Their major saluting Sir Patrick punctiliously and gesturing to his men.

'All yours, sir.'

'Thank you, Major.' The politician turned to look at the assembled marines. Then walked into the middle of their formation, no more than a few feet from the front rank. Mickey shook his head at his fellow officers, gesturing them to stay back.

'Good morning, gentlemen. It's to be hoped you feel a

little more human than I do right now. I also hope you have more good fortune in avoiding the various biting creatures that infest this otherwise delightful part of the world. When I was last here in uniform it was the bullet ants that worried us most, because those nasty little bastards are a good deal more prevalent than spiders and snakes. Trust me, if a bullet ant sinks its teeth into you it'll feel like a red-hot poker. For about a day.'

Mickey shot the major a glance, seeing the same look on his friend's face as that of most of the listening marines. Sutherland was tapping into a shared heritage. And politician or not, it already had his audience on his side.

'I was just a wet behind the ears lieutenant, of course. And things were perhaps a little less professional in my day, although the old sweats wouldn't entertain such a suggestion. Every generation thinks the next won't deal with life's challenges as well as they did. And every generation, gentlemen, is wrong. I'm sure your senior NCO's would share my view, if only privately. While, of course, telling anyone that'll listen that just isn't like it used to be.'

A ripple of quiet laughter greeted the comment.

'Good, isn't he?'

Mickey nodded at Cavendish's whispered comment.

'Now I'm sure you know why it is you're really here.' The soldiers were suddenly visibly more attentive. 'The official story is that you're here to undertake jungle training. And that's true. But there's more to it than that. HMG is sending a message to its competitors in the region. Foreign powers who would dearly like to snap up this small but determined country. And that message is a simple one: keep your hands off. If the people of Belize were to vote to unify with their Guatemalan neighbours, so be it. But until that happens, the UK has undertaken the role of guaranteeing their independence. You are following a proud tradition, whether you know it or not. Britain might not always have been the most beneficial of nations when it came to foreign policy, but by God we're on the side of right now. And I know, if it comes down to the use of force, you'll do your country proud.'

He turned to the officers, standing off to one side.

'Thank you, gentlemen. On behalf of your country and your government. And now, Major Cavendish, perhaps we should be on the move?'

The drive to their hotel was a short one through empty streets. Cavendish apparently sharing Mickey's approval of the low profile that was being adopted.

'This visit hasn't been publicised. The PM hopes that Sir Patrick's speech to the national assembly will come as something of a surprise to the other side.'

They installed the politician safely in his room. Carbine-armed Prot officers standing guard on the door and outside terrace. After which Cavendish outlined the visit plan to Mickey, and Wade.

'The speech to the national assembly is scheduled for 11.00. Nicely timed for the evening news bulletins in the UK. He makes the speech, we get in the cars. Back to the airport and airborne by twelve. Which will put us back in the UK in time for breakfast TV and radio slots. In which Sir Patrick will repeat our absolute commitment to resisting China's attempts at global dominance. With Belize as the front line in that resistance.'

Putting himself on the side of the angels, Mickey thought.

And possibly, just possibly avoiding the executioner's axe at the next reshuffle.

'We'll maintain a two-man guard on the room overnight.' Mickey turned to Wade. 'Relieve the guys at 03.30 and give them a chance to get their heads down. Don't know about you, but there's no way I'm going to get any sleep before that. Fancy a turn around the grounds?'

Wade grinned, having known all along this would be Mickey's intention. His skipper not being famous for his ability to sit around and relax. They left the major to his own devices, walking out through a side door and into the darkness of the hotel's unlit grounds. Mickey lowering his voice to a soft murmur.

'Get veiled up.' He took the British army-issue face veil from around his neck. Draping it over his head and tucking it into his clothing. The perforated scrim loosely woven. Covering his white face while allowing him unhindered vision. 'Right, let's do this like they taught us in Hereford. Bounds and overwatch. Thirty-metre spacing. Off you go.'

He sank into the undergrowth and watched as Wade patrolled slowly forwards. Staying in the shadows and moving slowly through the grounds. Sinking into the darker shadow once he'd covered thirty paces. Becoming invisible to the naked eye. Waiting for Mickey to move up and pass him. The two men patrolled slowly around the hotel, seeing and hearing nothing other than the incessant buzz of insects. Mickey paced slowly up to where Wade had taken cover in the shadow of a large bush. Squatting down slowly beside him.

'This place is as quiet as the grave. I think we can go and get an hour's kip before—'

'No sudden movements, gentlemen.' The woman's voice in his earpiece was whisper quiet, but authoritative. Stilling his urge to go into a compromised comms routine. 'We're your guardian angels. Do not react, do not turn around, do not start looking for us. When I tell you, both get up and move off towards the hotel. Make it look like you've completed doing your sneaky-beaky turn and all you want now is to get into your pits. Don't look back, and don't go for your weapons if you hear anything out of the ordinary. It'll only make the men stalking you nervous. And we don't want them shooting you, do we? One click if you understood all that.'

Mickey pushed his transmit button briefly.

'Good. OK, get on with it. We've got your backs.'

Mickey nodded. Stood up, muttering to Wade to follow his example. Walked at a steady pace towards the hotel. Not looking back. And feeling vulnerable in a way he wasn't sure he'd ever felt before. Resisting the temptation to look back only by force of will. Until the gunshots.

Suppressed fire. No louder than a rumour of a distant war. Subsonic ammunition, at a guess. Two shots, with less than a second between them. Followed a moment later by a long burst of the same from the near distance. A full magazine's worth on full auto.

The two men turned to see a pair of camouflage-dressed figures wearing night-vision goggles running across the grass towards them. And a pair of sprawled bodies a few paces from where they stood. The newcomers grabbed hold of the bodies by their collars, dragging them towards the closest foliage. Both men were undeniably dead. Headshots. And equally undeniably Far Eastern in origin. Both corpses with an unfamiliar design of suppressed machine pistol strapped to body harnesses festooned with kit. Spare mags. Stun grenades. Medical kit. The full special forces Christmas tree.

'Get their knives.'

The woman's urgent whisper brought Mickey back to the here and now. Snapping off the amazement that had him frozen where he stood. He stooped, picking up a pair of wickedly sharp fighting knives from the close-cropped turf. Blades that had been intended for him and Wade. Following the woman into the bushes, he realised that he recognised her from the flight in. One of the so-called BATSUB personnel Cavendish had been so dismissive of. She pulled a spray bottle from a pouch on her belt. Handing it to Mickey.

'Follow us. And spray this on the ground we pulled them across.'

Mickey and Wade followed the pair as they dragged the corpses across the open ground to the hotel's fence. Mickey spraying a fine mist of something odourless across the grass behind them. They stopped at a gate in the property's boundary. The woman taking the spray bottle back and using it to mist the grass around the corpses.

'Enzyme mix. Digests the blood as if it was never there.'

A moment later the other two men Mickey had spotted on the flight in appeared out of the darkness. Each of them dragging another identically equipped body. Both riddled with bullet wounds. The man who seemed to be their leader nodded to Mickey.

'Sorry we had to do that in front of you. Your night-time wandering didn't give us much choice.'

'Who the fuck are—'

'All in good time.' The other man held up a hand. 'Alpha One to Bravo, immediate extraction. Team plus four hostile KIA. Location two.'

He listened to the return traffic for a moment before looking up at Mickey.

'I know, you have a thousand questions. And you've got about a minute before we're out of here. So you'll get more out of us if I just talk?'

Mickey nodded.

'What can I tell you? Not much. We're freelance. Contractors. Paid to come out here, deal with these people and then fade back into the landscape. As in that old "we were never here" trope.'

'Shouldn't the regiment be doing this sort of thing?'

The other man shook his head.

'That's hot war stuff. Whereas this is a very cold war indeed. These poor dead bastards are probably equally deniable. We use ex-special forces; the Chinese just don't give a shit. If they'd managed to slot any of us then HMG could happily deny any involvement. Having counted our men back in again with no losses. Although the boys who are about to pick us up are from the regiment. They've been tracking this hit team for the last couple of days.'

'So they flew you in just to make the kill. But...'

The sound of car engines disturbed the night's quiet. A pair of vehicles coming along the seafront road.

'How did they know you'd be here, when the visit was only briefed to you guys yesterday? Good question. I'll have to leave that one with you though. It's time we weren't here.'

A pair of Defence Force Land Rovers pulled up at the kerb a few feet away. Two pairs of obviously British soldiers jumping out and setting to dealing with the dead Chinese soldiers. Zipping each of them into a body bag, weapons and kit included. Then pitching each one into the rear of the vehicle. Spraying the grass where the corpses had lain with the enzyme mix.

'What will you do with them?'

'Not my need to know. Dump them in the jungle, probably, without their kit. That'll go back to Hereford for analysis. The bodies will be unrecognisable inside a week, bare bones within a month. Just another unexplained disappearance. But the other side will be in no doubt what happened. Right, we're off. Alpha team, embark front vehicle.'

'But...'

'We'll see you on the flight back. You can buy me a beer and see if I can answer the other nine hundred and ninety-nine questions, eh?'

26

Mickey relieved his colleague Franklin, standing guard on the hotel's balcony. Unable to sleep as the full realisation of what had just happened sank in. Just how close he and Wade had come to a violent death.

'Skip...' Wade had been equally bemused, his tone that of a man who wasn't quite sure if what had just taken place had really happened. 'Those two Chinese guys were after killing us, right?'

'Looked that way to me.'

'And those contractors had our radio freqs.'

Pronounced like freaks.

'Yeah.'

'So I guess the major was in on the whole thing.'

'That's what I'm thinking.'

He sent Wade off to at least try to get some sleep. And took a seat on the room's terrace. Joined shortly before dawn by Cavendish. Who, freshly shaved and with his uniform pressed, had clearly been briefed in the meantime. Raising a hand to forestall Mickey's comment.

'I couldn't have told you even if I'd known. The first rule of sneaky-beaky being...'

'You do not talk about sneaky-beaky?'

'In one. Sounds like they saved your bacon though.'

'But you knew there was a Chinese hit team coming after us?'

The major shook his head patiently. 'No, Michael. I did not. I wouldn't have allowed you to go wandering around the hotel grounds if I had. I did know that there were MI6 intelligence operatives tasked to oversight the visit. But until I was briefed on how close you and Constable Harris came to being killed I had no idea that there was any sort of threat. It does rather seem as if they intended to get their retaliation in first though, rather than waiting for Sir Patrick's speech. Doesn't it?'

'And what now?'

'Now?' Cavendish shook his head. 'Nothing much. The minister wakes up, has a shave and gets into his best bib and tucker. And we, for the avoidance of doubt, tell him nothing. The release of any information with regard to this matter is an MI6 decision. Which makes it a matter, I've been told, for the Foreign Office. So, we escort him to the assembly, you and your colleagues looking all business. He makes his speech, to general happiness from the elected representatives. After all, he's just about to promise whatever it takes to keep the country independent of a somewhat overbearing neighbour.

'And then we head for home. Easy. The difficult bit was stopping the Chinese from butting in. From here on, Michael, all you and your chaps have to do is make sure the minister doesn't get mobbed by well-wishers.'

27

To be fair to the major, Mickey was forced to concede, the rest of the morning went like clockwork. The move from hotel to the city's council building, barely half a mile away, was a simple enough job. Unlike the move from the airport, the vehicles provided were civilian. A pair of Chrysler Jeeps for the visiting dignitary and his escort. The cars slightly past their best years but still tidy enough. With a pair of Defence Force long wheelbase Land Rovers leading and bringing up the rear. Ex-British Army Afghan issue from the look of it. Each one loaded with half a dozen of the ferocious-looking local troops.

Mickey rode shotgun in the minister's car. Making a change to the usual SOP by ushering Sir Patrick to the front vehicle. Let any opposition think the rear car would be the one with the high value asset. His head on a swivel, checking left and right with metronomic regularity. Not even a hint of a threat. But unable to stop his mind drifting away to the minute that he heard the two muffled thuds. And turned to find the men who'd been hunting him dead. Neither of them even having known what hit them.

At the council building there was a small crowd waiting to greet the minister. Small, but vociferous in their evident support for yet another British intervention in their relationship with Guatemala. Cavendish discreetly indicated the cameramen lurking on the group's fringes.

'The press are here, Michael. Might I suggest two of you leave your carbines in the vehicle while the other two keep watch out here? I think the optics will be better if you escort Sir Patrick into the building with nothing more obvious than your pistols. I can imagine the headlines that the Chinese will come up with if you take him in with machine guns ready.'

Mickey and Wade walked the minister into the building without incident. Merging into the background as he took the podium and addressed a selection of the national assembly's representatives. Delivering a short but passionate speech touching on free speech, democratic rights and strength of collective defence.

All of which went down well with the assembled politicians. The same news crew that had broadcast their arrival recording the whole thing. Mickey realised that the speech had been exquisitely crafted to avoid gifting any verbal own goals to the other side of the argument. And, if nowhere near starting to relax, he sensed that the tension levels around the visit were subtly lowering.

Emerging into the sunlight he was about to usher Sir Patrick into the front vehicle again. But was prevented from doing so by the Belizean minister of defence and army commander. The two men flanking Sir Patrick and gesturing to the rearmost Land Rover. After a brief discussion. Cavendish turned to Mickey with a knowing smile.

'It seems that these two gentlemen would very much like a few minutes with the minister on the way to the airport. I'm guessing this is their last chance to lobby for even more British support, and they don't intend to miss the opportunity. I think they intend pointing out that the airport has a very long runway. Quite possibly wondering if the RAF would like to send its Typhoons to visit every now and then.'

Mickey thought for a moment. Then shrugged.

'Why not? It's a nice piece of sleight of hand. If he rides in the back of the rear Landie with them, Wade and I can double up in the front. James and Franklin can go in the rear Jeep as passengers. And the locals can fill the rest of the spaces with soldiers, make them look occupied. That'll work.'

With the convoy's occupants shuffled to match his hastily amended plan, the lead Land Rover led them out onto the street. Motorcycle outriders clearing a path through the traffic with a no-nonsense approach. Wade steering the Land Rover round the most obvious potholes. The two men exchanged wry grins at the state of the road.

'We might as well be in Croydon.' Mickey hanging on to the door handle as Wade navigated around another crater. 'Once we're onto the Northern Highway the ride ought to get smoother. We can only hope the guys in the back aren't getting too rough a—'

The windscreen was suddenly opaque, the heavy Land Rover shuddering as a blast wave hammered across it. Wade braked to a halt, his vision completely obscured. Mickey reacted as he'd been trained. A small part of him waiting for the shooting to start.

'Get the glass out!'

Both men wielded their carbines. Hammering at the

crazed glass with the weapons' butts. Punching holes in the crazed windscreen big enough to see through. Mickey reversed his weapon, ready to fire. Gaping at the scene of destruction revealed.

The street down which they'd been driving had been transformed. A thriving city thoroughfare reduced to carnage. A dozen corpses lying scattered around what appeared to have been a massive car bomb. The leading car and the Land Rover in front of it appearing to have taken the brunt of the blast.

The Jeep was on its side with its nearside bodywork and glass blown away. The Land Rover stopped, its bodywork engulfed in fire. Its occupants were apparently unable to move, dimly visible through the flames. The rearmost Jeep was sagging at the front on deflated tyres. The two soldiers in the front seats either dead or incapacitated. James and Franklin, perhaps shielded by their bodies, climbing unsteadily out from the rear doors. Their carbines ready to fire but lacking targets.

The panel behind them slid open. Cavendish shouting through it from the rear of the vehicle. 'Can we get through?'

Mickey looked at the rubble-strewn road surface. 'Not without blowing the tyres on debris! We'll have to go back!'

Cavendish's reply was crisp.

'This vehicle is ex-Afghan! Armoured tyres!'

Mickey leaned forward to shout through the ragged hole in the windscreen. 'Get in, guys! We're pushing through!'

The other two officers climbed hurriedly into the Land Rover's rear. Wade drove slowly past the wreckage of the other vehicles. Mickey's carbine was raised and ready as he searched for any sign of a hostile target. The sheer brutal power of the car bomb that had smashed the convoy becoming apparent. A twisted wreck, vaguely discernible as a pick-up truck, at the roadside. The cars parked beside it both ablaze, shunted into their neighbours. Shopfronts blown in, scattered dead and wounded in their dozens. And in the leading Land Rover, the stick-like figures of its occupants were engulfed in flames from the ruptured fuel tank.

The drive to the airport was conducted in silence, other than radio comms with the airport. Telling the Voyager's crew to be ready for immediate take-off. When they reached the airstrip the big plane's engines were already idling with a thin shriek of restrained power. Mickey stopped the Land Rover at the foot of the single stairway. Then told his team to debus and cover their arcs. He shot glances to his rear as Sir Patrick, still white-faced, got out of the vehicle's rear. His parting comments to the Belizeans shouted over the engine noise. Loud enough for Mickey to hear.

'Rest assured, this outrage will not go unnoticed! The United Kingdom is made of sterner stuff than our enemies seem to think!'

He shook hands with the two men and went up the steps. Leaving Cavendish and the Prot officers to follow him.

The aircraft was taxiing for the runway before Mickey had his belt fastened. Pondering the significance of Sutherland having completely blanked him as he'd walked past. The pilots throttling up to get airborne as soon as the turn onto the landing strip was complete. The Voyager's engines screamed, hurling the massive aircraft into as fast a climb as possible. Lifting the vulnerable transport out of man portable anti-aircraft missile range. With, Mickey presumed, its defensive aids suite ready to spit chaff and flares if needed.

Once the climb-out was complete Cavendish got out of his seat and beckoned to Mickey. Gesturing to a row of seats at the rear of the front cabin.

'Sir Patrick is furious. I had to tell him about the events of last night. Better he finds out now than when MI6 decide to brief him. And I'm afraid we're both somewhat the focus of his ire.'

Mickey nodded, grim-faced. Having guessed where this was going.

'No shit. We didn't tell him that the Chinese were trying to assassinate him. And now he's thinking that if he'd known, it could all have been different.'

'Exactly. And he's been busy on his telephone. I'm to be the subject of a departmental investigation led by the permanent secretary's tame hatchet man. And you, I'm afraid, are off his team. He "doesn't want to see your face again". Your colleagues can drive us back to the Hall; you and Constable Harris will just have to go back to London. I'm sorry, Michael, we both seem to be somewhat in the shit.'

Mickey thought for a moment. 'And presumably none of this can be divulged to my management?'

'It'll get out, eventually. But no, I doubt that SIS are going to want it made public that they've been running hit teams on foreign territory. It's a bit like masturbation I suppose. Everyone does it, but nobody ever owns up to it.' He sighed. 'The best-laid plans of mice and men, eh? I'll have a word with a couple of people when I can get a minute to myself once we're back on the ground. See if I can mitigate the damage for you.'

Mickey nodded. Wondering what he was going to be walking into the next morning.

'OK. I'll brief my guys accordingly. And then I think I'm going to need a beer.'

He brought the other three team members up to speed with the development. Thanked them for the sympathy offered. Knew it was bad when none of the usual jokes got wheeled out. Then left his men to get some sleep. Wandering down the length of the plane until he found the contractors in the rear cabin. One of them stood up, plucking a pair of bottles from a cool box. Then walked down the aisle to meet him. Gesturing to the seats beside them and passing Mickey the chilled bottle.

'Here you go, get that down your neck. Let's sit here, eh? Best if you don't get too much of an eyeful of the others. We tend to be a bit jealous of our privacy.' An inch or so below six feet, he had sandy hair and a knowing expression. Blue eyes set in a narrow, watchful face and a nose that had seen better days. Held out a hand to shake, the grip firm but not crushing.

'Ian Shaw. Ex-Regiment. Now what Tom Clancy used to call a shadow warrior. The prick. I hear you had a bit of unscheduled nastiness on the way out to the airport.'

'I'm Mickey Bale. Michael when I'm on duty. And yeah, you could call it that. Hence the scramble take-off.'

Mickey told him the bald facts of the car bombing. And the minister's reaction.

'Well, Mickey called Michael when you're on duty, I guess the coneheads running this mission ought to have seen that coming. The Chinese have never been famous for their subtlety when it comes to the close-in stuff. And they have a big enough embassy in Belize City for there to be a good few intelligence officers on the premises. Someone's going to get their arse kicked in for that. But it won't be you.'

'Why not?'

'Because you, Mickey, were bright enough to let the principal ride in the back of the vehicle least likely to be targeted. Which, I'll point out to you, is obviously the only reason he's still alive. You'll be fine. In fact I'll bet you a pint on it. You can call me on this number when you want to pay up.'

The card was plain white, with a single phone number.

'You don't overdo it with the details, do you?'

Shaw shrugged. 'You try doing what we do for a living, neither would you. The Chinese are probably trying to find out who slotted their hit team even as we speak. And were they to do so, I reckon our life expectancy would be measurable in days. So, no, we don't exactly throw names and addresses around.'

'So why give me this?'

Shaw shrugged, getting up to go back to his team. 'You seem like a decent guy. And probably good value for a beer. Whoever's paying.'

28

Dawn, rosy-fingered, tickling the rooftops. Joe, Eddie and Lewis in the Rhino, ghosting into town through light traffic. Heading for Smithfield.

Joe walked into the caff like he owned the place. Which, in point of fact, he partly did. Along with every other participant in the meeting he'd called. Neutral territory, the Bosphorus Cafe. Owned by an incorruptible Turk by the name of Sebnem. Who had been very happy when the proposal was made several years before. For her business to be the recipient of a capital injection from each of the big crime families. Given free rein to make the caff into a nice little earner. With a proper coffee machine, and all the right kitchen gear to boot.

Enough wedge to go out and recruit the best cooks going. Which had turned the caff into a bit of a destination, for the cognoscenti. There'd even been talk of a Michelin star, after Giles Coren had visited one morning. Lured in by Sebnem's advertising, the offer of "top nosh for not much dosh". And had then rhapsodised over his full English in the *Times*. Putting the Bosphorus in the papers and starting the gold rush.

Which was why a stream of punters were having to

be turned away this morning. A private engagement. Apologies for the lack of notice. Please go away and eat somewhere else. And no, it really doesn't matter whose friend you are.

Lewis entered the caff at Joe's shoulder. His trusty Smith & Wesson .45 auto tucked under the Rhino's driver's seat. Deigned to let the private security present pat him down. And not just any security. Proper hard men. With manners, mind you. Nobody wanted to get on the wrong side of these attendees. But if the need arose they'd close down any agg before it got serious. Every gang leader's bodyguard present was disarmed and proven so. For show. Because the first man to draw a weapon in this company would spark a bloody massacre. And besides, with Lewis to hand, Joe didn't need a gun.

'Joe! We were just wondering when you was going to show.'

Albie. The mouthiest of them. The flashiest too. Gold Rolex President, gold bracelet, gold neck chain. Old-fashioned gangster style. If you could call it style, in Joe's jaundiced opinion. His own white gold Submariner understated, but every bit as expensive.

'Nothing wrong with arriving dead on time, Albert. The big mistake is—'

'Arriving dead! Don't we know it!'

The remaining participants listened with an air of indulgence. The Joe and Albie needle being a constant factor in their negotiations. Like sonic wallpaper.

'So, we getting down to it?' Sammy Chin, speaking through a mouthful of bacon sandwich. And nobody could blame him, given how exceptional the cook's bacon sandwiches were. 'You called the meeting, Joe. Why not tell us what's on your mind?'

The rules being that each of them could call one meeting in each calendar year. Either on their own behalf, or for another member of the group, if favours were in order. To deal with petty disputes. Boundary questions. Accidental border clashes. And all the other small matters that might otherwise become a distraction. Or end up costing more than they were worth. On occasion they had even been known to ask Sebnem to mediate a solution. Respecting both her common sense and the fact that she gave no shits for any of them. All being sworn to respect her impartial decision.

But this was different. This meeting had been called by Joe, at short notice. And everyone present knew why. Joe looked around the table and then started talking. Looking at each of them in turn as he spoke. His voice level. No anger, perfectly rational. Sending some messages. One: this is just about business. Two: I am confident that I will deal with this. Three: I will be watching to see how you all respond to what I say.

'It doesn't take a genius to work out why I've called the meeting. You know that someone's been hitting my operation. Hitting it hard. One of my dealers was shot dead. Looking like a pro hit. Then one of my cash collections was ambushed. Five good men killed and the money torched. A lot of money. And now one of my facilities has been attacked. Employees beaten senseless. Then the police called. My people nicked and my merchandise confiscated.'

Merchandise. That got a few tight smiles around the table. Especially from Albie. Who preferred the old-fashioned term "toms" to describe prostitutes. No matter where they'd come from.

'You know that this was nothing to do with any of us. We all have equivalent facilities. We're all equally vulnerable to reprisal.'

Joe nodded at the speaker. One of the two women present. Neither of them apparently seeing anything strange in discussing the liberation of trafficked prostitutes in business terms.

'I believe that to be the case. These appear to be the actions of a single person. Male, age unknown. Highly proficient with firearms. A gunfighter, from the footage I've seen. Good at hand to hand as well. And well informed. Very well informed.'

'So you got a rat? Find the rat, kill the rat.'

Joe raised an eyebrow at the interjection. 'Yeah, thanks, Albie. When I find the rat I'll do a good deal more to the cunt than kill it.' Joe nodding his apologies to the women. Both of whom stared back impassively. 'But in the meantime I'd like some assurances.'

'Assurances?'

Joe looked over at his sparring partner with the barest hint of irritation. Lewis reckoning he was resisting the urge to ask Albie if he was a fucking parrot or what?

'I'd like to be assured, Albert, that this isn't one of you having a quiet chip at my organisation to see what I'll do. The answer, in case you were wondering, being sat behind me.'

Lewis kept his face stone-like. Not showing how much he gloried in being Joe's champion.

'It isn't any of us.' Sammy shaking his head to emphasise.

'We all know the madness that would lead to. Nobody here wants to go back to the mess we had ten years ago.'

When a relatively small dispute had escalated. Setting half the foot soldiers in London against the other half. Five months of killing and disappearances. Ending up with the Bosphorus Cafe peace accord.

'What I thought too. Hence the meeting. It's always best to be clear though.' Joe looking around the table again. 'And to tell you all one more thing. Which is that when I find out who's doing this to me, I'm having him. Or her. There'll be no protection for the bastard. No hiding from me. And whoever's turf they're on, Lewis here will be coming for them. And I... *request*... you all to extend him the courtesy of any assistance he might ask of you. Because an attack on any of us is an attack on us all. Right?'

Nods around the table. Perhaps a little reluctantly. Nobody really liking the thought of big Lewis rampaging around on their ground. Which, of course, would make helping him get what he wanted the quickest way to get rid of him.

'Good. And thank you. I appreciate your understanding... and your restraint... at this difficult time.'

Joe grabbed a couple of bacon sandwiches as he stood to leave. Because, for one thing, taking food off the table emphasised their shared interests. Breaking bread together a demonstration of their tenuous alliance. And, for another, because Sebnem's bacon sandwiches were the best in a ten-mile radius. And only marginally less feted than her baklava. Eddie was waiting in the Rhino's passenger seat. Looking at Joe as he got back into the car. Assessing his mood.

'How'd it go?'

Joe shrugged. 'How'd it go, Lewis?'

The big man fished his pistol out from under the driver's seat. Tucking it back into his shoulder holster.

'They all looked like butter wouldn't melt. The boss told them when we find the rat he's sending me to get the bastard.'

'What'd they say to that?'

'What can they say?' Joe, through a mouthful of bread, butter and bacon. 'They all looked like sheep. That isn't my concern though. My concern is finding the rat. Are we any closer to doing that, Eddie?'

The question Eddie had been waiting for.

'We don't have enough information to pin it down. Warren was known to enough people that whoever did him didn't need any inside information. The cash collection was probably known to forty, perhaps fifty blokes.'

'Yeah. I get that. Counters, guards, gang kids, all that. But add in Number 37...'

'Gets us nowhere.' The frustration evident in Eddie's voice. 'We never kept 37 a secret, not really. Half the organisation knew we had a training house, and half of them knew where it was, I reckon. One man with a grudge, that's all it'd take. He turns snout, the filth pass the information to whoever it is that's doing the hits. Did you see the co-operation that the *Clarion* got in getting inside?'

Joe was quiet for so long that Eddie was on the point of asking him what was wrong when he spoke again. With a thoughtful note in his voice.

'The *Clarion*. Is that the answer, I wonder? You, Eddie, might just have shown me where to look.'

Eddie sounded faintly surprised. 'I did?'

'Whether you know it or not, yeah.' A glint of delight in Joe's eyes. 'So we know that the Met have got a hard-on for gangs in general. And us in particular. Which is why we recruited that muppet Felgate in the first place.'

Eddie nodded. None the wiser. 'But how does that—'

'It all makes sense. The Met want to nail the gangs. That Chinese bitch is never off the TV. Telling everyone what a "corrosive influence" we are on London society, or some bollocks like that. So what if the Met was feeding information from some snout or other to a tame hit man?'

'A hit man?' Eddie strained every mental muscle not to betray his disappointment that they were back to that one again. 'It sounds a bit…'

'Over the top? Not a hit man then. Some bloke with a grudge. And access to weapons. Perhaps even provided by the Met.'

'But that'd be like the shoot-to-kill thing in Ireland.' Both men looked at Lewis, mildly surprised. Not expecting a constructive addition to the discussion from that quarter. 'There's no need to look at me like that. They made us learn about it in General Studies, and it was on the telly too. The army were right off their lead in the Eighties. Killing the IRA left, right and centre. All deniable and that, but everyone knew it was happening. And it was ignored, even when they shot criminals and civilians by mistake. Official collusion was what they said on Panorama.'

'Yeah.' Joe's tone thoughtful. 'Let's face it, they've got the information. They've got the shooters. And they're the biggest gang in London all right.'

'So what was that about the *Clarion*?'

Eddie's question snapped Joe back to his insight of a moment before.

'Yeah, the *fucking Clarion*. Which paper was the first to report about Number 37? And had a photographer in the house two minutes after the filth arrived? The *Clarion* did. How did they know where to be at that time of night? Obvious, really. Either the filth tipped them off, or this mystery hit man did. Either way, there's one person who can tell us for sure. Whoever took those pics. We find the photographer, then we find the killer.'

29

'Sergeant Bale. I was hoping to catch you before you went off duty. Please report to my office before leaving the building.'

Mickey had been minutes from leaving LX. Having beaten the early traffic into London. The Voyager having caught a tailwind and arrived at Brize an hour early. He'd ignored his in-box and typed up and submitted his post-tour report in record time. But his job phone had rung just as he was booking his Glock back into the armoury. Inspector Phil's number. His request politely framed, sending Mickey a message nonetheless. The formal use of rank a signal to expect something more formal than the usual. A meeting without refreshments of any kind. The burning hoop he'd have to jump through before getting to go home and unwind his tightly coiled psyche.

Which made it no surprise when he found the duty inspector's office rather more heavily populated than normal. What was surprising was the acreage of silver braid laid out to meet him. A very unhappy-looking Chief Superintendent Johnnie Palmer, head of Prot. Worse, standing next to him, his superior. Assistant Commissioner Jasmine Chen. Looking like she could shoot death rays from her eyes, given a sufficient excuse to do so. Mickey saluted, coming to attention and making his face blank. And behind them, Inspector Phil. His face pale. The result, Mickey guessed, of finding himself caught in the blowback.

'Ma'am. Sirs.'

And shut up. Being a firm believer that it was madness to pick up a spade when you were already in a hole.

'Sergeant Bale. Welcome back from your somewhat brief sojourn in Belize.'

AC Chen's words laced with acid. Mickey nodded.

'Thank you, ma'am.'

'Anything you'd like to share with us, Sergeant? Any detail that might have been omitted from your end-of-shift report?'

'No, ma'am.'

Jasmine's eyes narrowed, and Mickey wondered for a moment if this was death ray time.

'Your report detailed a High Risk Environment protection detail task to Belize. The flight out from Brize Norton. Overnight in a Belize City hotel. The principal delivering a speech to the national assembly. The drive back to the airport, flight home. All of which seems unaccountably sparse, to our uninformed eyes. Three lines of text. And yet Sir Patrick Sutherland's office has already been in contact this morning. Telling Inspector Green that you're now persona non grata on the minister's protection detail.'

She fell silent, fixing her gaze on Mickey. Who, having been beasted by the best, fixed his gaze on the wall behind her. Knowing never to volunteer an answer to a question still to be asked.

'Nothing to say, Sergeant?'

'No, ma'am.'

'No explanation as to why it should be that Sir Patrick no longer wants you protecting him? And no connection with the car bomb that was reported at about the same time you were heading for the airport?'

'I am unable to comment, ma'am.'

If it were possible, the assistant commissioner seemed to be reaching a new level of fury. Her face white with anger. Knuckles white too, placed on the desk before her.

'Sergeant Bale, you will now explain the circumstances of the events in Belize that have resulted in this stain on the department's reputation. In full. Omitting no detail. Do you understand me?'

'Yes, ma'am. I understand your order.'

A short pause. Long enough for it to become clear that Mickey wasn't going to start talking.

'Well then?'

This was it. No way to avoid it.

'My apologies, ma'am. I am forbidden to answer that question under the terms of the *Official Secrets Act of 1989*.'

All three officers stared at him, momentarily dumbstruck. Jasmine being the first to the counterpunch.

'Is this some sort of piss-take, Sergeant? Because if it is—'

'No, ma'am. No humour is intended.'

'You'd better start talking, Bale.' Mickey noted the abandonment of even vestigial politeness. 'Right now. Because if you don't, there will be a very prompt disciplinary board convened. Which will end your fucking Protection Command career with immediate effect. And send you back into front-line policing.'

Mickey looked up at the ceiling. Reflecting that it didn't get much more front line than the events of the previous twenty-four hours.

'And, with respect, ma'am, if I do, I will render myself liable to prosecution and incarceration. As will you, for forcing me to disclose an official secret. Under the terms of the act. Ma'am.'

Stand-off. Three very unhappy members of management stared back at him. One incandescent with rage. One dumbstruck, and probably wondering about the impact on his career. And Philip Green, just flat-out amazed. About time for a federation rep, perhaps? Mickey suspected it was.

But as he drew breath to make the request, AC Chen's phone rang. She looked at the caller display, thumb hovering over the red button. Saw who was calling and selected green instead.

'Good morning, ma'am.'

Oh really? There was only one ma'am in the chain of command above AC Chen. If, of course, the Queen was discounted. This was about to get interesting. She listened to her phone for a moment. Then replied, her voice emollient by comparison with the moment before.

'Yes, ma'am, I have him in front of me now.'

Here it came. Orders for the defenestration of Sergeant Michael Bale, most likely. Mickey braced himself for impact.

'Put the phone on speaker? Yes, ma'am.'

She placed the telephone on the desk before her and pressed the relevant button.

'You're on speaker, ma'am. In the room are myself, Chief Superintendent John Palmer and Inspector Philip

Green of Protection Command. And Sergeant Michael Bale. Recently returned from duty in Belize.'

To everyone's surprise, Mickey suspected, the voice from the phone's speaker was cheerful. A "job well done" voice, if Mickey was any judge. Even if he'd never actually met the commissioner in person.

'Good morning, gentlemen.'

He found himself returning the greeting along with his superiors. Wondering how many more turns were left in this insanity.

'It isn't very often that I get a call from the Chair of RAVEC, and even less so before I'm even in my car. So when I saw his number on the caller display, you can imagine that I was more than a little surprised.'

Jasmine Chen gave Mickey a look that he decided to interpret as "now you're really in the shit". Death rays poised to strike.

'Imagine my further surprise when he told me that he was calling to congratulate me on the conduct of one of my protection teams.'

Wait. What? Jasmine Chen's expression was caught somewhere between relief and horror.

'Specifically, he named Sergeant Michael Bale as having behaved in an exemplary manner. And being responsible for a decision that probably saved the life of the principal. And went on to add that while Sir Patrick Sutherland no longer wishes to be protected by Sergeant Bale, this should in no way reflect poorly on his competence or professionalism. Sergeant Bale, it seems, was part of what might best be described as a national security incident yesterday. An incident the detail of which Sir Charles wasn't able to share with me. But which he assures me has reflected in a tremendously positive way on Protection Command. And indeed the Met more generally.

'And he asked me to pass his thanks on to the officers in question, and to Sergeant Bale in particular. I can't offer a formal commendation of course, given the somewhat delicate location and circumstances. But what I can do is offer you my personal thanks for a difficult job. Well done, Sergeant Bale.'

'Thank you, ma'am.'

'No, Sergeant, thank *you*. Have a good day.'

Had there been a hint of amusement in those last few words? Mickey pondered the likely chain of events. A call from Cavendish to his mentor, then one from Sir Charles to the commissioner. And realised that he owed James Cavendish his thanks. Without his quickness of thought, Mickey would be twisting in the breeze now. Instead of which, behind his immaculately maintained deadpan, he was beyond smug. *Let's see you get out of that gracefully, Assistant Commissioner.* Jasmine Chen stared at him for a long, hard moment. Making her true feelings on the matter completely clear, albeit non-verbally.

'It seems that you're to be congratulated, Sergeant Bale.'

Already have been, Mickey thought. *Just not by you.*

'Thank you, ma'am.'

And shut his mouth. Nothing more to say.

'I'll bid you good day then, gentlemen.'

And with a last glower around the room, AC Chen was gone. Presumably to pull the arms off whatever hapless officer caught her attention first.

'Dismissed, Sergeant Bale.' Johnnie Palmer, at least

partially human. 'And allow me to add my congratulations to those of the commissioner.'

And not the assistant commissioner, Mickey noted. Nothing like being loved by your subordinates.

'Thank you, sir.'

'We'll have to reassign you, of course. Now that the minister's made it clear he never wants to see your face again. For reasons which I'm sure you'd tell me you couldn't share with me, were I to ask.'

Give the poor bastard a break, Mickey thought. Or as much of a break as the rules allowed.

'If AC Chen had asked that question, sir, I'd have given her the same answer I'll give you. The minister saw some things that were somewhat disturbing. Part of the national security incident the commissioner mentioned. And I think that my continued presence would remind him of what he saw. Sir.'

'Thank you, Sergeant. You and Inspector Green had better go and work out what duties we can use you on. It's not like we can afford to waste good Prot officers, is it?'

30

'Who the fuck owns that piece of purple shit. And what the fuck is it doing stinking out my drive?'

Lewis had parked the Rhino alongside a twenty-year-old BMW 3 series coupe. The antique motor painted in a fetching shade that Acɪd had informed Eddie was called Techno Violet.

'It's Acid's car.'

'Fair enough.' The curl of Joe's lip remaining curled, even as he acknowledged potentially good news. 'Let's hope he's got something for us. Something to make it worth pissing off the residents' association with that pile of spare parts.'

Eddie kept the usual commendably straight face expected of Joe's lieutenant. Reflecting internally that the residents of Cockfosters probably had bigger fish to fry. If indeed they ever did anything as vulgar or risky as to associate. The paps thronging Joe's gate, for one thing. Bringing down the tone of the neighbourhood. Or the fact that hard-faced men in camo gear were roaming the nearby fields, poking into every ditch and bush.

Inside the house Acɪd was sitting waiting in the hall. With news of the hunt for the mystery gun dealer. He set up his machine on Joe's desk. Opened his window into the dark web, then the chat room program through which he was communicating with their target.

'Steph says the MP5 is booked out for the next three days. We can have it after that. Want me to change the order and ask for something else?'

Joe thought for a moment. 'That's the only machine pistol on the list, right?'

Eddie leaned closer to the screen. 'Yeah. There's five other pistols. A couple of rifles. And a fucking Bren gun.'

Joe and Eddie sharing an amused grin at the hacker's incomprehension. Joe patting the kid's shoulder. Rare praise, albeit unspoken.

'You watch *Lock Stock*, you'll see what a Bren gun is. But nothing else like what we asked for. I think we wait. Change the order now and we risk spooking whoever's at the other end. And this might be the only chance we get at him. You're sure you can't trace him?'

Acid shook his head.

'This level of encryption cuts both ways. He can't see where we are, but he could be anywhere in the world. Of course if I had government resources, I might have a chance.'

'But you don't. So set up a meet for the morning of the first day that shooter's available.'

'Yes, Mr Castagna.'

Eddie was pleasantly surprised. Either the kid was taking lessons in manners or he'd just soaked up the idea of showing respect by osmosis.

'Hey, relax kid.' Joe was showing his magnanimous side for once. 'You can call me Joe. Just as long as you promise to replace that purple rust bucket when I pay you a nice big wedge for putting this Steph on a plate for me. Trussed up and with a lemon stuck up his arse. Ready to carve.'

He turned to Eddie.

'And you and me, Eddie my son, have a journalist to go hunting for.'

31

Tamara walked down the long line of desks to where Mark was sitting. The news team's semi-official turf at the heart of the *Clarion*'s office. No seat reservation allowed, of course. Not with hot desking even more rigidly enforced by social distancing. But the team's cut and no prisoners taken thrust of "witty banter" usually saw off intruders from those members of the features team adventurous enough to venture into the office.

The two of them were busy working out what their next reportage target should be. Having found themselves shot to stardom – of a sort – by the events of the night before last. Tamara still reeling from being appointed the title she had coveted. Reporter. The object of praise to her face. And, she was only too well aware, derision behind her back.

As she walked, she glanced across the office to where Anthea, their editor, sat. A malevolent spider at the heart of her web. From where she barked terse commands. Issued incandescent bollockings. And, Tamara suspected, occasionally ensnared the unsuspecting and injected them with venom. Liquefying their innards for later consumption.

It was a rare moment of perfect synchronicity. Her chance moment of observation had coincided with the exact spot from which Anthea's screen protector was ineffective. A micro-mesh filter across the editor's main screen. Designed to prevent a chance – or deliberate – oversight revealing anything that wasn't anyone else's business. Totally effective at preventing eyeballing of her screen from any angle but ninety degrees. But completely useless if a person was directly behind her. Precisely where Tamara was standing. With a startlingly clear view of who it was that she was talking to. Whereas, to the person on the other end of the video call, Tamara was just a blurry blob of pixels in the background over Anthea's shoulder.

'Isn't that…?'

Mark looked up from his screen. 'Isn't what?'

She beckoned him over. With enough surreptitious urgency in her gesture that he stood up and strolled over. Trying, and largely failing, to look innocent.

'Take a look at Anthea's screen – a good look – then keep walking. Tell me who you think it is, then go get us both a coffee.'

Mark played his part with just-about acceptable aplomb. Took a long hard look and then turned his back on Anthea.

'Yeah. It's that police officer. What was her name…? Jasmine?'

And, as bidden, sloped off to get them a coffee. Both of them regarding the woman on screen as "Jasmine" rather than "Assistant Commissioner". Mainly because, in a show of sisterhood, that was what she had insisted on being called. While she had shown them around Number 37. Not that the *Clarion* was to name her, or even hint at her participation, she'd instructed them. Telling Tamara that she wasn't doing it for the publicity, but for all the other victims. A statement which Tamara had met with a carefully composed expression of approval. Inwardly wondering whether the woman's rat-trap fierce intellect really had that sort of room for sentiment. A thought she'd instantly dismissed as unworthy, under the circumstances.

And yet there was Jasmine, on screen and talking animatedly. Something Tamara strongly suspected was against some fairly well-defined police service regulations. She looked around, calculating.

The news desks were sparsely populated. Part time of day, part continued social isolation by the older members of the team. Those few people present heads down and focused. Reassured of relative privacy, she thought hard for a moment. Knowing that what she was about to do could get her fired. Blackballed from the entire news media industry when it inevitably got around. As other people's bad news always does. No doubt about it, she was just about to risk tossing her newly heroic status down the shitter of principle. A line from Kipling that her father had frequently quoted at her sprang to mind. Making her smile, as she reached into her camera bag, muttering to herself.

'Treat those two imposters the same, eh Dad? I'll give it a try.'

32

It was Roz who spotted the headline. The two of them were making the most of a quiet weekend. Getting back in touch with each other after all Mickey's overtime of the previous weeks.

Saturday had been spent tidying up the house's small garden. Followed by a daring couple of hours in the only cinema left open for miles. A romcom, of course. And then dinner at Roz's favourite restaurant. An eye-wateringly expensive meal. The smirking sommelier having produced a bottle of something north of fifty quid a bottle and pronounced it to be 'madam's favourite, from your last visit'. The smug bastard then having to be rewarded both with showers of praise and a hefty tip for remembering to get Mickey's wallet opened once again.

Roz had guzzled a good two-thirds of the bottle. Consumption justified on the grounds that Mickey would be needing both his wits about him and a sharp pencil when they got home. A prediction which, partially thanks to the wine's lubricating effect, had proved well-founded.

Sunday morning, she'd compiled a shopping list. Rousted Mickey from his well-earned and not fully completed doze. Instructed him to drive them down to the nexus of all evil, as far as Mickey was concerned. A supermarket next to a DIY store. With the post-modern labyrinth of a branch of IKEA across the roundabout. Roz tended to manage shopping with Mickey as any intelligent woman would. By treating him like a grumpy toddler and showing him the alternatives. Outlining her plan to him as they crossed the car park.

'A nice easy whiz round an empty shop to get the groceries. And then a quick dip into Granddad World to get those screws you need to finish building my new worktable. Couldn't be easier. And if we get all that done timely, with you pushing the trolley like a responsible adult and not using it as a surfboard, there'll be no need for lunch over the road. Will there?'

Casting her gaze across the urban clearway at IKEA's forbidding presence. Knowing Mickey to regard it as a fitting stand-in for the seventh circle of hell. Mickey, about to reply with a one-liner to crush all potential for such an outcome through its brilliance and wit, had found himself abruptly ignored. Roz having suddenly left formation to stand and stare, frowning, at the newspaper stand. Papers piled high, ready for the Sunday morning rush. The *Clarion*, as usual, in pole position.

'What the...?'

She reached out and picked up a copy. Looking at it for a moment before turning back to Mickey with a frown. Holding up the paper for him to look at.

'Greece and Turkey square off over Cyprus?'

'Not that! This!'

Pointing at a secondary headline. Which Mickey read. Doing a bit of a double take. Reading again. A secondary headline, but still front-page news. '*Hero Cop Blasts Minister!*' He looked up to find Roz giving him an old-fashioned look over her specs.

'I think we need a sit-down and a chat before we start shopping, don't you?'

Roz bought the paper and sprang for two cappuccinos. Sat Mickey down in the store's restaurant. Generously allowing him time to read and digest the piece before reaching for her thumbscrews. Hero cop? It was a distinction that Mickey reckoned he could have done without, all things considered. Especially given that there was no commendation involved. And the ire that Roz was about to visit upon him. The paper quoting an anonymous but "well-informed" source. Yeah, right. Three guesses as to who *that* might be.

Not stating that their informant was a Met officer, of course. Although the story couldn't have come from anywhere else. That anonymity protecting whoever had provided the story, obviously. Since leaking to the press was only a Met sacking offence if you were actually found out. Sitting looking at the words, fuming, Mickey thought fast. Reckoning that he had a pretty good idea which senior officer had been responsible for the *Clarion*'s version of events.

Which was that the unnamed Prot officer in question had unleashed a barrage of retaliatory expletives after being sacked by the minister. Mickey's problem being that there was no way he'd ever get to refute the most contentious and salacious part of the story. The part where he C-bombed a senior member of the government.

Which, of course, would make him instantly notorious. Not a man any minister would want on their protection team, once his identity became clear. What was left of that bridge irrevocably burned to the water in the space of two hundred words. Jasmine Chen's revenge for him helping her make herself look stupid, he assumed. The article featuring a pic of an anonymous male Prot officer, suited and pistol armed.

The latter obvious because his suit jacket was open to reveal the butt of a Glock 17. Clearly not Mickey, who wouldn't have been seen dead in that tie. Adding, he mused gloomily, sartorial insult to libellous injury. And probably making the tie's actual owner an instant celebrity among the coffee-drinking masons. Masking tape sunglasses had been Photoshopped onto the unknown officer's face to cover his identity. And a minutely printed disclaimer added under the photo, reassuring the reader that the cop's picture was a stock photo. So far so *Clarion*.

The story being that, before being sacked, the officer in question had single-handedly foiled a "*foreign government's assassination attempt on a senior member of the government during a ministerial visit*". Providing, in the process, the perfect cover story for the contractors who had actually done the job. Which would have had the side benefit – for the Met, at least – of having made the Secret Intelligence Service happy.

So, everyone a winner, it seemed. Except for Mickey. Who knew that notoriety was a proven career killer in Prot. And that he was now pretty much doomed to being "that officer" for the rest of his career. Which in turn felt as if AC Chen had single-handedly pushed him right to the exit door. Opened it and pointed the way through.

'So. Mickey. Hero cop? A little more information, please?'

Roz, reminding him that the first woman he had to worry about was the one sitting in front of him.

'What can I say? It's a pile of shit. No way did I say any of that to—'

'Not the swearing, you muppet. That bit I could happily have lived with. In fact I'm a bit let down it's not true. What I'm asking about isn't "blasts minister", it's "Hero cop". What are they talking about?'

As expected. Mickey and Roz having replayed this discussion perhaps a dozen times over the past ten years. Roz's position on the matter being simple and, from her perspective, clearly defined: Mickey was free to ponce about playing 007 as much as he liked. But only as long as it was a Bond-girl-free existence. And, crucially, providing he took no unnecessary risks. To which Mickey's response had, over the years, been consistent. Bond girls, obviously, were both a definite no-no and, more to the point, exceedingly unlikely. Whereas the potential for Mickey to have to put his body in the way of flying metal to prevent the perforation of the principal was a remote but unavoidable fact of life. Albeit a fact that Roz had, over the years, steadfastly refused to accept.

Mickey had, of course, long argued that the likelihood of such an event occurring on his watch was beyond negligible. Firstly because of the simple odds. With five hundred Prot officers, the odds of Mickey being the bullet-catcher on the spot were far higher than one hundred to one. On top of which, he had pointed out, such an attack on a member of the government was highly unlikely. Because reasons. The Special Air Service, MI6 and the long-armed wrath of HMG not the least of them.

His argument having long been that the revenge for any such attack would be epic. Roz's response being equally dismissive of her spouse's argument. An attack, in her opinion being ever more likely, not less. Because suicide bombers, because lone nutters and most of all because explosive vests. An argument that Mickey sincerely prayed would never be properly tested.

'Roz, love, I'm simply not allowed—'

'Cut the crap, Mickey! What were you doing?'

And so, where the *Official Secrets Act of 1989* had succeeded in deflecting one powerful woman, another blew through that defence like it was smoke. Mickey told her as much as he could. Playing down the more explosive elements of the story. Such as a foreign government's assassination team having been frustrated by the militant arm of the Foreign Office. An event that could have seen the death of minister, equerry and all four Prot officers. Foreign government hit squads not being in the business of leaving witnesses to their kills. Not that Roz was fooled.

'So you were rescued by the SAS then? And then nearly killed by a car bomb!'

'Not what I said, Roz.' Mickey was becoming perturbed by both her intuitive skills and the volume at which she was expressing them. In a coffee shop full of people with nothing better to do than earwig interesting conversations like that. 'These were contractors.'

'Which is worse!' Roz leaning forward to whisper vehemently. 'That makes them disposable!'

'Don't you mean dispens—'

Mickey shut the fuck up as his wife ramped her death stare way past anything Jasmine Chen could manage.

'Don't you even dare, Mickey Bale! You could be dead now, and me a widow. And all for some stuck-up, privileged piece of—'

'Roz.'

She stopped talking. And just stared at him, half-raging, half-pleading. Raging because she knew she was right. And that, insouciant and obviously unjustifiable cool notwithstanding, her man had been in the line of fire without her even knowing it. Pleading because, just like a dozen times before, she knew he wasn't for turning.

'I know.' She spoke without looking up at him. Contemplating the chocolate-flecked milky ruin of her empty cup. 'It's what you do. And it's not going to change. But I tell you this, Mickey fucking Bale. The day I find out you've taken an unnecessary risk is the day you and I stop being a couple. You got that?'

And Mickey, just like he'd done a dozen times before, nodded soberly into her raised stare. And, somewhere inside him, the demon who had been unchained by his little sister's death, laughed knowingly.

33

Mark was still enjoying his moment in the sun, three days after the Number 37 story first ran. He was, after all, part of the team that had blown open a major scoop. Modern-day sex slavery laid bare. That and the discovery of a vigilante hero determined to set them free. A man of action, taking action. No matter what personal risks he – or, their story had obviously speculated, she – ran. Although three days seemed to be the limit of the slightly unnerving adulation from management.

He wasn't under any illusions that it was Tamara's success that had pulled him out of comfortable obscurity. Success based on her source. And her source's surprising willingness to bring her in on something so explosively newsworthy. Putting them both onto a bigger and faster hamster wheel. News editor Anthea already enquiring what they planned to scoop next. And only half joking.

He walked out of the *Clarion*'s office building with a jaunty step nevertheless. Life being a whole lot better now than it had been a week before. His elevation from so-so subeditor to part of a dynamic investigation team feeling better than just good. Feeling magnificent. Coupled with his strong expectation that Tamara had more than one rabbit in her hat. They were going places.

In the meantime, Mark was going to get the coffees. Neither of them caring for the machine sludge that was served by the in-house caterer. And so, preoccupied with his own thoughts, and looking at his phone for good measure, he ventured out onto the street. And was brought up short by the presence of a man standing in his path.

And not just a man. A positive giant of a man.

'Sorry, buddy.'

Pavement possession being nine-tenths of the law. Especially now that distancing was not just politeness, but outright expected. The last tenth being the other guy's frankly disquieting build. And so Mark stepped aside. Or tried to. The big man took a step forward, jabbing a fist into Mark's gut. Driving the air from his lungs hard enough that he was momentarily stranded. And helpless to resist as he was shoved across two feet of pavement. Manhandled into the abruptly opened door of an anonymous silver SUV.

Inside which he found himself restrained between the back seat's other occupant and the big man. His hands plasticuffed behind him. Just before they put the hood over his head he looked around helplessly. Surrounded by blacked-out glass so dark as to be virtually opaque. The street more or less empty. Most people still avoiding the city unless their jobs absolutely depended on it. The hood came down. Blocking out even that minimal view of the world from which he'd just been plucked.

The car pulled away, moving smartly through the thin traffic. Mark tried to keep track of the turns it made. But a hard smack on the side of the head distracted him for long enough to make that a worthless endeavour. As intended, he guessed.

'Who are you people?'

Silence met the question.

'I work for the *Clarion*. You can't just kidnap a journalist! The police—'

Another slap, harder than before, silenced him. A brutal voice speaking quietly in his ear. Quietly, but with a significant edge of menace. A threat that didn't sound affected to Mark.

'We know who you are and what you do. So shut the fuck right up. Now. Or I'll staple your fucking lips together.'

A threat which Mark would have viewed as dire enough in and of itself to have obeyed immediately. Which made the cold caress of his top lip by what felt very much like a heavy industrial stapler superfluous. But extremely convincing. Mark shut the fuck right up. Sitting in perfect silence while his captors took him who knew where.

It wasn't until the door on his left side opened that he realised they'd reached their destination. The big man hurried him through a door, which clanged shut behind him. Then pulled his hood off. Leaving Mark blinking in the artificial light of some sort of vestibule. His captors guided him through another door into a larger space, the ceiling arched along its length. An arch, forty yards deep. Lined with camp beds, each with a rolled-up sleeping bag. Looking like a barracks. Turning right, through another doorway, they entered another arch. Seemingly converted into a succession of storerooms. Their contents concealed behind frosted glass.

Halfway down its length he was pushed into a room.

The door closing behind him with a disturbingly quiet click. The walls seeming to eat up any sound, and the air itself hushed. And found himself face-to-face with a man in his mid-forties. Black hair, heavy stubble. If the big man who'd abducted him was daunting for his size and aggressiveness, something in this man's eyes was equally frightening. More so.

'Well now. Here he is. Mark from the *Clarion*.'

'You can't—'

The big man slapped his head. Hard enough to get his attention, not hard enough to dull his wits. His grating voice menacing in Mark's ear. 'That's a warning. The next one will put you on your knees.'

Mark mused unhappily that with his wrists tied behind him, he'd land on his face. A disquieting thought. Made worse by the discovery that the floor onto which he'd faceplant was ridged with drainage channels. Leading to a grille in the middle of the room. Oh fuck.

'Thanks, Lewis. Now, where was I?' The man facing him affected a moment's thought. 'Oh yes... Mark, from the *Clarion*. The paper that's been haunting me for the last month.'

Watching Mark intently, he grinned evilly as the penny dropped.

'So, who do you think I am?'

'You're him. Joe Castagna.'

'Well spotted. Although given the number of pictures of me and stories about me you lot have published, I'd have been amazed if you hadn't sussed it.'

When he spoke, Mark noted the same strange, dull quality to his words that had reduced the door's click to a tiny sound. Joe noticed him looking around at the walls.

Sheets of plaster board riddled with thousands of tiny holes in concentric patterns.

'This is what we call the games room, Mark from the *Clarion*. Can you hear it?'

Mark nodded, realising that was exactly what he'd noticed. The complete lack of any echo or reverberation from the gangster's words.

'It's soundproofing. Me and my man Eddie there put it in years ago. When we realised we needed somewhere really private. A place where we could express our disapproval of our competitors' activities without their counterarguments being heard.'

The big man sniggered behind him. And Mark realised that he was holding on to the contents of his bowels only by dint of a considerable effort.

'I say "their counterarguments", when what I really mean is their screaming, of course.'

Mark now staring at him in horror. As he realised that he was in by far the deepest shit of his life.

'And now, of course, you're thinking: "He's told me who he is, he's bound to kill me". Aren't you?'

Mark nodding, reluctantly. Unwilling to even admit the possibility of what was staring him in the face.

'Doesn't have to be that way, of course.' The gangster, looking like butter wouldn't melt in his mouth. 'No harm done yet, really. I just wanted to talk to you. And it was pretty obvious you wouldn't have responded all that well to an invitation. Would you?'

'No.' Mark was starting to feel just a little emboldened by the other man's matter-of-fact attitude. 'So this was just a slightly more assertive way of saying you wanted a word?'

'You got it.'

'I see. So what was it you wanted to discuss?'

Joe gave him the "oh please" face.

'I think you know exactly what I want. But if you're going to make me spell it out, then so be it. What I want from you, Mark... all I want from you... is a name.'

Mark kept his mouth shut. Knowing only too well whose name it was that Joe wanted.

'Just one name. It'll take you no time at all to tell me. I know that you worked on that piece about Number 37. You need to have a word with your bosses about IT security, I reckon.'

Implying that there'd be an opportunity to chastise the *Clarion*'s IT team. Which raised Mark's hopes, just a tiny bit.

'Fair enough.'

Joe raised an eyebrow. 'What, you're going to tell me what I want to know just like that?'

Mark shrugged. 'If I don't tell you then you're going to torture me. Aren't you? I mean, this place isn't subtle. And I've got eyes.' He gestured to the welding gear neatly racked behind the gang leader. With a circular saw beside it, along with a selection of hammers and other handy tools. 'No, I'm not up for screaming out my last breaths while that big bastard behind me carves lumps off me with a gas torch. I'll tell you what you want to know.'

Joe raised an eyebrow, seemingly surprised. 'Bugger me, Lewis, perhaps you were right after all? And there was me thinking we'd have to encourage Mark here quite vigorously. Perhaps the persuasion won't be necessary after all.'

He returned his attention to Mark. Whose fear had only

been ramped up by being discussed in the third person.

'Go on then, let's have a try. Who was it that took the photos and wrote the article? The one about my sex workers being *liberated*.'

Keeping his face straight, Mark looked him in the eye. 'Anthea Hall. She's a colleague of mine.'

Knowing that he might be condemning his editor to an unpleasant fate. But saving Tamara. Seeming like a fair enough trade.

'Anthea Hall. Let's see who that is. You stay here, and I'll go for a chat with my hacker.'

His hacker? Mark stared after Joe as he went out through the room's heavily insulated door. The throwaway comment about IT security suddenly making horribly obvious sense. Shit.

34

Mickey was out for a run when the WhatsApp message arrived. Saw it was from Nemesis. Stopped running and took a moment to get his breath back. Feeling the suppressed fear and rage in the words on screen.

'Joe has the journalist's colleague. He will be talking by now. Joe's hacker will find her through her phone and he will send Lewis for her. She needs to hide. And the *Clarion*'s systems are compromised, so make it somewhere that's not on record. Make it happen. now.'

Shit. His mind raced. Working through his options. Narrowing them down to one. Typed in a reply.

'I'll have to make the next kill earlier than we planned. It's a risk.'

Got a terse reply.

'You taking risks caused this. Now you can take some more to get us both out from under.'

Fair point. Well made. Mickey went to kill the app. And start making phone calls. But the phone buzzed again before his finger touched the screen. A one-word message.

'Improvise.'

35

'So, we've established that you lied about the name I want. This Anthea isn't a reporter. She's the paper's news editor.'

Joe was sitting on the room's only chair. Smoking a cigar that he'd lit up on returning to the room. Making sure it was properly lit before pronouncing judgement on Mark's attempt to protect Tamara. He looked down at Mark, who'd been dumped out of the chair onto the ridged floor, with an expression that spoke of irritation. Intimidation and torture looking over irritation's shoulder with evident eagerness. Mark could see the psychology being employed, however crudely. And knew that he was totally unable to resist it. That he was totally in the shit.

'Not that the name's not useful. Given the bitch has been mounting some sort of campaign against me. Encouraged, it seems, by the filth.'

The filth? Mark took a moment to make the connection. 'The police?'

'Yeah. We got access to her emails. Seems like there's a senior copper who might have been a very naughty girl. And we'll have her as well, in due course. Put her on the payroll, without the option to decline.' Joe grinning triumphantly. 'It's amazing what these hackers can do. I should have got myself one years ago, but better late than never, eh?'

He took a puff at the cigar smouldering in his hand.

'And that's not all my man can do. Did you know, for example, that he can make a video appear on a computer screen? Doesn't matter if the owner wants to see it or not. So I can shoot some film – of you having your fingers amputated with bolt croppers, say – and then make it open on this Anthea's screen. Just for example. Not that either of us really wants me to have to do that, of course. You don't want to have your balls carved off with a rusty carving knife. And I don't really want to reveal that I can do whatever I want in the paper's computer system. But I will, unless you tell me what I want to know.'

Mark swallowed. Not doubting Joe's willingness to do exactly what he was threatening. His mind racing. On the one hand, he could just name Tamara. The work of an instant. And, perhaps, avoid the fate Joe had outlined. But what if he did?

'Say I give you the name you want?'

'Which would be advisable.'

Joe, twisting the metaphorical knife by showing Mark the actual knife. Which was, as trailed, rusty. Although he hadn't mentioned what looked suspiciously like dried blood on the serrated blade.

'If I do...'

'What happens to you?' Joe leaned forward. Patting Mark's cheek in a manner that, under other circumstances, might have been fond. 'My old nonno... my granddad, that is... used to take me down the market of a morning, on a non-school day. He liked to walk around, looking at the produce. Buying whatever my nonna had told him to get for dinner. Although I reckon what he really went for was the respect.'

He took a drag at the cigar. Stretching out a deliberate silence that Mark instinctively knew he was supposed to fill. Help Joe's story along.

'Respect?'

'Yeah, that. He was a big man in the Fifties and Sixties, my nonno. A face, as they put it then. He ran half of North London in his heyday. Had a proper gang, not the watered-down imitation I have to put up with. No blacks either. All local boys, the Windrush kids not being properly on the scene yet.' He laughed at Mark's face. 'What, you think a thick bastard like me wouldn't know anything about post-war immigration policy?'

Mark shook his head. Denying exactly the thought that had flashed across his mind.

'Hard men for hard times, they were. And under his leadership they ripped up the rulebook. Overturned the old order. And made him a king, pretty much. By the time I was old enough to know what was what, he was retired. He passed the crown to my dad and allowed him to get on with business. Plus he was probably worn out by then. It ain't easy, being a king.

'Anyway, he used to walk around the market, with me holding his hand. Acknowledging the respect of his subjects. And I remember, one day he stopped at a fish stall. Pointing to the fish. I wondered what the old geezer was about, until he told me what was on his mind. And what he said was this: "Any other creature here – were it brought back to life – could run or fly away. But not them. And why's that?" he asked me. In Italian, of course, because he was determined that I'd speak it.

'"Well that's obvious, Nonno," I said. "They're out of water." And he nodded, all serious like, as if to acknowledge a point. "And there it is," he said. "They are out of their element. And you," he told me, "must never be out of your element." And then he spread his arms wide, gesturing to the market. "And this, young Giuseppe, this is your element. Our world."'

He took another puff at the cigar. Tapped the ash onto the floor, then blew on the tip. Holding it up to contemplate the cherry red ember.

'And as I got older I came to appreciate his wisdom. I was bright enough to go to university, but I chose to go into the family business instead. Even if I was a bit freelance at the beginning. I stayed in my element. Whereas you...' getting, Mark suspected, to the nub of his homily '...you left yours when you teamed up with whoever it was that wrote that piece about Number 37. You left your comfort zone. Of your own free will, mind you. Seeking fame and fortune. And you walked onto dangerous ground. What made you do that, eh? Ambition? Stupidity?'

'Both.' Mark, feeling that this lengthy story had to be leading somewhere. Wanting Joe to get on with it. Get to the point where he betrayed Tamara. Having already decided to save his own life. Even if that came at the expense of hers.

'Yeah, I thought as much too.'

Joe looked down at him. Almost sympathetically. 'So... you going to give me what I need?'

Leaving the alternative unspoken. Which, given the rusty blade in his hand, wasn't too much of a concession. And so Mark spilled the story. Tamara's name, of course. Description. Personal details. The mysterious man who'd called her. A policeman, Mark reckoned. Unable to add any detail to that supposition even under repeated encouragement.

And then the story of that night. Their summons to the house by the same mystery man. To find the carnage he'd inflicted on Joe's people. And Joe sat there, all the time Mark was spilling his guts. His smile slowly broadening as he realised that he had at least part of what he wanted. And, at length, when Mark was done, he nodded and stood. Giving Lewis a significant look. Then walked slowly around the prisoner, puffing at his cigar. Reigniting the red-hot tip.

'I said if you told me what I wanted there'd be no pain. And that was true. Almost.'

He bent with surprising speed, stubbing the cigar out on Mark's hand. The prisoner reacted predictably, clutching the hand with his face contorted at the burn's sudden agonising pain.

'Jesus! I—'

Distracted by the unexpected assault. Which meant he barely had time to register the sudden movement behind him. Lewis stepping up and levelling his pistol at the back of Mark's head. Looking at Joe. Who simply stepped away from the recumbent prisoner. Not wanting to risk getting any flecks of blood on his trousers. Primarily for evidential reasons, but also because it would be heart-breaking to have to burn well-tailored gear.

And nodded.

36

Lewis looked over the Rhino's steering wheel at the gym's entrance. Slid the seat back another notch to give his big frame a little more room to relax into. Then took a sip of his Red Bull. Relaxed, but alert. Because the journalist had to come out of the gym at some point. And when she did, he intended to be ready for anything. It was after eight in the evening, daylight fading rapidly. Not that Lewis was all that bothered whether it was light or dark. He wouldn't need to be able to see her car to follow her. Not since Acıd had joined the gang.

A weird-looking kid, but sharp as all hell when it came to tech. Five minutes after the journalist had given up his mate, Acıd had pulled her phone number off the paper's computer system. Set up a tracker on her phone, its location services handily enabled. And Lewis had been on the spot fifteen minutes after that. Almost two hours ago.

Presumably she was enjoying a lengthy exercise session. With a massage, perhaps. And even a bite to eat in the cafe afterwards. But eventually, no matter how long she took, she was going to hit the bricks. And he'd be waiting. Ready to follow her back to her apartment, where his de facto deputy Rocco was waiting. Ready to snap her up. One in front of her, one behind. No escape. Lewis's task was simply to follow her. Make sure she didn't spook and try to run for it. And if she did, to follow her to wherever she ran. Deal with anyone that got in his way. And get the one piece of information from her that his boss needed. Two words. A name.

His phone rang. Eddie.

'She's on the move. You see her?'

'Nah. She ain't come out yet.'

'Well her phone has. It's heading north, up the main road. Acid's tracking her. Keep the line open and we'll put you right on top of her.'

Lewis, liking the sound of that, jacked the Rhino round in a U-turn.

'How far ahead is she?'

''Bout half a mile. Going slow though. You give it the beans, you'll soon be on her tail.'

Giving it the beans not being all that easy, even at closer to nine than eight. But Lewis had a rep to maintain. Never having let the boss down. Not an image he intended giving up. He wove through traffic. Using the Merc's outrageous power to punch past the cars in front of him. Slotting it into the spaces in front of them, ignoring their protesting horns. Already knowing what the woman was driving. A white MX5. And there it was. Two hundred yards up the road. He relaxed and fell into a follow pattern.

'Yeah, I've got her. She's still going north. But she's going nowhere without me.'

Eddie, sounding bemused, said, 'That's not the way to her fucking flat. Someone must have tipped her off.'

Yeah, Lewis thought. That fucking rat. One of these days

Joe was going to work out who it was. And then Lewis would be the man to take some fingers and toes off with a hammer and a chisel. One at a time. Until the fucker told them everything. After which, he firmly expected, Joe would tell him to keep on chopping pieces off. Just larger ones.

At the next set of lights the white roadster went left. Leaving Lewis with a choice. Either sit in the queue like a good boy and wait his turn at the lights. Or pull out and monster the oncoming traffic. He chose the latter. Flooring the V8 and flicking on Joe's secret weapon. Blue lights and a police siren, behind the radiator grille. Totally illegal, but totally effective. Ploughed through a flock of cars, scattering them in all directions as drivers took to the pavement to get out of his way. A savage grin on his face. Game on.

He took the left turn as fast as he dared in the wrong lane. Tucking in to the left side once the road opened up. Having flicked off the blues and squawks as he came past the lights. A dot of white in the middle distance.

'Still got eyes on. Heading west.'

A hint of urgency in Eddie's voice.

'We've lost her tracker, must be in a dead spot! What road you on?'

'How do I fucking know? I turned left at a set of lights, now I'm going west. Just passing a chippy. Name's Codulike.'

'What was that? You're breaking up!'

Eddie's words frayed at the edges. Something interfering with his phone?

'Codulike. Cod! U! Like!' Silence at the other end. 'Hello?'

Nothing. Perhaps a vague whisper, but unintelligible.

'*Fucking* phone!'

He looked down at the Merc's screen. No bars of signal. Nothing at all. Useless bastards. Looked up again, just in time to see the Mazda turn left again. Floored the Merc, powering towards the junction. Took the turn with a screech of rubber, braking down to cruising speed as he realised it was a dead end. Bitch had a hidey hole, did she? Looking left and right. Searching for the tell-tale flash of white that would tell him where she'd run to.

37

Mickey waited. Quiet as a mouse. Pulse racing. Partly due to the run from the car. Partly because of the enormity of what he was about to attempt. His subconscious screaming blue murder at the risk he was taking. Like a caveman about to try taking down a sabre-toothed tiger with nothing more than a net and a heavy stick. No pistol. No Taser. No grenades. Crouched behind a wall, in a derelict warehouse. Hiding in the shadows like a hunted rat. Waiting for a very dangerous cat to make an appearance. Blowing a long slow breath out. Willing his body to stillness.

The warehouse was dark. And totally still. Mickey could hear the rustlings of rodents in the gloom. And, more faintly, the low-frequency rumbling of traffic on the nearby M25. The warehouse had been built thirty years ago, capitalising on the improved communications engendered by the new motorway. And had probably made its owners a lot of money, over the years. Until a year before, when a brief but intense fire had swept through it. A combination of highly flammable products, a faulty sprinkler system and a careless night watchman who liked to smoke.

Half of its framework had been declared unsafe. The

abandoned building now of more interest to lawyers than paying customers. Fit only to be pulled down and rebuilt. A process still pending the agreement of liabilities and compensation. First delayed, then postponed indefinitely by the impact of global events. Gas and electricity cut off. Reduced to a cold and lifeless shell. Nothing that a well-bribed moonlighting sparky couldn't solve, of course. Which was how come Mickey had been able to run a hundred-metre power cable across the darkened building.

The click of a car door closing got him up on his toes. So Lewis, if it was Lewis, had found the Mazda. Parked with a fraction of its back end visible from the road. Tamara's car. Bait. Mickey had walked past the Merc outside the gym fifteen minutes before. An easy stroll, not breaking stride. Sports bag over his shoulder. Making sure that it was Lewis that had been sent to watch the gym. Checking that the enforcer was alone.

He'd collected Tamara's phone and keys from the front desk. Where she'd left them waiting for him on production of his warrant card. After a terse conversation that had scared the shit out of her. Mickey still feeling guilty at having laid it on so hard. Telling her what would have happened to Mark. And what would happen to her if she didn't run. Telling her to leave her phone behind to avoid being tracked. To spend cash to get on the bus, avoiding both her car's tracker and her card being traced. And to go to a friend's for the night. Somebody not on record at the *Clarion*.

Car keys in hand he'd walked into the changing rooms. And straight out of the back, warrant carding his way through the staff exit. Finding her car where she'd left it.

And guessing that Joe's hacker would be able to track her phone. And put him and Lewis in the same post code. Both hunters. Both hunted.

He'd paced out the timings several times after setting the lights up. Before hurrying down the road to the gym. Twenty seconds from the Mazda's parking spot to the open side door that was the building's only easy entrance. Left deliberately ajar. Lewis would recognise a potential trap, of course. But he was Lewis. Armed, very dangerous and quite psychotic with it. He'd note the danger and bull on into it. Ready for anything. Almost.

Another minute of cautious progress across a floor littered with debris would bring him to the spot Mickey had chosen. Walking into the trap that Mickey had prepared, when Nemesis had nominated his next target. And told him just how dangerous Lewis could be. What he was capable of. What he'd done, over the years he'd served Joe. Why he needed to die. And how.

After a minute or so he heard the sound of approaching footsteps. Confident. Steady-paced. Without any attempt at concealment, other than a soft, careful footfall. Unsuspecting. Lewis still believing he was hunting a woman. A soft target. The steps paused. Making Mickey wonder if he sensed the ambush in the same instinctive way the tiger might have caught the caveman's scent. Not sure what was wrong, exactly. But knowing there was something not quite right. Then he saw the faint blue light of a phone screen. Smiled knowingly. That ain't going to help you much, buddy. And you just blew whatever degree of darkness adoption you might have gained in the last minute or so.

'*Fuck!*'

The light faded. Lewis's vehement whisper speaking volumes as to the enforcer's frustration at the lack of signal. His footsteps resumed, getting closer to Mickey's hiding place behind the wall. Mickey braced himself for action. The unseen figure stopped walking at the entrance to the section of the warehouse where Mickey's equipment was set up. The bath's chipped white enamel a pale, almost ghostly presence in the gloom. He knew that the other man would be able to see it. Question was, would he investigate?

The footsteps started up again, progressing more slowly from right to left. The rustle of a weapon being drawn. The hiss of oiled screw threads. A suppressor? Then the click-clack of a slide being racked. His victim suspected that all was not quite as expected, perhaps. Or just a sensible precaution. Either way, it made no difference. Because his quarry had just walked right into the middle of Mickey's trap.

Raising the heavy rifle, Mickey put the sole of his right boot on the foot switch. Took a long, slow breath in and pressed it down. Sending power to the powerful Nitesun floodlights positioned to either side behind him. Illuminating the warehouse interior as brightly as if a car's headlights had been flicked to main beam. In the middle of the debris-strewn floor, the powerfully built enforcer was caught like a fly in incandescent amber.

Gun raised, he turned to look straight into the lights. Tried to shade his eyes with his other hand. Fired a round off blindly, chipping a lump from the wall ten feet to Mickey's left. Mickey no more than a dark spot between the blazing twin orbs to his wrecked vision. Mickey made a fractional change to his point of aim and squeezed the rifle's trigger. Hurling a heavy nylon net across the gap between them, the corners and edges weighted with lead balls. The snare wrapped itself full length around the disoriented Lewis. Who took half a step forward and then tottered to the ground like a falling tree.

Mickey dropped the net gun and sprinted forwards. Pulled a heavy lead-cored rubber cosh from his belt. Raised it and stooped over the trapped man. The moment of maximum danger, if Lewis still had the gun in his hand. He struck down at his victim's head, hitting him once, twice, three times. Enough. He waited, cosh raised, but the other man was completely still. Either unconscious or feigning it.

Mickey threaded a heavy-duty zip tie through the net and trussed his victim's ankles tightly. Then did the same with his wrists. Sat back and looked at his prisoner for a minute. Lewis still unconscious. He stood, disentangling the lifeless man from the net, then used more zip ties on his legs. Further restraining his arms by tying them tight to his trunk. Twenty zip ties in total. Overkill, but prudent. More tensile strength than even the strongest of men could overcome. Rendering his prisoner immobile, even if he woke before he was properly in position.

He picked up the big, black automatic pistol. Handy. Then walked over to the forklift truck waiting on the far wall. Drove it across to the fallen man through a carefully cleared path. Raised the forks until they were six feet up, positioned over his prisoner. Getting out, he looped a nylon sling over the forks. Draped one loop over the recumbent man's shoulders and put his head through it. Pulled the other up his legs until it was under the top of his thighs. Ready to lift Lewis into his final resting place.

38

Eddie re-dialled. Getting the "this person's phone is currently out of service" message again. Shook his head at Joe, who had walked in from supervising the disposal of Mark's body to find his right-hand man looking worried.

'There's no answer. There's not even any signal, from the sound of it.'

Joe shrugged. 'Mobile phones, innit? He'll pop back up again soon enough. What was the last thing he said?'

'He was following the reporter north up the main road. Then we lost his phone signal and the tracker on hers at the same time. We think she turned at the lights and he followed.'

'Which way?'

'No idea. He had to use the blue lights to clear a path, I could hear the siren. Which meant he wasn't talking. Then when I asked him where he was he didn't know. Said something that might have been "chippy", then his signal went to complete shit.'

'What about the tracker on the Rhino?'

Eddie making it an article of faith always to know where all the gang's vehicles were. Basic security.

'Nothing. Must be in the same signal black spot.'

Joe's face creased in a frown. Not because Lewis couldn't look after himself. But because his best soldier was out of contact.

'Right. So get on Google Maps and look for a turn-off with a chip shop. And let me know when he surfaces. I want that name!'

39

Mickey looked down at Lewis. Waited impassively as the big man slowly returned to consciousness. Surfacing from deep with the bends. A grimace on the big man's face. Speaking of both pain and disorientation. Slowly, grim reality dawned on the enforcer.

First, the realisation that he was blind, a double-thickness mask over his eyes. Next, the dawning terror of total immobility. Pinioned by six lengths of heavy chain. Each five yards long. Their weight making it harder for him to breathe. Wrapped around his body while he'd been held up in the sling. His trousers perforated with a dozen scissor cuts, in between the zip ties.

He was lying in an old bathtub Mickey had purchased from a builder, out of a skip. Untraceable. His feet against the tap end, head level with the battered enamel rim. With padding either side to prevent him from even rocking from side to side. Nemesis having been very clear that this wasn't someone you took a risk with more than once. Hearing some minute sound, the captive stared sightlessly straight at him.

'When I get out of here I'm going to fucking kill you. Whoever you are, you're fucking dead meat.'

The statement matter-of-fact. Bored, even. Not even a threat, just a declaration of intent. A bravura performance, under the circumstances. Mickey rewarded it with a terse laugh.

'And what is it that makes you think you'll be able to get out?'

Mickey could have sworn that the big man shrugged. Even trussed like a turkey.

'You've taken me prisoner, right? You're looking to have my boss over. Except Joe don't take being done over all that well. So he's going to pull out all the stops. He'll find you. And then *I'll* kill you. Unless you let me go right now. In which case—'

'Nah.' Mickey enjoyed the slight shudder that his interruption generated in Lewis's body. Almost imperceptible. But there. 'You were almost convincing until that last bit about letting you go. When you were about to say you wouldn't kill me if I did.'

Lewis doubled down with impressive chutzpah. 'Fuck you then, buddy. That's your last chance done.'

Mickey found himself having to admire the bravado. But not particularly influenced by it either.

'Yeah. Right. Thing is, Lewis, no-one knows where you are.' He watched in silence for a moment as the gangster struggled to control a smirk. 'Of course you think he'll track your phone. 'Fraid not. You've been inside a jamming field since you turned off the main road. And before I switched the jammer off I took the SIMs out of your phones. Joe's phone and your own handset. Then powered the phones down and smashed them both with a hammer. Very thoroughly indeed.'

He paused for a moment. Allowing the other man to think that was all.

'Oh, and the tracker in that Merc you were driving?' I jammed the shit out of it along with your phone. After all, that's all it really was. Just a phone chip with a GPRS connection. So there's a micro-jammer in the car now. Just enough to make the Merc invisible to the tracking system. Not enough to make a huge signal black spot. Won't stop them finding you eventually. But you and me have all the time we're ever going to need. All the time I need to see this through to the bitter end. Bitter for you, that is. Tell you what, you just lie there and see if you can work out what I'm doing. Bet you get it in no time.'

He turned away. Switched on the cement mixer standing beside the tub. Then busied himself shovelling cement and sand into the rotating drum. Topped it up with water. With a load mixed, he switched it off. Squatted down by Lewis's head.

'Thing is, Lewis, you've been called to judgement. They say there's no God. And I was forced to agree for a while. After my little sister died. But now I've got a different handle on it. I'm not much of a believer in God. But I do believe in fate.'

'Just let me go, if you want money—'

'We'll get to that. So, for the sake of argument let's agree that I'm fate's chosen means of settling the score with you. Which means that my voice is the last one you will ever hear in this life. And, it occurred to me, that your departure from it should be… well, fitting.'

Silence. Lewis listened intently.

'And when I say "fitting", I mean fittingly drawn out and

painful. Agonising. Horrific. A hard death, by degrees, and without any mercy. There is an alternative, of course. Quicker. Cleaner. But you'll have to pay for it.'

And after a moment of silence. 'Go on.'

'Sensible. The hard way you've already guessed. And I'm pretty sure you've used it yourself, on occasion. Cement, eh? Marvellous stuff. Did you know there are Roman buildings standing today, built with cement? But it has a dark side, does the old grey stuff. A nasty alkaline bite. It'll burn the skin right off you. And when I fill this bathtub right up to the brim, there's another aspect to consider.'

Lewis had gone quiet again. And white. Understandably.

'Yeah, you know. See how pale you are. That good old fight-or-flight response kicking in. Pity you can't fight, isn't it? Bet you'd put up one fuck of a fight, now you know what I have planned for you.'

'What's the alternative?'

Lewis's voice was strained. Mickey waited for a moment before replying. Allowing the tension to ratchet up.

'I'm not sure I even want to offer it to you. I think you've earned the harder ride downstairs.' He put the barrel of Lewis's own pistol against the enforcer's left temple. 'I pull this trigger right now and you'll be standing in front of St Peter a second later.'

Lewis replied without hesitation. 'Do it.'

Mickey laughed tersely. 'Fuck me, Lewis, but you're some kind of realist! Fifteen minutes ago you were telling me you were going to strangle me with my own guts. And now you're asking for a mercy killing. But here's the thing, Lewis old son. It.' He tapped the gun barrel against his captive's head. 'Doesn't.' *Tap*. 'Work.' *Tap*. 'Like.' *Tap*. 'That.'

He waited for a long moment. Allowed Lewis to fill the silence. 'How does it work?'

'Thought you'd never ask. The thing is, Lewis, that over the years you've made a lot of money. A *lot* of money.' Mickey paused, ostentatiously. 'I say "made", when of course I mean you stole it. Other people *made* it. And then you made them your victims. Killed them and robbed them. If they were lucky. And now, by a quirk of some poetic justice, you've come to the end of your rope. How does it feel?'

Silence.

'Nothing to say? Is that because you're ashamed of what a vicious, murdering bastard you are?' Mickey paused again. 'Or because there's nothing in you that recognises what a vicious, murdering bastard you are? Or rather you *were*?'

He ground the pistol's screw-cut muzzle, designed to accept a suppressor, into Lewis's cheek. Pushed and twisted it into his skin until blood ran down his cheek. Deliberately inflicting pain to ramp up the pressure.

'There's nothing good in you, is there? Just a raving urge to hurt people. Because that's what Mummy and Daddy made you. You've had a good run, but it ends here. Tonight. One way or another. So what'll it be? Two or three hours of horrific agony, or a bullet from your own gun?'

'Shoot me.'

'Yeah, thought so. Because you've killed people with cement. Haven't you. You know what happens. The alkali burning their flesh off. The chemical reaction cooking them, slowly but surely. I'd take death by bark-chipper over that.'

Mickey sat back. Took a cigar from his pocket. Saw Lewis's nostrils flare.

'Yeah, you like a Cuban, don't you?'

He snipped off the end and lit the tobacco, taking an extravagant puff. Knowing that another half-dozen inhalations would have him puking.

'You want some?' Answered by a nod. 'Yeah, I thought so. So here it is. For the bullet, and the Havana, one low, low price. All I need is one little piece of information. Bank account name, sort code, account number and pass code.'

The prisoner fell silent. Saying nothing at all.

'Yeah, I know. Tough choice. That money's supposed to look after those psychopaths that made you who you are, right? And your girlfriend. And that little bastard... and I use the term deliberately because he's not just illegitimate, he's not even yours. Not from what I'm being told.' Watching Lewis's face harden.

'So now you're getting ready to tell me to just fuck off. You need that money, right? Why else would you have tortured a dozen men to death to get it? Fair enough. Time for you to find out just what you put them through.'

He stood. Tipping the mixer's drum over to pour its contents over Lewis's legs. And crotch. And waited for the screams.

40

'We've narrowed it down. We think he turned left here...' Eddie pointed to the map on screen. 'There's a chippy here. Might be the one he mentioned.'

'It's a clever choice. Look at all that light industrial.' Joe, in Eddie's opinion unusually reflective. 'So what now?'

'We tried the tracker. The Rhino vanished off the face of the earth just after it turned left at the lights. Still no sign, so either whatever's jamming it is still working, or someone's switched it off in the car.'

'So the odds are that he's got Lewis.'

Both men automatically assuming that this was the work of their mystery assassin. They looked at each other. Joe spoke, his voice thinly controlled rage.

'Get the boys out. Mob-handed and properly tooled up. I want every building within half a mile of that chippy eyeballed. Industrial units first, derelict buildings at the top of the list. Searched, if possible. With consent if we can get it. Get them to spin a story about a missing kid or something that'll open doors.'

'And if anyone resists?'

'I'm going out there too. Rocco can mind me until we get Lewis back.' Joe pointed at the screen. 'Anyone wants to keep us out, I'll have some meaningful conversation with them. I can be very meaningful, when I put my mind to it.' He stood, reaching for his coat. 'And tell the boys to come out ready for a two- or three-dayer. If this bastard's got the brass balls to take Lewis, then he's got the stones to come after me.'

41

'So, Lewis, my old mucker. How's it going?'

The enforcer was panting like a long-distance runner. His nostrils flared with the pain. Teeth clenched. Having screamed himself hoarse half an hour before.

'Looks like you're finding that hard work. If only you'd settled for the bullet, eh? You could even have smoked that nice cigar. Instead of which...' Mickey looked down the bathtub's length. 'Instead of which the skin's probably coming off your legs by now. And your prick and balls. You still have a choice though. Right now all I've done is inflict an ocean of pain on you. But it's going to get worse. A whole lot worse. I'm going to bury you up to your neck and leave you to fry. There's enough mix ready to fill that bath to the brim. And once I start pouring, I'm not stopping no matter what you say. And when you're done, I think I'll pay your parents a visit. If your victims don't get to benefit from all that money, neither should they. So. Last chance. Bullet or cement?'

The information he wanted spilled from Lewis's mouth so fast he had to wait until the enforcer had calmed enough to speak slowly enough to be understood. Mickey held a burner phone up to his mouth. Then talked to Martin at the other end while Lewis puffed and groaned at the pain.

'Did you get that?'

'Yeah, logging in now.' After thirty seconds of silence his friend spoke again, his tone reverential. 'Fuck. *Me*.'

'How much?'

'Two and a half million. Give or take.'

'And you can transfer money out?'

'Hang on…' Clicking, as Martin tapped at his keyboard. 'Yeah, but there's a check on new payments. Texts to his phone.'

Mickey shrugged.

'That's OK. I've got his SIM. One transaction and it'll be security-cleared. And there's no rush.'

Lewis's voice, hoarse but insistent.

'Kill me.'

'I'll call you back. Got something to finish up here.'

He cut the call off and looked down at Lewis.

'Well done, Lewis. You came through. Time for me to keep my end of the bargain.'

The helpless enforcer nodding. 'Do it.'

Mickey folded his arms. Looking down at Lewis. 'Thing is, Lewis, the things my source told me about you didn't make for enjoyable reading. The murders. The men you maimed. The women you raped. That was a favourite of yours, wasn't it? Put a man back in line by fucking his woman in front of him? And your favourite. Murder extortion. Get a victim into a position like this. Pay up or die slowly. And with a pitiless bastard like you staring down at them, of course they paid up. Expecting to be spared. Except you never spared any of them. Did you? Here, let's have a proper look at you.'

Mickey pulled off the mask. Waiting while Lewis's blinking eyes adjusted to the light.

'You never spared a single person you had at your mercy, did you? You laughed at them as they died. And so the question is, Lewis, what makes you any different to them?'

He stood up, putting a hand on the mixer's tip handle.

'You... you *promised*!'

Mickey nodded. 'I did. And yet...'

'Please. Kill me now.' Lewis's voice imploring him.

'Fair enough. You've earned some consideration. Let's compromise.'

He picked up the .45. Levelled it at the desperate enforcer's face. Then lowered his point of aim until the pistol's muzzle was aimed directly at his stomach.

'No! You prom—'

He squeezed the trigger. The heavy bullet blowing a hole in the enforcer's guts. Clanging off the bath's metal skin to lodge somewhere in his back.

'I promised you a bullet. And a bullet you have. And now it's time to finish this before your boss finds us.'

The sweating, gasping prisoner looked up at him. Eyes slitted against the pain that was racking his helpless body.

'Finish... me! You... fucking... promised!'

'Yeah, I did, didn't I? Problem is, buddy, so did you. Time and time again. And then let the cement do its worst to them anyway. Time to reap what you sowed.'

Lewis stared wide-eyed as Mickey, smiling sadly, tipped the drum forward. And then bellowed in pain and fear as a viscous cascade of liquid cement poured into the bath.

42

Joe walked into the dark warehouse. Ten men fanned out around him in a loose circle. Rocco walking next to him, with Lewis's matt black automatic in his hand. Having found it resting on the edge of the bath and claimed it for his own. Vowing revenge. Someone had found the foot switch and turned on the twin Nitesuns. Revealing Lewis, entombed in concrete up to his neck. Only his head remaining clear of the flat grey surface.

'Jesus *fucking* Christ!'

And for once, Eddie was inclined to share Joe's... well, whatever it was. Outrage. Anger. Horror. Disgust. All appropriate, given the state his former enforcer was in. White-faced, presumably from blood loss. Eyes bulging in their sockets from the heat that had cooked him. His mouth gaping wide, labouring to breathe as the concrete dried and crushed his lungs. Tongue, blackened, protruding between lips cooked cherry red.

'What the fuck did he do?'

A rhetorical question? Eddie wasn't given to ignoring Joe's questions. So, genuine request for information or simple railing at the heavens, he answered it with faultless logic.

'I'd say he shot the poor fucker. Possibly twice, there being two rounds fired from that...' gesturing at Lewis's automatic in Rocco's hand. 'Kneecaps, possibly. Or just in the guts. Made him bleed out, in case we found him before the cement hardened. But gave him time to feel the cement cooking him.'

He managed to ignore the look Joe shot him. It not being from his usual repertoire of death stares. More like amazement that Eddie could be so callous. Perhaps forgetting that Lewis had been the bloke who had shot his best friend.

'This is a message.'

Eddie nodded. Thinking that much was pretty obvious. Joe standing over his dead killer with an expression that said his temper could go one of two ways. Ice cold or apocalypse.

'He's sending a clear message. To me. Saying that he could just have shot the poor bastard. But chose not to. And that he'll do the same to me.'

Eddie nodded, feigning thoughtfulness while marvelling at the man's sheer self-centredness. Joe shook his head decisively.

'This has gone too far. I want another meeting with the other families. Fuck the rules. Anyone who doesn't agree to talk will be making a very clear statement that they're against me. Tell them all that.'

'Yes, Joe.'

Joe nodded. Putting a hand on Eddie's shoulder. 'You and me, brother. You and me. We have to be ready to go to war. Because if we don't find out who did this, and put them on display, the other gangs are going to lose patience.

See the balance of power shifting away from me. And they'll move on us, you mark my words. So we go to a war footing, right? We have the troops mobilised, so we keep them mobilised. Get the camp beds out and operate as an army, from the arches. And when the time comes to strike, we strike first and hardest. I'm minded to show that loose-mouthed twat Albie the error of his ways. Send Rocco to take him out. Decapitate his gang, consolidate his territory into ours and face the rest down. Change the balance of power permanently.'

Eddie nodded. Ruing the day that Joe had picked up a copy of Sun Tzu. Suddenly seeing himself as a scheming warlord. Using words like decapitate and balance of power. His phone buzzed. WhatsApp. A message on his private group with Acıd.

'Steph's agreed to meet tomorrow. With the weapon.'

He showed Joe the screen.

'Good. Because that bastard is our last hope to catch the fucker that did this.' Waving a hand at Lewis's remains. 'Get him out of that before it sets hard. And put him on ice. Somewhere private. No publicity at all. I want him as a threat I can use to unbalance the other gangs, when the time comes. Tell them all he's coming to their turf for the rat. Have them all looking the other way when the hammer falls on Albie. And when this is all over we'll have a Viking funeral and pay our respects properly. But for now I've got a war to plan.'

43

'**G**ood morning, Michael! Welcome back for your first day on the dark side!'

Mickey couldn't help but smile at Philip Green's cheerfulness. And bathe in the warmth of being addressed by his first name. Rather than his rank. Even if the bonhomie wasn't likely to be replicated at any rank above Philip.

'Thank you, sir. I presume I'm on the replacement rota for the day?'

Suited and booted, and with a Glock holstered, he was fully expecting to go straight into the pool. To be sent wherever a Prot officer wasn't available due to holiday or sickness. More likely than reassignment to a new principal. Ministers preferring the presence of bodyguards known to them. Although the moment when whoever he ended up guarding realised that he was "that" officer had potential to be amusing.

Inspector Phil shook his head.

'On a normal day you'd be spot on. But not today.'

Mickey guessed what was coming. Not hard to do. Given half the emails he'd read that morning had started with the same title.

'Operation Rampage?'

The inspector nodded tersely. With the look of a Sunday cricketer who'd fielded a ball only to find out it had rolled through dog excrement on its way to his hands.

'Quite possibly the most appropriate choice that's come out of the random name generator in the last five years. Good guess. William Nichol's gone sick as of two minutes ago. A pretty serious case of food poisoning. Get yourself over to St John's Wood and his constable will pick you up from the tube station.'

Putting his firearm and belt kit into a daysack, Mickey left LX. Taking a face mask at the door. Headed for Lambeth North tube station. Got on a Bakerloo train and headed north. Changed lines to the Jubilee at Baker Street. Rode north one more stop and came back above ground. Looked for, and found, what he expected to see. An illegally parked Mercedes people mover, waiting for him to emerge. What he wasn't expecting was the person driving it.

'Skipper! Fancy seeing you here!'

Mickey shook the extended hand as he climbed into the vehicle. Shaking his head in amusement.

'Wade Harris. There was me thinking I wouldn't be seeing you again for a while, and inside a week here you are playing taxi driver.'

'I know! I'm not sure which of us is the luckier!'

Mickey turned to look at the younger man as he pulled away from the kerb, heading for Winfield House. The US Ambassador's London residence. Home to the leader of the western world during his state visit.

'It's you, Wade. And speaking of lucky, how's it going with the girl you met just before that nastiness in Belize?

Still going strong?' He leaned forward and made a show of inspecting his former partner's eyes. 'Pale skin. Sunken eyes. Bags the size of holdalls too. Looks like you're still burning the candle at both ends.'

Wade grinned. Clearly unable to contain his happiness any longer.

'It's amazing, Mickey! It's like we've been together for months!'

Mickey, shaking his head, pronounced sentence. 'That's you done then. Set the date yet?' And then did a double take at the lack of any denial. 'Whoa! Wade, mate, obviously you've been smitten, but surely not that hard?'

''Fraid so. She's the same. Worse, even.'

'And she knows what you do for a living? That you'll be going missing for days on end to fulfil your 007 fantasies?'

Their airwaves beat Wade to the counter punch.

'All Rampage callsigns, Rampage Bronze Commander. Moving in five minutes, positions please.'

Wade turned into the Outer Circle. Showing his ID to the AFOs standing guard on the crescent. Who examined it with microscopic care. Despite having seen him drive out fifteen minutes earlier.

'Christ on a bike, but you can tell when there's a president in town, can't you?'

Wade laughed. 'You haven't seen the best of it yet. Sally Williams is Bronze Commander for the day. And you'd better believe she's taking this one seriously.'

'So would you be, if your promotion was on the line. I'd better go and pay my regards.'

Leaving Wade to three-point the Merc, he found the uniformed Prot Bronze Commander standing beside her vehicle. Directly behind the hulking eight-tonne brute that went by the name of the Beast.

'No time to talk, Michael. POTUS will be out of those doors in thirty seconds. Thanks for standing in; you're in charge of the four-man support team in position fifteen. The Mercedes van being driven by Constable Harris.'

'Yes, ma'am. I'm on it.'

As Mickey turned away she added a parting comment. Presumably having had a quick look around to check that POTUS wasn't coming out of the big house behind her.

'Oh, and Michael…?'

He turned back, half-guessing what was coming from the mischievous look on her face.

'Ma'am?'

'No exercising of your Tourette's today please.'

Mickey resisted the urge to reply with a crisp "Fuck off, ma'am" to firmly cement his place in Prot folklore. Contenting himself with a raised eyebrow.

44

'Operation Rampage' was just about right. Straight from the automated random word generator it might have been, but the potential was definitely there. Routing a full-scale presidential motorcade through London? Mickey would have loved to have a word. Seriously. A twenty-vehicle convoy? In Central London? In New York, sure; close the streets off and drive a simple grid. Child's play. Whereas in London it would probably have been lower risk to just put the bloke in a taxi. But at least he wasn't in command of the whole bloody awful mess.

Jasmine Chen was Gold Commander in the LX Ops Centre. It being Mickey's dearest hope that she was sweating bullets. Which was probably pretty much the truth. Because getting such a huge and unwieldy automotive leviathan into Central London was the easy part. And very soon now they would have to get it out again. At three in the afternoon, with the traffic getting heavier by the minute.

To be fair, all had gone well on the journey in. With the morning rush hour over, the journey from St John's Wood to Clarence House had been smooth enough. With a path cleared by the Special Escort Group's motorcycle outriders. Making the roads down into the city a relative breeze. Even

Mickey could work that route out in his head. And he was nowhere near SEG's legendary black cab level of London mastery.

'Oi! Mickey!'

He strolled over to the row of SEG BMWs. A dozen bikes parked in a precise kerbside formation. Their riders standing around in their usual operational teams. Smoking, those that did. And gossiping, which all coppers did. The oldest of them walked out to greet him, hand held out. Grabbing him by the shoulder and walking him back to his little gang.

Silver-haired now, and a bit more solidly upholstered. But still the same old Kev. One-time beat copper, now king of the Easy Riders. Mickey's mentor, so to speak, on the streets of North London. Before he'd managed to wangle a transfer into Traffic. And from there to the golden fleece of motorised policing. The Special Escort Group. Within which he had risen to the height of his chosen branch. At least in terms of both skill and respect.

'Here we are then! This is the Prot skipper I was telling you about! The one who told a certain government minister to get fucked!'

Mickey holding his hands up, protesting his innocence. 'Never let the truth get in the way of a good story, eh Kev?'

His protests ignored by the SEG boys and girls. Who shook his hand and clapped his shoulder. Generally lauding the mythical deed. To be fair to his former colleague, it wasn't just gossiping coppers who were building the legend of his exit from Sir Patrick's protection team. AC Chen, via the *Clarion*, having presumably played her part as well.

Kev prodded him in the chest with a finger. Grinning fit to bust. 'Come on, Mickey! You know the truth of it! Just what did you say to that berk? Must have been juicy, you having just pulled his nuts out of the fire and that.'

Mickey shook his head. Firmly denying the assertions. 'Just because it's in the papers—'

'Bollocks! Come on, there's donuts on this.'

'I wondered why you called me over. There was me thinking it was for old times' sake.'

The older man patted his cheek robustly enough for it to sound and feel like nine-tenths of a slap.

'Spill the beans, sunshine! If you don't tell me I'll be forced to set Maisie on you!'

Mickey looked past Kev at the aforementioned Maisie. A tall female officer in her mid-thirties, ginger hair cut short over a face full of freckles. She shook her head at the older man, her expression fond. Nodded to Mickey. Nodding being the new Met handshake.

'Maisie Blake. And ignore my granddad, Skipper. He does like to embarrass us when we bring him out.'

'Oi! I resemble that comment. Anyway, the words, Michael. Give 'em up! Or we'll tie you to a bike and drag you back up the road to London Zoo in front of the Beast. See what POTUS makes of that, eh?'

Mickey raised his hands. 'All right. If you have to know, I never got the chance to say anything to him. He sacked me through his private secretary.

Kev glared at him.

'What, nothing? I've got a tray of Krispy Kreme riding on something with the word "fuck" in it!'

Mickey, simultaneously amused and exasperated, spread

his hands wide. 'He's a minister, Kev! What would *you* have said to him?'

'Me? With days to go 'til my thirty? I'd have told the bastard to fuck right off!'

'Yeah.' Mickey shrugged. Part of him wishing he'd had the chance to tell Sutherland exactly what he really thought of him. 'But I'm six years short of mine. And six years in the salt mines didn't really appeal much, at the time. Although it could have been worse. I could have ended up as a glorified knowledge boy in the Special Escort Group.'

'You ain't got the patience, boy!' Kev turning to his teammates with a knowing smile. 'You think it's all just riding around and blowing whistles, dun'cha? I'd like to see you try getting your head around the—'

'Rampage Bronze to all Rampage callsigns, five-minute warning.'

The veteran officer winked at him. 'Saved by the bell, eh Mickey?' He waited until the vehicle teams had finished acknowledging the alert, then keyed his own airwave. 'Rampage Bronze, Easy Rider. All received.' And turned to his colleagues. 'Saddle up, boys and girls!'

The riders dispersed to their machines. Kev taking a moment to look Mickey up and down.

'You all right, Mickey? Not too pissed off?'

'Me? Yeah. I was a bit disappointed when it happened. And with the way the press got hold of it. But worse things happen, right?'

'That's my boy.' Kev pulled his helmet on, adjusting the strap. 'And let's face it, given you'll be sat scratching your arse in a car, I know which one of us I'd rather be for the next hour.'

Mickey watched as the bikes formed up at either end of the convoy. Two of them zipping away up the Mall to perform an advance route check. And shaking his head in fresh wonder as he looked down its length. First up, a Special Escort Group Jaguar leading the parade. Next, three heavily armoured Chevy Tahoes. Senior presidential staff and Secret Service agents. Behind the initial group, a Prot Range Rover leading the convoy's heart. After that, the Secret Service ID car. Another hulking Tahoe, but festooned with aerials. Scanning for threats, and probably capable of talking to any American military unit on the planet. Then the Watchtower. Another SUV, with aerials to detect radar and a full-on laser detector built into a glass dome on its roof. Behind them a pair of Beasts. Each weighing in at eight tonnes, twice the weight of a bulletproof Rangie Sentinel.

Mickey couldn't help admiring the armoured monsters, despite their pig ugliness. Five layered glass and polycarbonate windows. Bulletproof, and proper heavy-calibre bulletproof to boot. Five-inch-thick composite armour. Like a tank. Layered steel, titanium and ceramic plate. Bombproof, rocket-proof, and pretty much invulnerable. At least for as long as it would take the pair of Apache gunships, currently waiting on hot standby on Horse Guards, to get overhead. Once the convoy got moving there'd be a president in one of the brutish limos. The man Mickey and his colleagues were sworn to protect, in defence of the realm.

Behind the Beasts was a Prot Land Rover Discovery. Rampage Bronze Command's mount. The woman with the unenviable tactical responsibility for the convoy package. Her eyes on the prize at all time. Followed by a pair of

Toyota Land Cruisers, already crewed. Both vehicles four up, SCO19's Counter-Terrorist Specialist Firearms Officers. Taking the place of the Secret Service's Hawkeye Renegade quasi-special forces team in the order of march.

Mickey was still amused by the fact that the Americans, clearly unable to choose between two names, had decided to go with both. Whereas the CTSFOs gloried in no code names whatsoever, if you didn't count their unit designation. Kitted out in grey special forces uniform, their eyes just visible over face masks. Oozing fast-rope cool. Deliberately, of course. Each with a 5.56mm SIG MCX assault rifle. Capable of full-auto if needed. Their participation being the Met's way of telling the Secret Service "we got this". Mickey suspecting that the Secret Service's gun club wouldn't spare them a glance, in the event of a threat.

Behind SCO19's Toyotas were a pair of BMWs. Each four up with Harriers. The Met's potential response to any civil disorder issues. Non-lethal intervention a speciality. Big coppers, with muscles on their muscles and plenty of attitude. Trained to defuse any situation not involving the use of weapons. Picked for their physique and ability to intimidate. Whereas the counter-terrorist boys were selected for their ability to make fast decisions and take fast shots accurately. Brains, and the shooter's trained eye, over brawn being their version of the truth.

Counter Terrorism and the Harriers didn't enjoy the closest of relationships on the back of that dichotomy. Harrier officers prone to implying that their CT counterparts were at less than their physical peak. At which point CT usually replied with references to knuckle dragging. Much glowering and disdain resulting, on operations.

And behind all that muscle was a Mercedes people mover containing four more Prot officers, one of them Mickey. Just in case. The convoy topped off with three minivans of support staff and favoured members of the press. Plus a full-on ambulance with combat experienced medics. A Special Escort Group Rangie brought up the rear to keep traffic at a distance.

Twenty vehicles, some of them distinctly difficult to manoeuvre in a London street. Which was why the convoy would ideally be routed on roads wide enough for tactical freedom, in the event of a disruption. Led by Kev, Easy Rider calling the shots to his Working Bikes. Their job being to clear the route ahead. And keep it clear, until the convoy was through.

'Rampage Bronze to all Rampage callsigns, two-minute warning. All callsigns prepare to move. Two minutes.'

Mickey climbed into the passenger seat of the Prot Merc van waiting behind the Harrier Beemers. Exchanging knowing glances with Wade. The other two officers waiting next to the vehicle, watching their arcs.

'Everyone's talking about you, Skipper.'

Mickey smirked at him with a bravado he wasn't entirely at home with yet. But which he knew Jasmine Chen's presumed leak to the *Clarion* would make his default setting for the rest of his career. The copper who told a government minister that he was a cunt and to fuck right off? If you say so, Assistant Commissioner.

'Goes with the turf, Wade mate. Do me a favour, don't burst their bubbles, eh?'

Wade nodded with a knowing smile. 'I won't spoil the story. I only wish it were true.'

Mickey pulled a lopsided smile. His "jaundiced cynic" face.

'It already pretty much is. And give it another month or two and it'll be the only version that anyone other than you and me remembers. But in the meantime, Wade, I'd focus on not driving into the back of the car in front. I don't think the Met would thank you for buggering up their no claims discount.'

'Rampage Bronze to all Rampage callsigns. POTUS and FLOTUS are travel ready.'

Prot officers and Secret Service mounted up. The latter in their long coats and special black glasses. Wraparound, and, Mickey suspected, with some sort of head-up display linked to their weapons. Kev led them away, taking the turn onto the Mall at ten miles per hour. Knowing that the secret of a London motorcade was to keep it as slow as needed to avoid the vehicles getting strung out. And, God forbid, leaving spaces into which other vehicles might be inserted.

'Easy Rider, Romeo Control.'

Uh-oh, Mickey thought. A call straight to Kev from LX could only be a traffic problem.

'Easy Rider. Go ahead.'

'Easy Rider, be aware, major accident Hyde Park Corner. Reports of a pedestrian under a bus. Off-duty medic on scene is advising that the casualty cannot be moved until ambulance service reaches the scene.'

'Romeo Control, all received. Working Two, Easy Rider.'

Kev nipped nimbly into the gap before Bronze Command decided to have an opinion.

'Easy Rider, Working Two.'

Maisie was equally quick coming back. Knowing what her skipper wanted. A chance to get the convoy rerouted before they drove into the back of the resulting jam. And before management tried to prove their value by offering help. Time to let SEG do what they did best.

'Working Two, is there any way through?'

Kev cutting to the heart of the matter. A binary question, no messing.

'Negative, Easy Rider. We're just on-scene, carriageway is completely blocked. Looks like the bus tried to avoid the casualty and hit the central barrier. Plus multiple collisions behind the bus blocking all four lanes.'

'All received, Working Two. Break break. Rampage Bronze Command, Easy Rider. Recommend switch to secondary route.'

'Easy Rider, Rampage Bronze Command, secondary route approved.'

Smooth as a greased weasel, Mickey thought. Allowing the breath he'd subconsciously been holding to hiss out. Out front Kev was taking the convoy round the Victoria Memorial in a slow one-eighty. Talking fast to his Working Bikes. Doing what he did best.

'All Working callsigns, Easy Rider, rerouting to secondary, repeat rerouting to secondary. Turning right, right, right, Mall eastbound.'

Mickey grinned, imagining the clenching sphincters at the change of plan. Senior officers hating little with more passion than circumstances spiralling out of their control. The advance riders would now be blue lighting their way east across Mayfair, heading for Regent Street. While Kev's front running Working Bikes were haring back up the Mall towards Trafalgar Square. Never the easiest of junctions to close at the best of times.

'Secondary route, Skip?'

Mickey shot Wade a disgusted look.

'Really? Presumably you were on the nest all night. Which would explain the lost brain cells where the route plan should be residing.' The two officers in the back sniggering. 'The Secondary, Constable Harris, is Mall, Trafalgar Square and left Cockspur Street, Haymarket Street, Coventry Street, Regent Street, Langham Place, Portland Place, left Park Crescent, Park Square West, left Ulster Terrace, Outer Circle, right Winfield House.' Putting on a passable Aleksandr Orlov voice. 'Simples.'

The motorcade progressed north smoothly enough. Carving a twenty-vehicle path through London's afternoon traffic. Working Bikes doing their assertive whistle and raised hand act at every junction. Momentarily freezing cars and buses in place at the sight of an armed copper on a fast bike staring them down. Palm unequivocally held up. All progressing well until, without warning, it suddenly wasn't. The traffic in front of the lead Working Bikes going from moderate to solid in thirty seconds.

'Easy Rider, Working Three. Portland Place is jammed. Cause unclear.'

'Working Three, Easy Rider. Determine cause of blockage and attempt to resolve.' Kev's brain probably doing somersaults by now. 'Break break. Working One and Two, Easy Rider. Backtrack to Portland Place and clear blockage from the northern side.' The veteran skipper thinking faster than anyone else could. 'Break break. Romeo Control and Bronze Command. Easy Rider. Next cross street is New Cavendish Street, potential dogleg west.'

Giving management the options. Their job to make the decisions, Kev's to execute.

'Bronze Command, Easy Rider. Your recommendation?'

Mickey and Wade exchanged knowing glances. Not every day that Prot management asked for advice. Perhaps Sally Williams was destined for great things.

'Easy Rider, Bronze Command. Potential for further blockage if we turn off route is significant.'

Yeah, Mickey thought. Like playing snake on your mobile, with the longest snake in the game. And you try three pointing a Beast in a two-lane street with parked vehicles on either side. See where that gets you.

Kev was still talking. 'Recommend hold in place and deploy appropriate personnel as required.'

Put like that, it made perfect sense. Other than the fact that it left the President of the United States going nowhere. With the Polish Embassy on one side and Pret A Manger on the other. And the great British public on both sides, of course. The latter being what would be bothering Bronze Commander. And putting the shits right up Jasmine Chen, Mickey reflected happily.

He looked out of the window. Seeing a pretty even distribution between two different sorts of people on the pavement. One half of them getting on with life. Mostly oblivious to the twenty-vehicle convoy, just traffic and therefore ignored. The other half having realised what was happening. And displaying their interest in a variety of ways. Phones, obviously. Pictures would be hitting social media with a range of comments from humorous to disgusted. Some looking more interested in expressing their amusement or angst at POTUS's presence in a more physical manner. The Beast's windows capable of being fully opaqued, of course. And just as well, because of the sorts of behaviour the man inside the vehicle inspired. But no-one likes to see a nose ring giving him the finger from two feet away. Whether the nose ring in question can see their target or not.

'All Rampage callsigns, Bronze Command.' The woman on the spot. With a decision to make. 'All Rampage vehicles will hold position and await route clearance. Harriers, deploy and maintain public order. Remaining Rampage callsigns, await further instruction.'

Oh great. Mickey looked in the wing mirror next to him. Seeing the Harriers debussing from their BMWs as ordered. Eight big men, identically dressed in combat boots, black trousers, blue T-shirts and midnight blue bomber jackets. Only needing neck and face tattoos to look the full Combat 88. And not, he noted with interest, wearing the yellow covert caps he knew they carried as identification. Marked with "Police" in strong black lettering. Experts in crowd control and "violent person tactics" they might be, but maybe a little common sense?

And as if to prove him right, the Secret Service deployed from their SUVs to face them. Not giving much of a shit about being told to await instruction. Their long dark coats and futuristic black glasses like Matrix wannabes. And looking very much like they'd like to air their weapons. Go bullet time. Their attention firmly fixed on the Harriers, the most obvious threat as seen through those lenses.

The closest of the muscle men started to reach into his

jacket. Possibly, belatedly, realising that his covert cap really ought to be on his head. Then thought better of it, as half a dozen Secret Servicemen put hands on the butts of their pistols. Mickey held his breath, seeing the Counter Terrorism Land Cruiser doors crack open. Eight assault-rifle-equipped firearms officers; 240 rounds of 5.56mm ready to rock and roll. Getting ready to debus onto a London street. In front of Secret Service officers not used to either their uniform or methods. Way to ratchet up the tension, guys.

'Bronze Command, all callsigns, *hold position*. Harriers, lower threat profile and focus on any obvious public disorder.'

Potential crisis averted. Everyone breathed a sigh of relief. The Harriers set to dissuading the more bolshie passers-by with their sheer intimidatory presence. Quietly putting on their yellow caps. Belatedly announcing themselves as 'Police'. Once they thought they could do so without being shot, that was. And the Secret Servicemen and women, denied a bullet to catch, stood and watched them with poorly concealed amusement. Another two minutes of vigorous direct intervention from the dismounted working riders cleared the road. Kev sitting impassively out front on his BMW R1000, ignoring the camera phones and catcalls.

'Romeo Control, Working Two.' Maisie, sounding smug. 'Carriageway will be clear in thirty seconds.'

The blockage, it turned out, having been caused by a delivery vehicle and a mobile crane. The former parked in an urban clearway to drop off office furniture for a development. The latter too big to make the turn out of a side street with a furniture van parked in its path. Its driver having got halfway round and realising there was no way he was going to make the turn. And then found himself boxed in by half a dozen honking cars behind him.

The vehicle at the heart of the problem now closing its rear doors and getting ready to go round the block. Maisie having threatened the site foreman with arrest unless the delivery driver presented himself within sixty seconds. Thereupon pointing out to Jerzy, from Krakow, that the Met could just as easily confiscate his waggon as wait for him to move it. And do him for obstruction. Words which, once translated into Polish by his mate, had made him see the light in double-quick time. Frayed tempers were soothed. Secret Service and Met muscle starting the phased fall-back to their vehicles. Counting down the seconds, Mickey grinned as Kev came on the air twenty-eight seconds later.

'Rampage Bronze Command, Easy Rider. Rampage is mobile.'

Sounding like he'd stopped for an ice cream. Rather than stuck in the middle of a London street, powerless to do anything other than wait. Mercifully, the remainder of the run to St John's Wood was uneventful. Delivering POTUS back to the ambassador's residence in time for his afternoon nap. And with a couple of hours to kill before the next move. All Prot officers not tasked with standing guard on the vehicles stood down.

'Fancy a cuppa, Mickey?'

He turned to find Kev and his crew beckoning him over. And since Wade had guard duty, as the most junior Prot copper on the team, he went with it. Promising to bring Wade something back.

The caff they had in mind was a rare find in North-West London. Both relatively cheap and decent quality. Tea from a pot, properly brewed. And with pukka home-made fruit cake. After a few minutes' appreciative silence Kev pushed his empty plate away. Gazing at the ceiling and blowing out a long slow breath. Looking around at his SEG colleagues and then shaking his head in amusement.

'I don't know about you lot, but I think I've stopped finding that sort of thing funny. Time I hung up my whistle and left you lot to it.'

'You know you'll miss us.'

He nodded at Maisie's comment.

'For sure. But I won't miss *this*.'

'What are you going to do instead?'

Mickey, with the question that most coppers got round to if left together long enough. Working One, Sean, the next most experienced of Kev's working riders, reached into a pocket. Dropped a card on the table in front of Mickey.

'That'll answer your question.'

Mickey looked down at the card. A stylised image of a bike, two up.

'Lightning Transfers? Not Black Rat Bikes then?'

'Does what it says on the tin. We get the punter from Central London to any London Airport in half the time the best black cab could do it. Which means that people who like to stay in meetings longer than they should can still make it to their plane on time. Plus we discreetly let it be known we're SEG. The rich punters lap that up, right enough.'

'So when are you starting this?'

Sean picked the card up. Waste not, want not, Mickey presumed.

'We already have. Websites are cheap, and after that all

you need is a decent bike, with a fairing, and three sizes of waterproofs and a helmet each. Plus we got a blinding deal on the bikes and kit, all buying together.'

'Does the Job know you're working on your off days?'

Kev shook his head.

'You know the rule, Mickey boy. What the Job doesn't know won't hurt it. Once I'm out I'll run the bookings, and do some runs to keep my hand in.'

Mickey nodded, impressed.

'Nice to see a Specialist Ops copper planning on doing something other than bodyguarding.'

'Yeah.' Kev took a slurp of his tea. 'Especially when most of you lot are already too fat and old to do it properly by the time you get out. Present company excepted, naturally.' He gave Mickey a level stare. Taking him back to his early years in uniform. 'But what are *you* going to do, eh son? No way you're going to make your thirty, are you?'

Mickey thought about that for a moment. Really thought about it. Kev's bald question having been, he guessed, the first time anyone had asked him that directly. Including himself.

'If you put it like that...'

'Look Mickey, if your Uncle Kev can't be brutal with you, who can? And the world's at your feet. You've got a cracker of a wife, undeserved but there you are. You're a bright boy too. Smart enough to do whatever you put your mind to. When you're not being a lazy bastard and tossing it off sitting around and drinking tea in Whitehall. And you know bloody well that the top brass have got a hard-on for you, after that thing in Belize. And the story in the papers.'

'But they *put* the story in the bloody papers!'

'Cause *and* effect. Clever. Still game, set and match though, isn't it? Face facts, Mickey, if the Job wants you out, the Job will have you out. One way or another.'

He finished his tea and stood up, reaching for his wallet.

'This one's on me. And you can stop pulling that surprised face, young Maisie. I know you're doing it even when you're behind me. Time we got back to let the rest of the team have a turn.' He dropped fifty pounds on the counter and raised his hands to refuse the change. 'And you, Mickey boy, need to start thinking about the future. Because it's going to slap you in the face sooner than you think.'

45

Martin approached the early morning meeting with the contact he knew as Neutralise as cautiously as ever. Took up his post on the high ground overlooking the meeting place an hour beforehand. He always insisted on meeting early, to minimise the number of people in the park. Making every single person obvious. Always got there first. Used the high ground up the hill. Watched the park's activities for an hour or so before the meet.

Looking for body language and pattern incongruity. The latter a term he'd learned from Mickey. Who'd picked it up during his Prot training. Suspicious behaviour, in the language that Martin understood. Because, in his experience, it wasn't hard to spot an undercover copper. The vibe they gave off was unmistakable. Unable to divest themselves of that bone-deep feeling of power. Their body language that of the master race. In control. Whatever, Martin could spot the feds a mile off, he reckoned.

One time, he'd almost pissed himself laughing. When Mickey's old mucker Jase Felgate had appeared in the vicinity of a meet. His presence giving Martin enough warning that he was half a mile away before the alleged customer had even got out of his car. A bit lucky, of course.

Martin knowing Jason from a few pub sessions back when Mickey and Jason had both been probationers. But Martin definitely had the nose for trouble, he reckoned. And so he took his time. Scoped out the various people who'd come to use the park. And decided that the pitch was clean. Went down to his usual bench to meet the new client. After a few minutes' wait a skinny youth in a faded Metallica tee and leather jacket strolled up and took a seat. Keeping his distance, obvs. No point in taking needless risks.

'Neutralise?'

'Yeah. You Steph? We weren't sure if you were a bloke or—'

'A woman? Yeah. Makes it easier for me to slide out from under, if anyone I might not want to meet is looking for the opposite sex. Gives me that little bit of extra time, if I need to leg it.'

Metal Boy nodded. Looking confident enough to Martin, if a little on edge. But hey, who wouldn't be just a little bit edgy the first time they met their arms dealer, right?

'Had me fooled. Until I realised this is the bench we agreed. You're not really called Steph though, right?'

'Nope. And before you ask, my name's not important. Let's get down to—'

'Your name's pretty important to me though.'

Martin would have been away on his toes, if he'd been able. Having been in the game long enough to know that people making a soft-footed approach from behind weren't usually well intentioned. But for one thing, where was the risk? He wasn't carrying. His modus operandi being to meet and suss out the client. Then go back to his stash and return with the desired equipment. Once payment had been made.

And for another thing, a heavy hand had clamped onto his shoulder. And so, taking the path of least resistance – and less likely to get him twatted, he suspected – he subsided back onto the wooden slats.

And looked round, to see who was manhandling him. Ready to protest his innocence.

And saw Joe, grinning down at him.

'Gotcha.'

Fuck.

46

Saturday morning; 11.30. Roz off getting her roots done, then down to the shops. Having promised Mickey a nice bit of steak for dinner. And Mickey pretending to himself that he was reading the paper. While his subconscious kept on playing clips of Lewis's hate and pain-contorted face as a torrent of liquid cement poured over his bloody torso. Wondering if he was showing symptoms of PTSD. His personal phone buzzed. Number withheld. Probably a marketing call. He'd been getting two or three a week over the last couple of months. Fuelling his belief that nothing was private when there was money to be made.

'Mickey Bale.'

'Police Sergeant Bale.'

So much information in those three words. The word "police" spoken with an edge of malice. Telling Mickey that "filth" would have been more to the speaker's taste. The word "sergeant" told him that whoever had called him knew exactly who he was. And his name articulated with an edge of deep satisfaction. A tone that said "at last". Mickey's instincts went to red alert in the time it took to digest them.

'You don't know me, Mickey.'

Almost gleefully expressed. This wasn't going to be good, Mickey already knew that much. Subconsciously desperate to hit the end-call button. But he knew the other man would simply call him back.

'But you're going to know me. And you're going to regret it for the rest of your life.'

Oh shit. The man on the other end paused for a moment. Clearly relishing the moment of confrontation.

'A period of time that is going to be very short, brutal and ultimately very fatal. Guessed who I am yet?'

Jesus fucking Christ.

'Joe Castagna.'

Mickey managed to keep his voice level. Just.

'Yeah. Who's a clever boy? Although not quite as clever as you hoped, eh? I'm going to say a name to you. Let's see if it rings a bell, shall we? Martin Hyde. Your arms dealer mate. We took him off the street about three hours ago. And do you know what, he spat your name out in less than the time it took to chain him to the lifting tackle in my games room. Gave me the lot. Everything.'

Almost everything, presumably, Mickey thought. Prayed Martin hadn't told him about Nemesis. At least not yet.

'So there's nothing I don't know about you. And what you've been doing. And of course now that I know all that, I've got you by the fucking bollocks. Your nuts, Mickey Bale, are in my left hand. And there's a knife in my right hand. You're proper fucked, son. And so is everyone you care about, literally fucked. Unless you do exactly what I tell you. You listening?'

'Yes.'

'Good. You've got a day. Six o'clock tomorrow morning,

you're going to surrender yourself to my boys down on the estate. In the same car park where you shot up my cash crew. They'll be waiting for you. And they'll be tooled. So no getting ideas about going out in a blaze of glory. Although of course you don't have any weapons anymore. Do you? Because I emptied out your mate Martin's little stash.'

He chuckled, and Mickey knew beyond any doubt he absolutely meant every word.

'They're going to bring you to me, my boys from the estate. And I'm going to be ready for you. With a video camera. And whatever assorted delights I decide to use to demonstrate the error of your ways. Not to you, of course, but to all the others. You're going to be the star of a film that'll show my rivals what happens to anyone who tries to tip me off my throne. Does that sound good to you?'

'No.'

'I thought not. You'd rather not walk onto the set of a snuff movie.' Joe sounding almost chatty. Unable to hide his glee. 'But you're going to. Because the alternative ain't worth even thinking about. Your wife. Roz, isn't it?'

He paused. Forcing Mickey to answer.

'Yes.'

'Yeah, Roz. Not bad-looking for an older bird. My hacker located her for me, and I had her picked up outside the salon. Amazing how easy it is to break into a person's phone these days. She'll go down well with my rougher punters, once she's drugged up and ready to be used. I reckon we'll get two or three years' use out of her before the smack kills her. It kills them all in the end, the ones we get properly hooked. You didn't think it was all just imported kids did you? I have to cater to all tastes, Mickey. And your

Roz will most definitely go down well on the ropes and bruises scene. Come to think about it, perhaps she'll enjoy it more if we don't bother with the drugs. And then there's that reporter. Tamara.'

Again the silence.

'Yes.'

Joe laughed. 'I can tell you're enjoying this. So, this Tamara sort. She can't hide forever. We'll get hold of her too, eventually. She's a bit younger. And a bit of posh totty, from what I screwed out of her mate Mark before he went into the cement. More likely to put up a fight. Too much of a fight, that is. So it'll be smack for her for sure, when we find her. And we will find her. I reckon I could make a thousand a night off her. Add in what your Roz could draw, and I might make back a hundredth of what you've cost me over the last three months. But then it's not about the money. Is it?'

'No.'

'So what is it about, do you think?'

Mickey laughed. Having found sufficient equilibrium to fight back. However weak his position. 'Revenge?'

Joe's tone was condescending. 'No, son. It ain't about revenge. That was what *you* came here for. Blaming my dealer for your druggie sister's stupidity.'

'I didn't blame him, I blamed *you*. Warren was just a way to send—'

'I literally couldn't give a shit. Not about you, and not about Warren either. Or the cash crew. Or the people you pasted at Number 37. I don't even really care about the product you took from me.'

Mickey needed a moment before he could translate "product" into "trafficked women".

'I cared about Lewis, of course. He was a diamond. A rare find in a sea of shit. And he'll be hard to replace. But even Lewis ain't the point of this. So no, I'm not about revenge. I'm about *respect*. You kill my people, you chip at my respect. You burn my money, you burn my respect. And I'm here to take that respect back. Problem is, I reckon I'll have to dig it out of you with a rusty fucking spoon.'

Enough. Mickey was back on his game. Shock absorbed, ready to fight. 'So why the twenty-four hours? Why not now?'

Joe laughed softly. 'You're a hard one, ain't you? Most blokes would be pissing themselves by now. Asking for mercy. But you just want to understand your sentence. All right, we can do that. Just as long as you're clear that you're done. When a man goes down, I keep him there.'

He paused, and Mickey heard the faint crackle of burning tobacco. The inhalation of smoke, then a gust of breath caressing the phone's microphone. The bastard was smoking a cigar. Probably with his feet up on the desk. Celebrating.

'Thing is, you must have had inside knowledge. A nasty little rat inside my gang. Someone who wanted you to chop off my limbs, one at a time. Make me so weak that my peers in the business would have no choice but to move on me. Eh?'

Another draw on the cigar.

''Course, I couldn't blame them if they did. 'Cause if they didn't, my organisation would go down under the weight of a hundred little gangs. Like rats on a mastiff. Causing chaos. Costing lives. Hurting their businesses as much as mine. So obviously they'd step in. Stabilise my turf. Either exile me or just kill me. And my family. Because it's as true now as it was two thousand years ago. You kill the king, you kill his heirs. Leave no risk of revenge, twenty years down the line. And I'm not having that.'

Joe inhaled again. The exhale followed by the sound of his cigar being ground out.

'So I'm going to entertain you in my soundproof playroom. And you're going to tell me everything you know. You play nicely, take what's coming and give me the rat, I'll free your Roz. Leave the reporter alone, if she promises to behave. But if you don't show, everyone you ever cared about is going to suffer. Wife, friends… fuck, I'll even track down your ex-girlfriends and have them as well. Which is why the twenty-four hours. I want you to have the time to reflect on just who's going to pay the bill for all that if you don't. I think you're out of choices. And I reckon you'll walk in, just like I said. Don't you?'

Mickey paused for a moment. Making the eventual concession sound even more painful than it was. 'Yeah.'

No other choice.

47

'That's got the Met's hit man put in his place.'

Joe cast an eye over Eddie and Richard. The former looking determined, the latter queasy. The ponce.

'Right, so me and Acid are staying here for the day. No way that fucker could come after me inside these walls. And with this much firepower it'd be a bloody short gun battle if he did. If he could even find a gun at this notice.'

Eddie nodding agreement. Having warned the half-dozen men he'd ordered to stand guard to stay on their toes.

'He'll spend all day trying to decide whether to top himself or not.'

Joe shook his head. 'He won't. He'll already have decided to come in to take his punishment like a good boy. Because he knows my reputation. He knows I'll make everyone he cares for regret the day he was born.'

'And you're going to spare them if he does?'

Richard. Who sounded a bit too shaky for Eddie's liking. Not temperamentally suited to this game, he'd always thought. And here was the proof. Likely to start winding Joe up if he didn't pack it in. Joe shrugged, with that "couldn't really give a fuck" look that he wore when he actually really wanted to hurt someone.

'Dunno. I might. Depends on how good a show he puts up for me. He shows the right respect, and takes his punishment in the right manner, I might let it go.'

Joe missed the two men exchanging glances. Lost in his own thoughts of just how hard he was going to punish Mickey Bale.

'As your lawyer...'

Joe turned a baleful stare on Richard.

'What? You're not going to try talking me out of this? Because if you are then you're a bigger prick than I thought you were. Consiglieri? You don't even qualify as cannelloni.'

'No. But as your lawyer, I need to have no knowledge at all of any criminal act, if possible.'

Joe smirked. 'Like you ain't known all about everything I've done over the last ten years. I wonder what ever made me take a gutless twat like you on in the first place.'

The answer to that question being clear enough to Eddie. Richard having impressed the shit out of Joe, in his early days with the firm. The mistake having been to expand his responsibilities from the legit business contracts with which he was so clever. Involving him in the questionable side of Joe's empire. Slowly but surely dragging him down into the moral cesspit that Eddie had been enduring for over twenty years. Richard went quiet. Avoiding Joe's angry stare. And for a moment Eddie wondered if the poor bastard was going to get on the properly wrong side of their boss. And then Joe, in one of his typical mood swings, hooked a thumb at the door.

'Go on. Do one. Now, before I change my mind. You're not cut out for this, are you?'

Richard didn't need telling twice. Bolting for the door

past an amused Rocco. Who, Eddie noted, was still carrying Lewis's .45 auto. Those were some shoes to fill though, he mused. And having the big man's shooter didn't make Rocco a fit replacement. Not in Eddie's opinion.

'I'll go and make sure he knows to keep his mouth shut.'

Joe nodded at the suggestion. 'Good man, Eddie. Although I can't see him ever turning Queen's on us, can you?'

Eddie shook his head. Being of the firm opinion that Richard wasn't that sort of geezer. Not brave enough, for one thing. Only too well aware of the bestial ferocity Joe would visit on him and those he loved, were he ever to rat on the family. And too much addicted to the good life, for another. If he lost the money that came with Joe's service he had a long way to fall, financially. And a lot to lose on the way.

'Nah. He'll keep his mouth shut. I'll just go and make sure he knows what'll happen if he don't.'

48

Mickey stared at the wall of the living room for a good fifteen minutes. Then stirred himself to action. Pretty meaningless action, but better than nothing. Headed for Martin's flat. Because what gun dealer wasn't going to keep something on the premises to defend himself?

Without the first clue as to what to do. But he knew he had to do something. Quickly. And so he focused on reviewing his options as he drove the short journey. Or rather on trying to come up with any different course of action to the one he knew was inevitable. It all came down to one question: how to stop Joe carrying out his threat.

The way Mickey saw it, there wasn't any sure way other than to put a bullet through Joe's head. The problems with that option being firstly that he wasn't in possession of any firearms. And wouldn't be getting any help from Martin.

And secondly, that with his threats delivered, Joe would go silent and deep. Knowing that if he stayed undetected then even the craziest end-run attempt on his life couldn't be attempted. Allowing the clock to run down on his ultimatum. A threat that Mickey was pretty sure Joe would order to be carried out without a second thought. Or even carry out himself.

All of which meant that he only really had one realistic choice. The defeated warrior's dilemma. To surrender. Trust that Joe would limit his revenge to taking as many pounds of his flesh as he deemed appropriate. The problem with that being that it probably wouldn't stop there. Revenge, he guessed, not being a dish Joe believed was best eaten cold. Probably more like a running buffet. And one to be consumed with gusto, for all to see. He could hear the gang leader's boast in his head. 'You've seen the video of me gutting the bastard who was killing my people? Now you can watch his wife pay the price as well. And the bitch reporter who put my fucking face in the papers.'

He'd want to send a message. Tell his rivals, his enemies and the police the same thing: you can't beat me. And if you try, this is what I'll do to you. And the people you love.

Put starkly, there was no good way out of the catastrophe. He could kill himself publicly enough for Joe to know about it. An act of seppuku, in front of Joe's house, perhaps? A samurai blade being a good deal easier to come by than a 9mm. A dignified, and necessarily painful way out. Rip his own guts open with a short sword. And then dying of the resulting blood loss, without anyone to give him the mercy stroke. With the hope that Joe would be assuaged by the fearsome suffering involved. And not take his disappointment out on Roz and Tamara. And Martin, of course. It was either that or surrender himself to who knew what torture before he died. But still without knowing if his wife and friends were safe.

Some choice.

He parked his car a quarter mile from the flat. Approached carefully. Taking time to be sure it wasn't being watched.

Nothing out of the ordinary to be seen. Perhaps cleaning out Martin's armoury had been enough for them. He listened at the door for five silent minutes. Heard nothing. Put on a pair of latex gloves. Then let himself into the flat with the key Martin had given him years ago for emergencies. Stopped in the hall and listened again. Breathing tidally. Every sense alert for any sign that there were men waiting for him. Again, nothing.

Moving quietly, he lifted the rug at the bottom of his friend's bed. To reveal a floorboard fastened in place with wood screws. Sprayed black to match the others. But brand new. Removed them with his penknife, lifting the board to reveal a long green bag. Heavy too, a proper lift. He knew what he'd find inside it. Useful, but not ideal. Heavy firepower, but useless for close quarters. He sat on Martin's sofa contemplating the weapon. Better than nothing, but almost guaranteed to get him killed if he went after Castagna with it. Condemning all around him to Joe's vengeance. Back to square one.

A spark of light in his peripheral vision caught his attention. His phone's notification light blinking. A message received. Another threat, probably. He leaned over and picked it up. From… *Nemesis?* Mickey's attention snapped down onto the screen.

'You only have one chance to get through this. Numbers 7, 8 & 9 are the key.'

Along with a postcode. Mickey took a look on Google Maps. E1. Bethnal Green. Wondering for a moment why the hell Nemesis had sent him the postcode of a railway line. Until the penny dropped. Railway arches? He clicked through into street view, orienting the view to look at the row of arches beneath the line. Various business uses. Baker, car repair shop, bathroom sales. Decorating supplies, insurance broker, a couple of print shops. Inevitably, several cab companies.

And there, numbers seven, eight and nine. Without any signage. Seven and nine with their doors bricked up, the frontage painted a nice dark green. The paint unspoiled by any hint of graffiti. Enough of a clue as to who owned those arches in itself. A gimballed CCTV camera casting its impassive stare down at the middle arch. The proverbial dollars to donuts that was one camera that had never been vandalised.

He clicked on it, zooming in to examine the central arch. A heavy-looking door. Probably steel-lined. Electric bolts to lock it into the brickwork, as well, most likely. No keyhole, numeric pad or any other obvious means of locking or unlocking. Which implied twenty-four/seven occupation. Always someone there to open the door.

The text notification light flickered again. No words, just a picture. Mickey tapped it, waiting while the file opened. Hand-drawn. A floor plan of the three arches. Showing how they connected to form one large space in three segments. The left-hand arch, number seven, labelled 'STORAGE'. The middle arch accessed by the front door. Which was labelled 'STEEL-LINED, WILL NEED EXPLOSIVES'. Explosives? Who did this guy think he was?

The door separated from the rest of the arch by a full-height internal wall. Keeping the draft out and maintaining privacy, Mickey guessed. The arch space behind it labelled

'GUARDROOM/LIVING QUARTERS'. Probably enough space for a couple of dozen men, if they slept on camp beds. An army, if Joe chose to mobilise. But it was number nine, the right-hand arch, that was the most interesting. A thick black line closing it off from number eight. And labelled 'DOOR – HEAVY'. The word 'heavy' underlined. And number nine itself was labelled 'COMMAND CENTRE'. With a hastily added further comment: 'JOE'S BUNKER – YOUR GUN DEALER FRIEND HELD HERE.'

He sat back and looked at his phone screen for a long moment. Whoever Nemesis was, he – or she – clearly knew about the threat to Mickey and those around him. And was offering the one way he could remove that threat at a single stroke. Except it would take a demolition expert to blow the doors open. And expert close-quarters battle skills to clear out Joe's army...

An assault squad.

Mickey reached for his wallet. Pulling Shaw's card out and looking at it. Just a phone number. He shrugged. Dialled the number. Which was answered at the second ring. Whoever had answered saying nothing. Waiting for the caller to self-identify.

'Mr Shaw? It's Mickey Bale.'

A moment more of silence. Thinking time, perhaps. Or just the call going through whatever filers and security Shaw deemed necessary.

'Mickey known as Michael at work. I seem to remember reading somewhere that you're not Sir Patrick's protection officer anymore. They made it official then?'

'They did.'

'But that's not why you're calling, is it?'

'No.'

'So…?'

Mickey took a breath. And dived in. 'You said I'd be fine. And to call you if I wanted to pay up on that pint. So I'd like to pay up. And see if there's a way I could also pay you to do a job for me.'

Another moment of silence.

'Do a *job* for you? You do know what my team's services cost?'

'I've got a pretty fair idea.'

The next silence longer. Definite thinking time.

'You're not proposing some sort of bank job, are you? I've heard the stories about you lot having fun planning how to carry out armed raids with police weapons in your lunch breaks.'

Mickey nodded subconsciously. It was a game he'd played in his time. Not that he or any of his mates had ever had the balls to follow through. Which, given what he'd done of late, would have been darkly funny. Except for his current circumstances.

'No. This is something riskier, truth be told. But without the danger of the Met coming after us.'

'Us? You want to participate?'

'Meet me and I'll explain it to you. Over that pint. But the job has to be done in the next…' Mickey took a look at his watch. 'Eighteen hours.'

Another silence.

'Better make it a coffee then. Where are you?'

49

The ex-soldier met him an hour after their call. Friendly, but sufficiently brisk for Mickey to know that this was business. He sipped at his cappuccino, nodded appreciatively, then stared levelly at Mickey and issued a simple command.

'Talk. Tell me *everything*. If I doubt what you're telling me I'll walk away without looking back.'

Mickey, having subconsciously repressed the events of the previous month, uncorked the bottle. And told Shaw, quite literally, everything. Warren, the car park ambush, Number 37, Lewis. No detail spared, nothing held back. Shaw sat and listened. And if he had been surprised or shocked at any point, his face stayed remarkably composed. Eventually, an hour and a half and two more coffees later, Mickey ran out of steam. Looked across the table at Shaw questioningly. *Your turn.* Shaw lifted his cup before speaking, draining it. Looking disquietingly like a man getting ready to leave.

'So, to summarise, you've carried out four hits on this man Castagna's organisation. Killed seven of his men and bitten a fair-sized chuck out of his reputation. And now that he knows who you are, he's got you by the balls. You gambled that you could put him down before he caught up with you. And you lost that bet.'

'Yeah.'

'So go on then. Tell me how you think we can pull your nuts out of the fire.'

Mickey started talking again. Showed Shaw the last text from Nemesis. The pictures he'd pulled from Google Maps. The rough floor plan of the arches.

'Jesus.' Shaw sat back again, shaking his head. 'And you have no idea who this Nemesis is?'

'None at all. There's probably a long list of people with the right motivation. Although there can't be too many people with the sort of information he's been giving me. If Nemesis is a man.'

The ex-soldier grimaced. Clearly unhappy with the degree of uncertainty involved.

'He could have twenty or thirty men in those arches. The odds are less, of course. Probably more like five to ten, given he has no idea you know us. Or what we can do. But the risk you're asking us to take is pretty fucking full-on.' He thought for a moment: '250k. Sterling. Even at that price it's still possibly more risk than my team will want to take. Do you have a quarter of a million pounds available at short notice?'

'No.'

The former soldier shrugged. 'Then I can't see what—'

'But Martin does. Lewis's money. We just have to get him out of there alive.'

'And if he gets killed in the attack? That leaves us empty-handed.'

Mickey shrugged. Tossing his last card onto the table.

'You want a quarter of a million? There could be ten times that much in used notes in there. And whatever else

passes for ready cash for a man like him. Gold. Drugs. I
don't know, diamonds, bearer bonds, crypto… A man like
that always needs to be ready to make a sharp exit. Which
means he always needs assets to hand. Portable. And liquid.
Easy to carry, easy to spend.'

'So, what are you suggesting?'

'A five-way split. Simple as that. Whatever we find gets
shared between us.'

Shaw stared hard at him. Pursing his lips.

'You *clever* bastard. You're offering me the chance to
get my team retired. One more job, against a bunch of
amateurs. Kill this goon Castagna. Clear out the valuables.
And we're on the beach.'

Mickey said nothing. Waiting. Knowing that nothing he
could say now would tip Shaw's decision either way.

'Wait here.' Shaw stood up. 'Make yourself comfortable,
because this could take a while. I'll be watching you through
the window, so don't touch your phone. I see any sign that
you're talking to anyone else, I'll walk. From now you're
comms dark. I don't care if the commissioner herself calls
you, ignore any incoming.'

He went out onto the pavement. Put in a pair of wireless
earbuds and leaned back against a lamppost. His eyes fixed
firmly on Mickey through the glass. Who, not wanting to
stare back, pretended to read a copy of the *Clarion*. Which
was running the story of a missing subeditor. Although
more from the "missing in London" perspective than with
any concern for foul play. After ten minutes of discussion
with whoever had been at the other end, Shaw walked back
in. Bought himself a bottle of water and sat down facing
Mickey.

'My team are sceptical, to say the least of it. But we're all realists. The sort of money you're saying might be in those arches is a powerful incentive.'

'*Might* be. I can't guarantee anything.'

'Yeah. That's part of the scepticism. But there's logic in what you say. And this has to happen before 06.00 tomorrow, right?'

Mickey nodded. Holding his breath while Shaw pondered the question one last time. Before he either agreed to help or just got up and walked away. Leaving Mickey to decide how he wanted to die.

'We *might* be in. But...' Shaw raised a hand to forestall any comment. 'From this moment on you're under strict conditions. Give me both of your phones. If either of them ring you'll answer with me listening in. No outgoing calls. From now on you don't leave my sight. So I hope you've had your morning shit.'

Mickey was somewhat relieved that he had. Although summoning a bowel movement after his call with Joe hadn't been very difficult.

The two men returned to Shaw's apartment. Picking up his car keys and legally held pistol, registered under his protection business. Then he drove them to a location in South London, Mickey blindfolded for the last mile. Inside a small light industrial unit, Shaw's team were waiting. Familiar to Mickey from Belize. Their expressions neither friendly nor hostile. Shaw gestured to a chair. Tossed Mickey a small bottle of water from a half-consumed brick of twenty-four.

'You've met the team. That's Jenny.' Pointing to the woman who'd shot the two Chinese who'd been stalking him and Wade. Short cut blonde hair and piercing blue eyes. 'The best CQ shooter I ever met. That's Rick.' A big man, hard-faced. As far from being "grey" as it was possible to be. 'Demo expert and medic. We used to call him Doctor Dynamite in the Regiment. And Darren.' Pointing to a slim, hatchet-faced man with close-cropped black hair over alert brown eyes. 'Literally ambidextrous. Which means he can actually do the computer game thing and use two weapons at a time. He's our comms and kit man.'

He pointed to a chair at the end of the table.

'Take the weight off. And tell them what you told me. Spare no detail. Just because I think this is a risk worth taking doesn't mean that we all will.'

At the end of his second telling of the story, occasionally prompted by Shaw, Mickey felt wrung out. Increasingly uncertain as to whether he was wasting his last day of freedom or not. He drained the water and looked around at each of Shaw's team in turn. Unable to read their closed expressions. At some shared signal all four of them stood. Shaw raised a hand to Mickey.

'Stay here. We need to make a decision.'

Huddled in the other corner of the unit, they talked for a few minutes before walking back over. Faces still unreadable. Shaw addressed Mickey in a matter-of-fact way. No more animated than if he'd been reading a shopping list.

'We're in. Which means we need to go and get some weapons.'

Leaving Mickey reeling with relief. Light-headed as they'd boarded the Discovery and headed out to the west. He listened, from beneath the blindfold, to their sporadic, clipped conversation. Professional talk about the task at hand. Discussion as to the required equipment. The best time to hit the target. Someone using a tablet to surf Google Maps. Approach route, egress route, secondary and tertiary routes in the event that the police made an appearance. And the need for some sort of distraction. Something to keep the police looking the wrong way at the right time.

Sometime around four, Shaw turned off the road. The rougher ride telling Mickey they were on a track of some sort. Up which they'd driven for a few minutes before stopping. Shaw's team heading off into rolling countryside. Pistols cocked and ready in their shoulder rigs, hidden under outer jackets. Not expecting any problems, but ready for them.

'Seems like a long way to go to pick up your gear.'

For a moment the terse laugh from the man beside him had confused Mickey. Then Shaw's dry reply had made him smile.

'It's not *our* equipment.'

'I see. So just whose gear is it you've come all this way to collect?'

The ex-SAS man grinned at him. 'As I've said before, Sergeant Bale, that's need-to-know stuff. And you don't need to know. Because what *you* don't know can't hurt *us*. But I'll tell you this much. If the people who own the kit we're going to borrow ever find out it's been used without their permission, they're going to be properly pissed. And it doesn't pay to upset that big a player.'

'Christ, this is spook-level stuff, isn't it?'

Shaw shook his head. 'Like I said, the less you know the better. And the advantage of this procurement route...' the last two words spoken with an edge of humour '...is that the weapons involved are clean. Whiter than white. Serial numbers erased. We could leave the whole lot in those arches, when the job is done. Because they're untraceable. Good kit too. Only the best for some intelligence services. And none of the crap their domestic industry turns out.'

His comrades came back to the car after an hour. All three laden with heavy tool bags.

'It was all still there.' Darren talking to Shaw as he lifted his bags into the Discovery's capacious boot. 'And the bugs we planted for our client are still working.' Passing Shaw a small black box. 'The jammer worked perfectly. This is all still perfect black.'

Mickey pondered that statement and decided to keep his mouth firmly shut. Shaw laughed softly at his carefully neutral expression.

'We'll put them back when we've finished with them. Minus whatever ammunition we use, of course. The odds are that they'll never notice a few missing bullets. And besides, what are they going to do. Complain to MI5?'

50

'So what the fuck's so important we all had to meet tonight? And who's your new friend?'

Deano, pint in hand, gave Shaw a hard stare. That clearly troubled him not the slightest. Mickey, knowing there was no time for any other approach, dived straight in. Having called all three and requested their presence in the Carpenter's as a matter of urgency.

'I'm going to tell you something. Something I've done. Something I need your help with.'

Deano snorted in a knowing tone of voice. Probably thinking Mickey had been caught over the side. And that Shaw was his lawyer or some such.

'Yeah, you've fucked up. Whatevs. Just spill it, we'll deal with it.'

'No, hang on.' Den, his eyes narrowed. 'This is something proper serious. Isn't it?'

Mickey nodded, grim-faced. 'Yeah. If killing gangsters is proper serious, then yes, it is.'

Steve was first to get it. He leaned forward with a look of dawning comprehension and disbelief. 'That *was* you?'

'What...?' Deano shook his head disbelievingly. 'You're

trying to tell us that you're the fucking Car Park Killer? It's been you going after...'

Den raised a hand. 'Keep it down, Deano. You keep ramping up the volume, the whole pub's gonna be listening.'

Which got him a glare from Deano. But which also lowered Deano's volume several notches.

'That was actually *you*? You shot Warren? You did the Car Park thing? You raided that tom training house?'

'Yeah. And I killed Lewis Dearlove too.'

Steve, freshly incredulous. '*Lewis?* We didn't even know he was missing.'

'It was less than forty-eight hours ago. And Joe isn't going to advertise that he's lost his enforcer when he's worried about a gang war breaking out.'

'Never mind that shit!' Deano, struggling to hold the volume down. 'What the fuck did you think you were doing? I told you, here, at this table, that whoever was doing it was going to get their ticket punched! And you sat there and nodded! Knowing that you were putting all our lives at risk?'

'Yeah. I did it for Katie.'

'I reckon you did it for yourself.' Den and Deano turned to look at Steve. 'I reckon you've always wanted to match yourself against a real target. You saw this as your chance to find out for yourself, didn't you?'

'Yeah. There's that too, to be fair.'

'And where did it get you?'

'I don't think it's where I want to be either. But now I have no choice.'

'And now you want our help. And it's something to do with him, right?' Steve pointed at Shaw.

'Yeah. I need your help.'

'And why would we do that?' Deano and Steve silent, as Den cut to the heart of the matter. 'When Castagna finds out we were involved, won't he come after us?'

Mickey conceded the point. 'There is that risk. Unless we kill him first.'

'So what do you want from us?'

Shaw stepped in. Looking at Steve. 'You're ex-army. Ever fired the old Bren gun?'

'Yes. We had a few, vehicle-mounted. We called them LMGs, but it was the same gun. I know my way round it.'

'Good. And all we need is a distraction. A few minutes without interference. I can't tell you any more unless you're up for it.'

'One question.' Deano, hungry-eyed.

'Go on then.'

'Do *I* get a go with the Bren gun?'

51

Two in the morning. Eddie was doing his rounds. Unable to sleep. Joe, by contrast, was happily sparko in a camp bed in his office. Eddie's guys were joking about it behind his back. Telling each other that the boss was giving off his "it's quiet – too quiet" vibe. Like some geezer out of the war movies their granddads used to watch, innit? The more perceptive shook their heads with a mix of bemusement and pity. But they waited until Eddie was well outside earshot before sharing their thoughts.

Which were that Eddie being unable to sleep fitted a bit of a pattern. Because, they reckoned, he wasn't looking forward to the next day. Everyone who worked for the man respected his intelligence. No flies on Eddie when it came to thinking. Everyone knew that. But when it came to good old-fashioned gang leader brutality, he just wasn't at the races.

Joe, they told the younger guys, would have the end cut off a bloke's finger with no more thought than if he'd asked for sliced bread. Immune to all the blood, and the noise, and the frenzy. Although it was a wise and fortunate man who could take his punishment and keep his mouth shut. In which case Joe was sometimes happy to accept their stoicism as a form of atonement. Yeah, weird mofo and all that, but it was what the man did. Whereas the blokes who made a lot of noise, or had to be held down while punishment was delivered? Likely to get it doubled. One poor bastard actually losing three finger joints before Joe decided he was bored of the whole thing.

Whereas Eddie? Eddie always approached the inevitable fact of punishment – any punishment – with all the relish of a twelve-year-old faced with triple maths. Put his head down and bulled his way through the whole sordid ritual. Because that was his job. And in fact, one older and sager head argued, perhaps respect was due? Arguing that Eddie was deserving of more kudos for hating it, but still doing it? Opinions were divided on that. But on one thing they all agreed. Eddie wasn't going to stop pacing the arches until later in the night. When it was almost too late to sleep.

And so they watched him with a mix of respect and pity. Respect for standing the pressure of working for Joe for as long as he had. And pity for just the same reason. Wondering, in their quieter moments, what might happen when his ability to soak up the stress reached its limit.

52

Three in the morning was the witching hour, according to Shaw. The team were preparing their newly acquired equipment, while Shaw laid out his plan for the assault.

'You're a gang banger standing guard at this time of day, a few things are certain. One, you're pretty knackered. Unless you've been at the go pills, of course. But why would you do that when there's not a war on? You get forty-eight hours of hyper-performance. Then you sleep for two days. Too risky taking that stuff until the very moment you're ready to pull the trigger. So these people are going to be in less than sparkling condition by now.

'Two, you don't believe anything's going to happen. It never has before, so why should it now?

'Three, even if it does happen there's no way any bastard's going to get the better of you, right? After all, you're carrying. Got the big man shooter. And that lump of metal gets you all the respect you need back where you came from. You're a king amongst men to the civilians, and you know it.

'And four, in this case, you're behind locked doors, steel-reinforced. Inside a brick shithouse of a railway arch that was built to hold the weight of those old iron trains. Nuke-proof.'

Mickey pondered his opinion. Finding it hard to argue with the logic to a point. That point being…

'OK. But how do we get inside? I mean yeah, they'll be half asleep by now, but they've still got CCTV watching the street. The second they see us they'll wake up and tool up. Won't they?'

The former soldier grinned at him. 'Simple. All I need is a bottle of urine.'

Mickey raised an eyebrow in gentle disbelief. All right, special forces and that. But all the same…

'You're going to open a locked door with a bottle of *piss*?'

'Yup.' Shaw raised a hand to forestall his incredulity. 'Has to be fresh, mind you. The cold stuff isn't half as effective.'

'I see.' Mickey still feeling incredulous. 'How does it work then?'

The ex-soldier looked at him for a moment. A question in his eyes.

'Before I tell you, I need to know that you still want to do this.'

'Of course I do. Unless I can knock Joe over before six he'll go to work on people I care about more than I care about myself.'

'Yeah, you said that. But there's a big difference between "need to" and "capable of". You're sure you want in on this?'

Mickey pondered that for not very long at all. 'In the last few weeks I've shot a drug dealer dead.' Raising a single finger. 'Ambushed a cash collection crew and shot five of them.' Two fingers. 'Beaten the living shit out of a houseful of people traffickers, and—'

'Yeah, we saw that in the papers. Nice work.'

'Thanks.' Three fingers. 'And then I took out his number-one enforcer. I'm not proud of the way I did it, but he had it coming.' Raising the fourth finger.

'I take your point. I really do.' Shaw nodded, pursing his lips in approval. 'But those were all set pieces, weren't they? All four of those actions were planned. But this, Mr Bale, is different. This is going to be chaotic. With an unknown number of opposition players, equipped with who knows what. We're not even sure about the floor plan either. And that's where *we* live.'

He gestured at the two men and a woman sitting at the table.

'You didn't offer us a share in whatever we find just to pull the trigger. You offered it because we've got the skills to get in there and shoot our way through to your target. That's CQB, right? Close quarters battle. And it's what we do. We've all done this a thousand times. Only for real half a dozen times, of course. But the other nine hundred and ninety-four times were just as stressful even if they were practice. Because we were shooting real bullets. At targets which we had to kill immediately we saw them. Fail to do that, people start looking at you funny. Like you're not good enough. Worse, put a round into a friendly, even if it's just a cardboard cut-out, and *you* start thinking you're not good enough.'

Mickey nodded, rubbing a hand across his face. 'All of which makes sense. But I have to go in with you. Because if there's a chance for me to put a bullet in that bastard Castagna, I want to be the one to do it.'

'Fair enough. Just don't say I didn't give you the chance to do the sensible thing.'

Mickey grimaced at that. 'You sound like my wife. Probably ex-wife. And she's usually right too.'

Shaw nodded, straight-faced.

'Very well. In that case, here's how we're going to do it.'

53

Eddie took a look into the games room. Checking that Martin hadn't managed to loosen his restraints.

'Comfy, are you?'

The gun dealer shot him a dirty look. Not bothering to answer. Eddie, bored and in need of something to distract him from contemplation of the horror to come, strolled into the room. Better insulated than its predecessor in the warehouse. Completely soundproof. He pulled up a chair. Putting it within a couple of feet of the captive.

'Pardon me for invading your social space. I just thought you might want to get used to the idea of it. Because when your mate Mickey surrenders himself, there's going to be quite a lot of intrusion going on. And I can guarantee he'll make you watch.'

Martin just stared at him. Probably uncertain as to whether any retort was even worth the effort. Eddie shook his head with apparent regret.

'See, Joe's not a man who takes this sort of thing lying down. And especially not when he loses this sort of face. Killing Lewis was pretty much the final straw. You pair of pricks are going down the sewers in pieces. Very small pieces. First he gets to watch you die. Just about as slowly as you can imagine. His new man Rocco being a total fucking psychopath. You two did him a right favour baking Lewis alive. Because it made Joe realise that he's going to *need* a right fucking psychopath if he's going to see off his rivals. Lewis was a nasty bastard, all right. But he was an attack dog. He could be restrained, when the need arose. Rocco doesn't have that ability to restrain himself. And so this is where you get to reap the whirlwind you've sowed. You, your copper mate and his women.'

That got Martin's attention. Not that they'd be able to find anyone he cared for. Given that his sexual predilections concentrated mostly on one-off use of hookers. But, knowing Mickey, he also knew Roz.

'I thought he said that—'

'If your mate gives himself up then the women get left alone? You mug.' Eddie shook his head sadly. The battle-weary general of a victorious army. Explaining the facts of life to the defeated population. 'Joe ain't going to miss up on those opportunities. Not if I know him, which trust me, I do. All too well. You two get to experience the reality of chainsaw art. On video, of course. He'll probably put it on YouTube. Bale's wife gets herself a starring role in a Joe production. Titled "My enemy's woman pays the price for his mistakes." And the reporter gets delivered to the *Clarion*. In pieces just large enough for her to be identified. Eventually. Sending a message for them to think twice next time. Before they try to sharpen their claws on him again.'

Martin shook his head. His expression part resignation at the hopelessness of his position. Part terror at what was to come. Eddie's evident resignation to having to watch him die badly more terrifying than any of Joe's threats.

'Yeah, well fuck him.'

'When the time comes, my advice would be to be penitent. Good word, that. You had no idea what your mate was doing. He took the guns from your store without telling you. If you'd known, you'd have coughed him up to Joe straight away. Might go easier on you, if you make a show of respect.'

'How much easier?'

A hint of entreaty in Martin's voice. An ocean of entreaty in his eyes. The gateway to the soul, Eddie remembered reading years ago. And Martin's soul was jumping out of his eyes like an old-style cartoon character with their foot flattened by a mallet.

'How much easier? Nine mil to the back of the head easier. Which, when you consider the wide range of alternatives, has to be the better choice. Easier on all of us.' Eddie stood up. Stretched. 'Think about it, eh? Right, I'm off to do my rounds.'

'Wait! There is something else!'

Martin, broken. Ready to spill the rest of what he knew. But Eddie waved a dismissive hand. Genuinely no longer interested. And perhaps a little broken too, on his side of the life and death divide.

'No, mate. I don't want to know. Save it for Joe, yeah? Gift-wrap it for him. Perhaps it'll earn you that bullet. Perhaps he'll start carving you anyway. 'Cause that's just the sort of psycho he is.'

He shut the door on the prisoner. Replacing the prisoner's entreaties with perfect silence. If Hyde started shouting the odds it wasn't going to go down well with Joe. Who was lying on a camp bed in a room at the other end of the arch. Theoretically far enough from the captive to remain asleep. But Eddie knew just what a light sleeper his boss was. Bringing true meaning to the cliché of sleeping with one eye open.

He walked down the arch to the back wall. Checking that the emergency exit was still tightly closed. Joe's escape route, in the event of a police raid. The Rhino parked on the semi-derelict estate behind the arches. The growth of a thicket of willow and alder between arches and estate posing a seemingly impenetrable barrier between the two. But Joe, with an eye to any contingency, had long since had a winding, hidden path cut through the dense, compact sliver of urban woodland. A path that was regularly checked and cut back.

And if the filth tried to block his path, Joe would be carrying the assault shotgun waiting by the door. Loaded with solid slug rounds. Eddie knew that nothing and nobody would come between Joe and a clean getaway. Or a blood-spattered getaway, if that was what it took.

54

Deano opened the door to the rooftop cautiously. Knowing it was the thing you didn't predict that tripped you up, nine times out of ten. Stepped out onto the flat surface with slow, careful steps and looked about him. No sign of security, courting couples or anything else to put a spanner in their works. He turned back to the stairwell where Steve and Den were waiting.

'All clear.'

The two men emerged from the shadows, Steve laden down by the machine gun's twenty-five-pound weight. Den carrying the bag containing the ammunition. They moved across the flat expanse to the parapet. Taking in the view over East London from the tenth floor.

'That's Castagna's site, down there.'

Deano pointed to a brightly lit compound packed with heavy plant. Having performed a walk-past an hour before and engaged the bored Polish security guard in conversation.

'All that kit's his. And all probably bought with dirty money. Must be two or three million quid's worth.'

Den leaned over the parapet. Looking down at the yellow-painted machinery with a wistful expression.

'I always wanted to be a digger driver. It was my old man made me put in for the police.'

Deano shook his head. A derisive tone to his reply. 'Thank fuck for your old man then. You'd had your way, you'd still be driving one of those. Earning next to bugger all and no pension either. Anyway, how long we got?'

Steve looked at his watch. Carefully zeroed against Shaw's, before they'd parted.

'Eight minutes. Let's get set up.'

Getting set up was the work of less than thirty seconds. Unfolding the machine gun's bipod support. Inserting the first thirty-round magazine and pulling back the cocking handle to chamber the first round. Laying the other four magazines out, ready to use. After which the three men were left looking at each other.

'You sure I can't have a go? You know, brass up a few diggers?'

Steve shook his head firmly. 'It's not like the movies, Deano. Where explosions are just powder charges and no-one ever gets cut in half by shrapnel.' Steve adjusted his position, rubbing at a sore knee. 'Fuck, I'm way too old for this nonsense. Should have brought my garden kneeler. If I let you get behind this thing you could kill some poor bastard just by twitching the wrong way.'

'You said you killed some blokes in Bosnia. What was it like?'

Both men looked at Den with disbelieving expressions.

'Fuck me, Den, you must be right up the far end of the spectrum.' Deano, shaking his head in admonishment. 'You simply do not ask those sorts of questions, mate.'

'Yes…' Steve speaking over Deano. 'As it happens, I have. Five of them.'

'You don't have to—'

'It's all right, Den. I've been waiting the best part of thirty years to tell someone who wasn't there about it. You pair of pricks can be my confessors. I was only nineteen at the time. Fresh out of training into Operation Resolute in what used to be called Yugoslavia. A battalion of us, armoured infantry, shoved in between the Croats and Bosnian Muslims. Keeping the peace. It was never as bad as it got for those poor Dutch bastards at Srebrenica, but we had it hard enough. The Croats didn't like not being able to have their fun with the Muslim civvies, so they took it out on us instead.

'And there was one guy, a sniper, who used to like taking pot shots. He had this big silenced rifle, with a home-made suppressor. Like a length of drainpipe, it was. And so we couldn't ever get him localised. Most of the time he missed. But every now and then he got close enough to make for a brown trousers moment. And twice he shot blokes. Wounded one badly enough for a medvac to the UK. The other was dead before he hit the deck. Straight through his right eye socket and out the back. So we were getting pretty bad-tempered about it. Some of the older blokes talking about cutting his balls off, if they ever caught him.'

He shook his head in dark amusement.

'It was all bollocks of course. For one thing we were never going to catch him. And if we did, no way the YeahRuperts would let us keep him long enough for any torture. They were just blowing steam off. A bit like you would have, wouldn't you, Deano?'

Raised middle finger from Deano.

'Anyway, one day my platoon got sent up to a village near the front line. Check how the inhabitants were doing, show our faces, that sort of thing. Three Warriors full of squaddies. Fully bombed up, because you just never knew what was going to happen next. Commanded by a salty old warrant officer because our lieutenant was away on emergency bereavement leave. We drove up into the hills, got to the village and put the Warriors into all-round defence on the edge of the settlement. No more than thirty houses, a right one-horse town. The boys debussed and wandered off, all very non-threatening, caps rather than helmets. The usual "what the British Army does better than anyone else" routine. Leaving me in Juliet's turret to keep an eye on things.'

'Juliet?' Den, somewhat baffled.

'My Warrior's nickname. Our officer was a bit of a frustrated actor on the side, so he called them Romeo, Juliet and Paris.'

'Paris?'

'Not now, Den. Read the play. Anyway, there I was. Ready to lay down some proper fire support if things went sideways. In theory. So I stood in the turret, smoking a fag and using the machine gun as a leaning post. Just enjoying the sunshine and listening to the birds. After a few minutes something made me look round. I don't know, instinct, or a sound, or just a flicker in the corner of my eye.

'And there they were. Bold as fucking brass. Five of them, all armed. Coming out of the trees, down a hunter's path. All of them with weapons slung. AKs mostly. But one of them had this great big rifle barrel sticking up over his head. Thick as your wrist, over a metre long. And I knew straight away it was him. The sniper. The stupid bastards were so deep in discussion they hadn't even seen the Warriors. Must have been a right shock when I racked the cocking handle of the Gimpy.'

'Gimpy?' Den, increasingly confused.

'GPMG. General Purpose Machine Gun. A nasty big bastard that was just like a bar of nutty.'

'Nutty?'

'For fuck's sake, Den, chocolate with nuts in it. Even I know that much.' Deano thinking for a moment. 'But why was it like a bar of—'

'Because when you pulled the trigger you didn't get a nice straight stream of bullets. Not like this little honey.' Steve patting the Bren gun's butt affectionately. 'The Gimpy was an area weapon. Designed to generate a spray of rounds. And produce a beaten zone. It was a brave bloke who'd run at a Gimpy, because there was no way to dodge. Whichever way you went was going to get a healthy dose of 7.62mm, sooner or later. If they'd put their hands up they might have lived. Although matey with the big gun would have had a warm old time of it. But they didn't. They started unslinging their rifles and generally making it clear they were hostile. So I did them.'

'You machine gunned them?'

'Yes, Den mate. I gave them a full two-hundred-round belt of ammo. Once I popped, I couldn't stop. Seemed to go on forever, although they were all dead inside the first two seconds. Smashed into offal. The lads came charging back, all ready to go to war, but they were well too late.'

'Bloody hell, Steve!' Deano nodding newfound respect. 'You must have got a medal for that!'

'No.' Steve with a knowing expression. 'I got a big pat on

the back. Fast-tracked to lance corporal. And mentioned in classified dispatches. But as far as the world was concerned, nothing happened. We buried the bodies five miles away, in the middle of nowhere. And as far as I know they were never found. Got me a lot of respect, at the time. Gave me a few nightmares, later on. Nothing compared to what we saw the next year though. When the shit properly hit the fan.'

He took a deep breath.

'And that, boys, is why we're doing this. Because that bastard Castagna has all the same evil in him they did. And if Mickey's mad enough to go and clean house on him, I'm up for it.' He looked at his watch.

'Ninety seconds to go. Good enough. Let's light up some diggers, eh? When I shout mag change, Den, you hand me a fresh one. Deano, you take the used one from me and put it in the bag. I want to be out of here in two minutes max. Because when the Met responds to this one they're going to send every Trojan unit this side of London.'

55

03.10. The assault team were on the street around the corner from the arches. Fully equipped for CQB. Monochrome mottled coveralls, black ballistic helmets with built-in radios and ear protection, black combat boots. Faces hidden under depersonalising skull masks, eyes protected by goggles. Body harnesses loaded with special forces assault gear. Plate carriers loaded with forty pounds of titanium-backed Kevlar apiece. Frag, smoke and stun grenades. Extra magazines for their machine pistols. And first aid kit. Trauma treatment, mainly. Bleeding control and pain relief. Plus a SIG-Sauer pistol and a fighting knife apiece. Weapons of last resort.

As their main weapon, each of the four had a suppressed Heckler & Koch MP7 machine pistol. Loaded with long forty-round clips for almost three seconds of sustained firepower apiece; 4.7mm high velocity. Small rounds, but no less effective when applied generously.

Shaw was wearing additional clothing over his equipment. A voluminous coat, several sizes too large for him. His machine pistol hanging, muzzle downwards, from a harness strap across his back beneath it. The garment was pungently noisome. And covered in a range of stains that had probably taken years to accumulate. The elbows worn thin, one pocket hanging loose. Purchased from a tramp an hour before, for enough money to get him a hostel place for a month. Or, more likely, high, or drunk, or both, for a week.

The hat was his own, an old commando cap comforter that had seen better days. With the coat buttoned, he fully looked the part of an alcoholic tramp. An impression topped off with hypertension-red face make-up. A half-empty bottle of paint stripper own label scotch in his hand.

The team leader looked at each of his people in turn. Asking a silent question. Each one of them answering with a nod. He looked at Mickey, raising his eyebrows in the same, unspoken challenge. Mickey nodded with equal certainty. Understanding his role perfectly. Shaw raised a hand, the universal signal for them to wait. And staggered around the corner, into full view of the CCTV. Which, if whoever was watching the screen had been paying attention, might have been the moment of maximum risk.

He slumped against the arch's front wall, dragging himself along the brickwork. Raised the bottle and took a hefty swig of the cold tea that had replaced its previous contents. Stopped where he was, raising the bottle to salute the moon. Belched loudly, then tipped the bottle back and finished it. Tossed it away, laughing uproariously as it shattered. A shower of glittering crystal shards spilling across the arches' tarmac forecourt. Enough to get even the most dilatory operator's attention. He took another half-dozen steps, right to the central arch's door. Tracked all the way by the camera's one-eyed stare.

Throwing his arms back theatrically, he staggered unsteadily. Turning slightly so that the camera was forced to look over his shoulder. Shielding the view of what he was doing with his hands. Which was to pull out the still-warm squeeze bottle of urine he'd filled two minutes before from an inside pocket. Jetting warm, steaming piss onto the door. Aiming for the joint between door and jamb. Then eased up on the flow, leaving enough in the bottle for one last squirt.

56

Satisfied that all was well, Eddie walked back up the arch. Looking in at Rocco in the cash room. Joe's new enforcer looked back at him levelly. Lewis's .45 disassembled on the table in front of him.

'Eddie.'

Respectful. But watchful. The two men not aligned yet. Their places in Joe's empire not entirely clear. Both of them knowing that succession to a role like the one Lewis had filled was complicated. Replacing a man who'd spent ten years becoming Joe's left fist, where Eddie was his right, couldn't be achieved overnight.

'Rocco. You and me need to talk, when this is over.'

The enforcer nodded. 'Yeah. I'm going to do Lewis's job. I need the same status.'

Eddie shrugged. 'Status has to be earned. Like I said, we need to—'

'Eddie?'

He turned to find the man assigned to camera watch in the doorway behind him.

'What?'

His disdain for Rocco momentarily forgotten.

'There's this bloke. A tramp.'

'And?'

'He's making a right fuss. Hammering on the front door.'

'And?'

'What if the filth come and—'

'What if they fucking do?'

Eddie, baffled at such stupidity, walked quickly to the screen. Seeing the tramp in question – who to be fair looked pretty revolting in 4k – throw an empty bottle into the road. Distracting Eddie's attention with its crystal spray in the camera's floodlight glare. When he looked back the tramp was huddled over the door. Obviously having a piss. Which made Eddie smile. Dirty old bastard. But what he saw next made his blood run cold.

57

With an abrupt clank of electric bolts retracting, the door opened. A single irate figure bursting through it, careless of any risk. A big man. Physically confident. Shouting at the dirty old bastard to fuck off. Raising a hand to take the tramp by the throat. Only to receive a face full of warm, steaming piss. The last of the bottle, sprayed straight into his eyes.

And then, while he was still blinking, Shaw whipped the fighting knife held in his other hand up into the hapless guard's throat.

58

'What the fuck?'
Eddie stared at the screen in horror. Instantly making the connection. The men camped out in the middle arch had their own screen. No controls, but a clear view of what the operator was seeing. And some idiot had decided to intervene in the tramp's urinary exploits. Looking to give him a kicking for pissing under the external door. Instead of which he had been expertly knifed. Swift, cold and professional. Then pushed aside, dead or dying. The knife handle protruding from his jaw. The tramp threw off his coat to reveal what looked like a machine gun strapped to his back.

He stared, aghast, as a group of what looked like heavily equipped soldiers stormed through the open front door. Someone opened fire in the central arch. Single shots. The shooting reduced to distant pops by the thick brickwork. Eddie, no fool, knew what had to be coming next. Threw himself at the connecting door between the two arches. Hitting the lock button just as the solid sheet steel reverberated as if it had been kicked by an elephant.

59

Shaw's team moved fast. Running down the front of the arches, weapons held ready. Their plan entirely dependent on getting into action inside the central arch quickly. Before the occupants had time to muster and bring their weapons to bear.

If the camera was still manned, then whoever was watching it would be staring in disbelief at the screen. And then shouting a warning at the men behind the inner door.

Shaw pushed the doorman's crumpling body aside and shrugged off the coat. Grabbing a grenade from his harness. Pushing the exterior door wide and striding forward into the walled lobby. With the team crowding in behind him, weapons ready.

He turned the inner door's handle. Finding it mercifully unlocked. Opened it wide enough to post the flash bang through it. Then pulled the door shut and ducked away from its flimsy protection.

'Flash bang!'

The exterior door clanged closed behind the team, bolts re-engaging with a loud clack. Someone inside the central arch started shooting, a series of holes punched through the wooden inner door. Shaw shot a knowing glance at his teammates. The fire aimless. And effectively pointless. Even if it felt like some sort of counter-attack to the men on the other side of the door.

Shaw and his team covered their eyes with crooked left arms raised to their faces. The central arch was pounded by a series of muffled cracks that they felt through their booted feet. Explosions that would be ear-splitting on the other side of the door. Accompanied by the release of three high-intensity flares. Lighting the room on the other side of the door like the brightest floodlight.

Lines of what looked like sunlight strobed through the bullet holes into the lobby's gloom. The flares burning for no more than a second. But bright enough to momentarily blind anyone with their eyes open.

Jenny pushed the door open and went through it shooting. Crisp three-round bursts rapping out. Each putting a triple hit of high-velocity ammunition into a fresh target. Knocking down Joe's soldiers as they struggled off their beds. She went left and crouched. Clearing the door and minimising herself as a target for return fire.

Darren came through the door behind her and went right. Added his firepower to the scourge raking across the hapless Castagna gang members. Turning the central arch into a deadly shooting gallery. Each gang member attempting to rise from their camp bed being engaged and put down. The two shooters stood and stepped in. Still firing. Shooting into the supine bodies to deal with anyone faking it.

Shaw and Rick followed up. The team leader tossing another stun grenade into the open tunnel that led into the left-hand arch. Waited for the ear-splitting bang and then hurried into the next section with fast but cautious steps. His MP7 raised and ready.

Rick aimed his weapon at the sealed doorway leading into the right-hand arch. Ready to fire if it opened. A final rap-rap-rap hammered three bullets into the last of the guards. The stricken gang member slumped back onto the camp bed he'd just risen from. The mechanism collapsed under his slumping weight and dumped him on the concrete floor.

Sprawled and silent or writhing in their death throes, every man who'd been set to guard the arch was down. At least half of them already dead, to judge from their contorted immobility. The two shooters simultaneously shouted 'mag change' and reloaded. Empty magazines into waiting pouches, so as to leave no evidence.

Jenny went into overwatch on the strewn bodies of the gang members. Darren turned to cover the door into the right-hand arch. Twenty seconds into the assault.

'Clear!' Shaw, coming back through the tunnel into the left-hand arch. His weapon unfired. He pointed to the door into the right-hand arch. 'Breach!'

Rick reached around to a pouch nestled against his back. Pulling out a fifty-centimetre-wide shallowly domed disk and slapping it onto the door. Placing it next to the lock.

'Fire in the hole!'

60

E ddie saw the demolition charge being placed. Drew his
pistol. Put it on the ground in front of him and got on
his knees. Hands behind his head. Knowing all too well
what was about to happen. Joe bursting out of the office
behind him, phone in hand.

'I got a call! Someone's shooting up one of my...' He
stopped, double-taking at the sight of his right-hand man
on his knees. 'What the *fuck* you doing, Eddie?'

The overwhelming thought in Eddie's mind, as he looked
back over his shoulder, was that of freedom. Of never
having to fight the urge to empty his bowels whenever the
man who was supposed to be his friend looked at him. And
suddenly, blissfully, he was at peace.

'Give it up, Joe! They're special forces! There's no way
even you can stand against this!'

Wincing as Joe's face contorted into a murderous,
betrayed glare.

'You *fucking* traitor! Do him, Rocco!'

Eddie shook his head as the enforcer stepped forward.
The reassembled .45 in his right hand. And just had time to
reflect on the irony of being shot by the same gun that killed
Nigel before the first bullet hit him in the chest. Blowing a

spectacular gout of blood out across the floor behind him. Then went over backwards, a nerveless sack of dead meat, as the second shot blew the top of his head off. Joe was already running for the emergency exit, shouting over his shoulder.

'Come on, Rocco!'

Punching in the lock code to his emergency door. Grabbing his briefcase and tossing the combat shotgun to Rocco as his new enforcer sprinted for the exit. With an almighty bang the door from the central arch was blown open. The explosive charge used to open it loud enough to burst eardrums.

Ac1d shrieked in terror as the first urban-camo-clad figure came through the opening. A woman's eyes over a grinning half-skull mask. And made the fundamental mistake of grabbing his laptop as he turned to run. Which looked like he was reaching for a weapon. A reflex three-round burst dropped him, dead before he hit the concrete floor.

At the other end of the arch Rocco opened fire. Punching a spray of heavy shotgun slugs up the arch's length, fanning the shots from left to right. Momentarily sending the assault team into cover and then stepping back through the door. Giving Joe critical seconds to push it shut. A tattoo of gunfire hammering at its thick steel lining as Joe dropped a steel bar into the waiting bracket.

'That'll hold them long enough. Come on!'

Rocco followed him across the road that ran down the rear of the arches. And into the tunnel cut through the long, shallow urban thicket on the other side. Joe keeping up a non-stop commentary as he pushed through the spiky foliage.

'Eddie must have been the one selling us out to Bale! I'm going to get somewhere I can't be extradited and then turn the dogs loose on that cunt. You look after my wife and kids until I can get them out too, right? You do that for me, I'll set you up for life.'

He cursed, pulling his leg away from a thorny tangle of branches as he emerged from the bushes.

'Here, give me that—'

Rocco, momentarily framed in the copse's exit, staggered backwards and collapsed onto the hard-packed earth. His upper body torn apart by a dozen high-velocity rounds. The shotgun fell from his nerveless fingers. Joe, who had been reaching out to take the weapon from him, spun to face the hidden gunman.

Mickey. Dressed in black. Looking at him over the Rhino's bonnet. Down the thick snout of a silenced machine pistol.

'It's a good thing my informant told me you had this nice little escape route. You'd have been clean away, wouldn't you?'

He advanced around the car. Putting another three-round burst into the twitching Rocco. The shots no louder than clapping hands.

'It's a lesson I learned from you, Joe. If a man goes down, keep him there. Put the briefcase on the ground.'

Joe obeyed, his mind working fast.

'Mickey Bale, I presume. The Filth's killing machine. I suppose I should be honoured.' Mickey kept his mouth shut. Happy to let Joe play out his paranoid fantasy. 'You realise what happens if you shoot me? Your missus gets to spend the next few days on a crash course in drug addiction and being buttfucked. Your choice.'

Mickey shook his head. Stepping forward and levelling the weapon's barrel at Joe's face.

'Yeah, but you'll be dead. And not the easy way.'

Joe went quiet. Calculating whether Mickey had that much psycho in him. Mickey stepped a little closer, making the gun's suppressor-clad muzzle even more menacing.

'But I'm missing a trick here. What's in the briefcase?'

'Mind your own fuck—'

Having switched the machine pistol to single shot, Mickey put a round through the top of Joe's ear. Surprising himself by taking the shot despite the risk of blowing his brains out instead. The whipcrack of the bullet and sudden stinging pain making Joe piss in his jeans. Blood running down the side of his neck.

Mickey nodded at him. 'Must be your lucky day. Because I doubt I could make that shot again. So the next time I won't even try aiming to miss. Your choice. What's in the case?'

Joe snarled at him, one hand exploring the bleeding wound. 'What do you *fucking* think? Money. Tickets. Passport.'

'The holy trinity of the modern gangster, eh? Open it.' Something in his eye convinced Joe to play along, at least temporarily. 'Now step back five paces.'

Mickey watched as the gang boss paced slowly backwards. Gestured with the MP7's barrel.

'Far enough. There's about twenty-five rounds left in this thing. Take one step towards me and you'll get them all in the face. Turn to run, I'll put them all in your back. Don't think for one second I won't do it.'

He bent, reaching one-handed into the case and pulling

out a passport. Flipped it open and held it up to view, one eye on Joe.

'Nice work. Even looks right. But then it would, wouldn't it? Man like you, money to *burn*.'

'Ha *fucking* ha.'

The look on Joe's face murderous, on being reminded of the events that had led to his fall from power.

'Where were you going, I wonder? Let's have a look.' Mickey flicked the passport pages one handed.

'Is this a visa for Qatar? And open-ended from the look of it. And Qatar with no UK extradition treaty. Good choice. And how much money were you taking for travel expenses?'

Joe, recovering from the shock of a bullet taking the top centimetre of his ear off, started negotiating again.

'Ten million. Bitcoin and diamonds. Plus a hundred k's worth of credit cards. Leave me the passport and the cards, you can have the rest. It's only travelling money, but there's enough to make you a rich man.'

'And you've got how much offshore? Twenty million? Fifty?'

The gangster shook his head in amusement.

'What do you think? I've been getting ready for this since the day I succeeded my old man. He always had an escape plan; I just made it better. A lot better.'

'I bet. Except I heard what you were telling your dead goon over there. I let you get away, forty-eight hours from now you'll be hiring hit men. My name on the contract. Perhaps you just need to die here.'

He'd already guessed exactly what Joe's negotiating position would be.

'Maybe. But I've still got your wife. You want her to live, you let me go.'

'So what's the deal?'

'You release me, I release her. You keep the ten mil, I keep the passport and credit cards. Her life for mine, and enough money to mint you for life. And my word that I'll leave you in peace.'

'Your word? Bit of a devalued currency.'

Joe shrugged. Grinned wolfishly. Pushing hard. 'It's the only deal I have for you. And a very reasonable offer, I'd say. Take it or don't take it.'

Mickey shook his head. 'Not good enough. Free her now. Have the men holding her give her the phone you call to give the order. When I know she's away clean, I'll give you the car keys, passport and credit cards. Want to know why you're going to accept that?'

Joe shrugged. 'Go on.'

Mickey raised his left hand. Tapped his ear.

'Hear that?'

'What?'

'Absolutely nothing. No sirens. There might have been a few calls about noise to 999, but those arches are built like brick shithouses, aren't they? Totally noise-proof. And the nearest house is two hundred yards away. Which means there was no-one around to hear much in the first place. And trust me, the Met's got bigger fish to fry right now. I made sure of that. Which means we're not going to be disturbed for the rest of the night.'

And shut his mouth. Giving Joe time to think.

'And...?'

'And so if you say no to *my* reasonable offer, I'll put a

bullet in one of your feet. Good thing about the foot, from a damage perspective, there's lots of bones but not much blood supply. Then we'll drag you back in there and chain you up where you had Martin hanging from the ceiling.'

'What, and then torture me? I don't think so. You don't look like you've got the stones for it, for one thing. And you're a copper for another. Not the sort of thing you lot do, is it?'

Mickey laughed softly. 'Not these days we don't. And no, I'm not half the evil bastard you are. But then I don't need to be. All I need to do is put the word out that you're no longer the king of this little dung heap. And where you can be found. I'd imagine your competitors will do the rest. And what was it you said? If you kill the king, you have to kill his heirs?'

He waited a moment and allowed the threat to sink in.

'So, when whichever of your fellow gangsters gets here first, what do you reckon they'll do? Cut you down? Or cut you up?'

Joe stared at him in silence. Hating.

'And it's not just *your* life that's on the line. Is it? Because your rivals won't want to leave your family alive, will they. Why take the risk? Seems to me we both have something to lose. So here's the deal. My deal. The *only* deal. First you strip.'

'You fucking *what*?'

Mickey shrugged. 'You could hide a lot of bitcoin in a stick small enough to hide in your pants. So the only way you're getting away from here is buffo. You get in the car. You call your thugs. Tell them to free Roz. Then you give me the phone. I talk to her, and when I'm happy she's safe, you get the keys, the passport and the cards. And drive away. After that, I see you again and I'll kill you.'

Joe thought for a moment. Weighing the proposal. And, from the poker face he adopted, clearly liking it. Seeing a way to win the game, Mickey presumed. The gangster eased off his Armani jacket, dropping it to the ground at his feet. Unbuttoned his shirt and peeled it off. Kicked off his expensive trainers, then unzipped his jeans and stepped out of them. Dropped his boxers and pulled off his socks. Stood naked, shivering in the pre-dawn chill.

'Happy now?'

Mickey shrugged.

'As happy as I'm going to get. Step back another five paces. Stop.'

He fished Joe's phone out of his jacket. The car keys from his jeans pocket. Pushed the unlock button on the key's plastic body. Opened the car door and checked it for weapons.

'Get in the car. Leave the door open.' He thumbed the machine pistol's selector to full auto. 'Try anything clever. I'll dump the rest of the mag into you. And don't fool yourself closing the door will protect you. All that'll happen if you put it between me and you is that each round I fire will bring a chunk of sheet metal and sound insulation with it.'

Joe climbed into the Rhino. Wincing at the cold leather's touch on his naked skin. Mickey reached out and passed him the phone. Keeping the weapon's barrel levelled at him.

'Make the call.' And then leaned forward. Ready to unload the rest of the magazine into Joe at the slightest provocation. The gang leader selected a number from the phone's recent history and pressed the green button.

'It's Joe. Yeah, *that* Joe… No, just fucking listen. Release the woman. Now. And give her your phone.' He listened for a moment. 'Yeah, you *could* keep your phone. In which case I'll have to have Rocco put it in the cement?' And waited for the response. 'Yeah. With you still holding it. Do it *now*!'

He looked at Mickey. 'They'll do it.'

'I'm sure they will, given your unique motivational style. Give me the phone.'

Mickey kept his eyes and the weapon's barrel levelled at Joe. Waited for Roz to talk to him. Joe stared through the car's windscreen with a look of repressed fury. Unwilling to meet his gaze. Knowing he was beaten, or just waiting for his moment? Mickey wondered.

'Mickey?'

Roz. Sounding more angry than scared. The sound of her heels on the pavement, moving fast. Hopefully towards the nearest lights and traffic.

'You OK?'

'No thanks to you, yeah. They just shoved me in some shithole room and ignored me.'

'And you're clear of the place? Did anyone follow you?'

'Yes. And no.'

'Good. I—'

'The next time we talk, Mickey Bale, you'd better have a good lawyer! You lied to me, you betrayed our trust and you got me kidnapped! So fuck you! That's you and me—'

He closed the call. Not needing to hear his wife intoning the last rites on their marriage to break him any more than he was already broken. Especially not at 130 decibels.

'She not happy with you then?'

Mickey met Joe's sour grin with a hard stare. And realised

347

that his trigger finger was a twitch away from plastering the gangster across the car's interior. The temptation to do just that so strong it was an act of will not to. But he had a better idea. One that would salve his conscience. Handed over the car key.

'What about the passport?'

'I'm changing our agreement. Like you were going to kill me and then make an example of my wife and friends no matter what promises you made to make me surrender. Weren't you? Besides, you'll have more documents stashed. A man like you always does.'

He watched Joe intently. Not seeing a man whose world had collapsed around him with the denial of his means of escape. Rather one burning for revenge, presented with another obstacle. But surmountable. Already planning the revised means of his escape from justice.

Joe shut the car door. Reached down and started the car. Never taking his dead eyes off Mickey. Seemingly ignoring the machine pistol's threat as he put the gearbox into drive. Communicating without words.

Then goosed the accelerator, the Rhino surging away down the pothole-pitted road. Mickey reached into his pocket, finding the key fob lookalike Rick had given him earlier. A transmitter frequency keyed to two kilos of explosive and pre-notched heavy gauge copper wire. The Rhino braked to a halt a hundred yards from him. Joe's voice ringing out in the silence. Edged with the raw fury of the truly humiliated psychopath.

'I'll fucking have you, Bale! You, your wife and that photographer bitch! And everyone else you care about! You're all going to fucking die! Very, very fucking slowly!'

Gunning the engine again. Flooring it, screech of tyres as the engine's monstrous power momentarily overcame the tyres' traction.

Mickey raised the fob. Looking at the blinking red light. 'That's our agreement cancelled then.'

61

Late afternoon the next day. Mickey, having booked into a hotel to get a few hours' sleep, woke at one in the afternoon. Still bone-weary. Shaw's team had extracted at speed, taking Joe's briefcase and several heavy-duty bags of vacuum-packed currency with them. Dropped Martin and Mickey off at the former's flat. Where the two men had stood on the pavement, exhausted.

'They took my guns. All of them, except for the Bren.'

'Yeah. We used the Bren to create a distraction.'

'Oh. So that's my business down the toilet then.'

Mickey shook his head.

'Your business was down the toilet from the second you let yourself get fooled into meeting Castagna. So there's bad news and good news.'

'What's the good news?'

Mickey had handed him a small plastic wallet.

'Lewis's SIM card. You can empty his account out. It's yours. All of it.'

'And the bad news.'

'You'll have to vanish. And I don't mean moving to the seaside. Proper vanish.' He shook his head. 'I'm sorry,

Martin. I never intended for it to come to this, but you need to get out. Sharpish.'

'What, you mean like *abroad*?'

Mickey had nodded. Waiting in silence while Martin shook his head and looked up at the dawn sky.

'I knew this would end up with me getting fucked, one way or another. He sighed. 'Worth it, for Katie, but all the same… How long do you think I've got?'

'No idea. But you're probably on Castagna's computer somewhere. And the Met will take this as their chance to pull his empire to pieces. Starting with a raid on the house to search for illegal weapons. You probably want to be gone inside twenty-four to forty-eight.'

His friend had sighed.

'It ain't like I've got that much to leave behind. And I can't say I'll miss the business. Or emptying bins, for that matter. Got any ideas?'

Mickey had held out the plastic wallet containing Joe's fake passport and credit cards.

'This'll help. Get his pic replaced with yours and the passport will get you into Qatar and let you stay there for as long as you need to. Just make sure you pay enough to get a decent job done. It was a good choice by Joe, Qatar's probably the nicest country without a UK extradition treaty. Although there's always Cape Verde if it gets too much. There's a hundred grand of travelling money on the cards. Keep in touch with me through the usual email address. I'll let you know when it looks safe to come back. And don't spend it all at once.'

He'd tried calling Roz. Number blocked. Called Tamara

to tell her it was safe to go home and got fairly short shrift there too. Hardly surprising, given Mark's disappearance. And so there he was. Out from under the falling piano but surveying the ruins of his life. A wreckage for whose creation he had no-one else to blame. His wife thoroughly estranged. His best friend forced to go on the run. And his head populated by the ghosts of the men he'd killed. Waiting to terrorise his dreams. Just as he was wondering if he might be best just eating a bullet, his Job phone rang. The number instantly recognisable. LX, of course. Who else?

'Michael Bale.'

'Michael. Philip Green.'

Mickey, frantically stuffing his personal feelings back down where he could keep them under control.

'Sir.' Perhaps a little terse, but not bad under the circumstances.

'Apologies for calling on a Sunday afternoon. Please believe that I wouldn't be disturbing you if I didn't have any choice in the matter.'

'No problem, sir.'

Perhaps the biggest single lie he'd ever told. But Mickey was working hard at making it sound believable. Just another boring Sunday afternoon.

'How can I help you?'

A slight pause. Ye gods, Mickey mused, Inspector Phil actually didn't want to ask whatever it was he was going to ask for. Which meant it could only be one thing.

'We have a problem, Michael. Well, in point of fact it's me who has the problem. But it's one I'd very much like to share with you.'

Mickey laughed softly, despite himself. 'Let's halve that problem, shall we, sir?'

'You're a good man, Michael. The problem is this...' Straight to business then. 'I have to organise a very sensitive principal move from Beaconsfield to South-West London and back. Nine Elms. The principal in question being one you're very familiar with.'

Meaning it could only be one person. And one destination.

Green continued. 'And it has to happen tonight. No ifs, no buts. And, with one of the team having gone sick, I need someone to pair up with the remaining officer on duty. Someone experienced. Ideally a skipper, since the man on the spot is a constable. Major Cavendish will brief you however fully he feels appropriate. If you feel you can help, that is.'

You bastard, Mickey thought. Recognising the hook Phil Green had sunk into him. Respecting the man for the pro he was at reeling in the potentially unwilling.

'Under the circumstances, I think it would be churlish to refuse. Count me in, sir.'

'Good man.' And straight to business. 'Right, there's no time for you to come into LX, arm yourself and then drive out. Make your way to the Hall and I'll send one of the armourers over with something appropriate. The Special Escort Group team will be on site at 19.00 hours, and the package has to be on the move an hour after that. That's...' a pause, presumably to look at the clock in his office '...just under three hours from now. Think you can make it to the Hall in time?'

Mickey shot a glance at the Black Bay. Just past five. 'I can be there by 19.00, or soon after.'

'In which case, with thanks for your invaluable assistance, I'll leave you to get on the road.'

His duty bag, as ever packed with everything he might need was waiting by the door. More than enough suit and boot in there. He told reception that he'd be back the next day and paid for another day up front. Then went out to his BMW, threw the bag in the back and jumped in. Belted up, rolled his shoulders and stabbed a finger at the start button. Three litres of Munich muscle coming to life under his right foot. Crawled the car carefully out onto the road. Then put the gearbox into sport and stabbed at the accelerator. Went off up the road like a stabbed rat. Blue lights the only thing missing. And for sure Mickey planned to warrant card a collector's item traffic car. Challenge accepted.

62

He reached the Hall just before seven. Mainly thanks to some epic right-foot action. Wringing the Bimmer's neck when the road opened up or a gap beckoned. Leaving a trail of outraged civilians behind him. Getting out of the car, he realised that there was something rare lurking in the evening's shadows. Rare, but not exactly unexpected.

He strolled over and tapped at the Range Rover's windscreen. Inch-thick solid bulletproof glass. The bodywork making a dull thud when hit with a knuckle. A Range Rover of a different and rare breed. The Sentinel. Four and a half tonnes of bomb- and bulletproof armour. Thick enough to stop a 5.56mm rifle bullet at close range. Propelled by a 550-horsepower supercharged engine to make all that weight at least moderately spritely. Hearing footsteps behind him, he turned. Wade, walking across the small parking area and holding out his hand. Mickey took it with a fierce grin, hefting his bag out of the car's back seat.

'Evening, Wade. So what the fuck's going on that needs a skipper to supervise a big boy like you?'

Wade gave him that look.

'You don't know? Christ.'

'That bad?'

Wade spread his hands with the look of a man at the end of his patience.

'Bad enough that nobody's telling me anything. Seriously, it's like I've got the word *cunt* tattooed across my forehead.'

And Mickey, with more than enough reason to be at the end of his own rope, nodded his understanding.

'Right. First things first. Which one of the miserable bastards from LX is here with my firearm?'

Wade grinned. Frustration temporarily forgotten. 'Vic. And he's not happy. But wait 'til you see what he's got for you.'

Mickey opened the delivered gun case to discover a SIG MCX Rattler. A baby assault rifle. Chambered for .300 Blackout. A proper man-stopping bullet. Noting approvingly that the armourer had equipped it with simple flip-up iron sights. Mickey having no truck with the fancier holographic scope beloved of the coffee-drinking theorists.

'Nice choice, Vic. Thanks, mate.'

'Yeah, well the inspector told me to bring you out something special.'

'And the inspector…' Mickey checked all three magazines, already loaded, their transparent windows all showing twenty-five rounds on board '…was absolutely right.'

He grinned at the departing armourer's back. Then turned to Wade, handing him the weapon.

'Right, you can mind this until it's time to leave. No dribbling on it. I'll go and find out what the hell's going on.'

James Cavendish looked up as Mickey tapped on the frame of his office door.

'Michael Bale. Lord, but I'm pleased to see you.'

'Unlike a certain other person, I expect.'

James snorted derisively.

'He'll do as he's told. This is hardly the time for prima donna behaviour.'

'So what is it the time for?' Cavendish frowned at the question. 'What's this all about? A Sunday evening trip into London is one thing, but the American Embassy?'

'Ah. I see your point.' The major leaned back in his chair. 'Come in and close the door. This is most definitely for you and you alone.'

He waited until the door was firmly closed before continuing. 'HMG has bowed to the Americans' power of persuasion. Or to put it more accurately, their muscle. There being nothing quite so dangerous as a superpower on the brink of collapse. One of the items on the agenda when POTUS came to tea last week was their demand for Sir Patrick to testify to the CIA. Spilling everything he knows about the Chinese plan for world domination. Hard facts, all the things he learned in the twenty years he was courting the most senior members of the regime. Their plan to use currency devaluation to destroy Western manufacturing. And to supply the chemicals needed to make the opioids that are destroying our workforces. Nothing we didn't know already, of course, but the man who heard them boasting about it in pissed-up banquets will make a powerful witness.'

He stared at Mickey levelly.

'There's a war coming, Michael. And not just the usual financial sanctions and aggravated espionage. A full-scale shooting war in the Pacific. Like the last one, except it'll be hypersonic missiles and kinetic orbital bombardment taking the place of carriers and marines this time round. With the same sort of casualty count as eighty years ago. Or worse. Which means the Americans want to have right on their side. Sir Patrick's testimony being a small but important part of their case at the UN. We demanded justice for our victims of American crime and stupidity in the UK as a quid pro quo, of course. And we got absolutely nothing. In return for which we caved. All part of being caught on the fence between a pair of superpowers, it seems.'

'They both take turns pulling us off the fence and giving us a good hiding to show us who's boss?'

'Pretty much. As you can imagine, the PM was left without much choice in the matter. His only viable red line being insistence that Sir Patrick testifies *in camera*. So the Americans are flying over a team from Langley. Private aircraft to Heathrow, secure transfer to a chopper and straight into Battersea. Half the reason they moved the embassy to where it is, so they can piggyback off the flight corridor into the heliport. They'll be in and out with his evidence on the matter without anyone ever knowing they were here.'

Mickey pursed his lips. Already thinking through the route to the embassy. Choke points. Secondary routings. And hoping that the Special Escort Group were bringing their A game with them.

'And how does the man himself feel about that?'

Cavendish smiled wanly. 'He's a realist. The deal, I suspect, is that he gives evidence in return for being spared at the next reshuffle. Although he'll be left in Defence, which, let's face it, will not be a comfortable seat once the shooting starts, unless we can stay out of it. Which I very much doubt. All it'll take is pics of one of our carriers sinking to see the poor bastard thrown to the wolves. It's a war-time ritual, if you read the histories. All of which means that right now all he can do is put a nice suit on, arm himself with whatever dignity he has left, and do as he's told. As, Sergeant Bale, must we all. Although while I know this is duty for you, I want you to know that I really appreciate your agreeing to escort us tonight. There's nothing specific on the threat board. Or at least not according to Liaison. I'll just feel happier with some proper protection to hand.'

Mickey shrugged. 'I won't pretend I didn't consider saying no. Would have been simple enough just to say I had a bit of a cough.'

'But they told you I asked for you?'

'Yes they did. And I was always a sucker for being asked for help. So now, if you'll excuse me, I've got a package to set up. We leave at 20.00?'

'That's the schedule.'

Mickey went back downstairs to find Wade looking for him. Holding a phone. Which he put behind his back as he whispered a warning.

'It's AC Chen. Asking to speak to you.'

He put the handset to his mouth. 'Here's Sergeant Bale, ma'am.'

And handed the phone to Mickey. Sensibly choosing to walk away. Mickey walked into the lounge, taking a seat before speaking. Composing himself.

'Ma'am.'

'Sergeant Bale. Thank you for stepping into the breach.'

'Ma'am.'

Keeping his replies deliberately monosyllabic. Nothing

she could take offence to, but no encouragement to believe that Mickey didn't know exactly what she'd done.

'This visit to the American Embassy is a matter of extreme sensitivity.' Yeah, thought Mickey. Got any other revelations for me? Water is wet, perhaps? 'If it gets out that the minister has been questioned by the CIA then all sorts of rabbits will be set running.'

Jasmine was in the loop then. A strong indication that the commissioner had no clue just how loose-lipped her senior officer was. She continued, her voice hard with excited purpose.

'The PM has made it very clear that this needs to be conducted with absolute discretion.'

In which case, Mickey mused, why the fuck are we planning to run him into town in a three-car blue-light convoy? Why not just put him in the back of a boggo saloon car and make the whole thing invisible? Jasmine Chen had obviously thought that one through.

'And before you ask me, no, we can't do an incognito job on this. Don't ask me to get into the politics of it; we'd be here half an hour. Let's just call this a show of strength.'

Strength. Mickey rolled his eyes at the brilliance of the self-deception involved. And kept his reply neutral in tone. Not allowing the cynicism and disgust he was feeling to break the outwardly tranquil surface. 'Ma'am.'

'Is that all you're going to say all the way through this conversation?'

'Ma'am?' Mickey fighting the urge to giggle at the absurdity. But sticking firmly to his minimal communication line.

'Fine. You have your orders, Sergeant, carry them out.

You and I will have to have a different conversation once it's done though.'

'Yes, ma'am.'

Wanting to ask if there'd be a transcript for the *Clarion*, or would she brief them verbatim? But restraining himself by the skin of his teeth. Knowing that powder would explode most effectively if kept dry until the right moment. The moment when he needed it, rather when it would make him feel better.

'That's all, Sergeant. Just try to stay off the trigger this once? We don't need any more corpses.'

She ended the call without waiting for a response. Leaving Mickey wondering what the hell that last comment might have meant. Surely not…?

'Special Escort Group are here, Skip.'

Wade, breaking his chain of thought with an interjection around the half-open door.

'Excellent. It's about time I got the chance to talk to some normal coppers.'

Mickey went outside to find them arranging the package running order. Three bikes out front. Then a Jaguar saloon. After that the Sentinel Rangie, then another Jag. The tail being two more bikes. More like a warband than a protection team, really. Six uniformed officers in the two saloons, both three up. Driver, navigator and observer. And five fluorescent-jacketed riders. All armed. Enough firepower to front up to an infantry platoon, at close range. Mickey, recognising Maisie and Sean, waved a hand in greeting, then found himself engulfed in a Kev-sized bear hug.

'Mickey *fucking* Bale! I nearly told them to poke this job where the sun don't shine, y'know? I'm three days from my thirty, right, so why would I want to be out at this time of a Sunday night? Then they told me you was skipper for the whole thing. And I was in like a shot.'

Mickey saw his opportunity.

'Really? I only volunteered for this because they said you were Easy Rider for the night!'

Kev looked at him for a moment, unsure if it was true or just a wind-up. Then realised, a second too late, he'd been had.

'Smart-arse!'

The two men grinned at each other, then Mickey's mind dropped back into pro mode. 'We've got about half an hour to get the route sorted.' He beckoned to the Hall. 'Shall we? I reckon we can use the lounge, since it's unlikely there'll be anyone else in it. Wade mate, can you get the kitchen to rustle us up some tea and a bit of cake or something? It's going to be a long evening, by the time we get back.'

Sat in the lounge on sofas, chairs and pouffes, cups of tea and hastily cut slices of sponge cake going down nicely, Kev outlined his proposed route.

'Normally I'd be taking us straight into London, east as far as Marble Arch and then south down to Vauxhall Bridge. But given the *strongly* emphasised need for this package to be low profile...'

He shot a knowing look at Mickey. Who thought yeah, you know when you've been Jasmined.

'I'm recommending that we turn south earlier. Cross the river via Battersea Bridge, then east again on the A3205 to the embassy. Whose security, I'm told, will be ready for us. And won't leave us out on the road like a fucking great big target.'

He looked round the room, his gaze answered with nods and thumbs up. Universal agreement.

'OK, secondary route. Same route into London, but if the road south to Battersea is blocked for any reason then we'll cut down through Fulham. Everyone good with that?'

More nods.

'And if they both go tits up then we'll just have to find another way on the fly. Probably into town via Victoria, which would have been my first choice anyway. Mickey?'

'Cheers, Kev. Right, there's been no mention of any threat intel by Liaison. So I think it's safe to say that we can predict a quiet enough run into London on a Sunday evening. You're all the best at what you do, which means I don't need to remind you how to do it. Any questions?'

Kev, raising a hand.

'This had better be good.'

'Given you let me down with the last wager I put on you, do you think you see your way to throwing a few fucks—'

He fell silent, looking at the doorway. There's that famous James Cavendish sneaky-beaky, thought Mickey. Turning to confirm that it was indeed the major who'd caught Kev's eye.

'Thought I heard voices.' James smiling faintly at Kev's discomfiture. 'Do carry on, Sergeant Bale.'

Mickey nodded. 'Good timing, Major.' He gestured to the equerry. 'This is Major Cavendish. The minister's right-hand man and passenger two for this package. In the unlikely event that it does get sporty he's one of the two people I'd prefer you not to shoot.'

'Two?'

Mickey gave Kev a look that told him to act his age. The major raising a hand in greeting to the assembled officers.

'Do you have a moment, Michael?'

He slipped back out of the door, and Mickey stood to follow him. Ignoring the silent moue and snigger from Kev. Thinking: *That's easy for you to say, given you'll be "Mr" Kev before you know it.*

In the corridor Cavendish was sober-faced.

'We've had a second-level alert from Liaison. Some chatter among the cells of jihadist suspects in West London. Nothing to worry about, apparently. But they thought we ought to know. Arse covering, I suppose.'

Mickey waited for him to continue, sensing the intelligence to be a pretext to discuss something else. Unfinished business from before?

'I was about to ask you what the form is for arming private secretaries, when the principal is being moved in a bulletproof vehicle. Except your assistant commissioner interrupted before I got the chance to do so.'

Mickey smiled, shaking his head.

'This package is going to be escorted by enough armed officers to form a football team. In the unlikely event of it going to the races they'll be forming a disorderly queue to get some unexpected range time, I'd imagine.'

Cavendish nodded, apparently unfazed by the knock-back. 'No harm in asking.'

'And you'd have quite liked the feel of a 9mm in your hand again?'

The major shrugged. 'I'm long past getting any feeling of power from firearms. It's just that I'm used to having a little more control of my own destiny.'

Mickey shrugged. Not without sympathy. But simply powerless to grant the other man's wish.

'Even if I were minded to tool you up, I don't see how I could. Every weapon in the package is signed out to an officer. And we tend to be a little sensitive about signing for weapons and then letting anyone else get their hands on them.'

'Bit of a career-ending moment?'

'Pretty much.'

Cavendish nodded, smiling brightly as he shrugged. 'Oh well, you don't ask, you don't get. Never mind. Right, I'll go and make sure he's going to be ready on time. I don't imagine the Americans will be all that happy to be kept waiting.'

63

The package pulled out dead on time. With Mickey just about as on edge as he'd ever been in eleven years of Prot service. Although he wasn't quite sure why that was. Because if he'd ever been in a better-protected convoy, other than Operation Rampage, he was struggling to recall it.

At the heart of the package, the principal's car. Inside the Sentinel, Mickey, Wade, James Cavendish and a very glum-looking Sir Patrick. Collectively pretty much nuke-proof, behind armour and bulletproof glass.

In front of the lead car, Easy Rider. Kev led them through the route, in constant communication with his outriders. While the Working Bikes lived up to their name. Operating in pairs to a well-practised routine. Two riders blocking off the capital's moderate late evening traffic at each junction. While the other two followed the convoy through as rear-guard. Then rocketed past the Sentinel towards the next set of lights, their mates falling in behind. Brake lights glowing red, as the new advance guard came to a halt on either side of the junction. Blue lights flickering, hands raised. Whistles piercing the late evening's relative quiet. Rinse and repeat.

Progress toward the American embassy was proceeding at a steady fifty miles per hour. Wade driving while Mickey listened to the evening's radio traffic for any sign of trouble en route. His nerves soothed a little by having the MCX to hand.

Wade drove smoothly, keeping the talk to a minimum. Which, with a senior member of the government glowering at the back of Mickey's head, was almost monosyllabic. Mickey's earpiece feeding him the continual flow of information from the outriders, as they worked their routine. All trace of the usual Job humour erased. Just clipped commentary from Easy Rider as they sailed past momentarily halted traffic. A voice spoke in Mickey's ear.

'Romeo Four Six, Romeo Control. Be advised, Cromwell Road eastbound is closed. Suspected terrorist incident in progress, emergency services attending and road closed. Advise re-route to Secondary.'

The best laid plans, et cetera. Mickey didn't have the time to be irritated.

'Acknowledged Control, Four Six concurs, re-route to Secondary. Easy Rider, Romeo Control advise switch to Secondary.'

Kev, who'd been listening, acknowledged and started talking to his Working Bikes. Switching their route from the favoured Westway option to Mickey's second choice. Route One was urban clearway all the way to the turn south. And the A3220 wide enough to give plenty of room for manoeuvre. The Secondary routing? Not so much.

Off the Westway at the Hammersmith Flyover. South through the complex junction, the Working Bikes in box formation to warn off the unwary. Onto Fulham Palace Road, their blue lights and whistles clearing a path through the light traffic. Mickey ignored the minister's muttered comments as the convoy bulled its way down the road, blue lights strobing. Hardly low profile anymore.

They passed Charing Cross Hospital on the left. Mickey's dark sense of humour muttered in his ear that that might come in handy. Passed Fulham Cemetery. Mickey told his dark sense of humour to fuck right off. Kev was unflappable out front. The detour to the secondary routing all in a day's work, Mickey supposed. They were still doing an average thirty and already closing in on Putney Bridge. The goal in sight, pretty much. Mickey was starting to think through the route south of the river when the tone of Maisie's unmistakable voice got his attention.

'Easy Rider, Working Two, carriageway blockage left.'

He looked up, seeing a parked van blocking the bus lane two hundred yards ahead. A Working Bike, presumably Maisie, slowing to check it out. Anticipating Kev's instruction.

'Working Two, check blockage.'

Double click from Maisie. Wade braked gently without needing to be told. Increasing the amount of time available for a visual inspection from the saddle before the Sentinel arrived. The lead Jag allowed the gap back to the principal to open up. Its occupants probably readying themselves for an emergency debus. The bike almost stopped at the van's driver's window. Maisie standing up on her foot-pegs to look into the cab. Her words made slightly comical by the whistle gripped in her teeth.

'All clear.'

She sat down again and eased the bike back up to a brisk walking speed, waiting for the convoy. Working One, Sean, had already blocked the roundabout's first exit, a hundred yards further south. The lead Jag slowed to repeat the inspection, cruising slowly past the parked vehicle. Nothing much to see, the cab nondescript, its black paint scuffed and matted by age. Much like the vehicles Mickey had bought for his attacks on Joe's operation, he mused.

A flatbed lorry cleared the roundabout a hundred yards distant, coming in the other direction. Just visible behind it, a van was lurking on the roundabout's other side. Waiting at the dotted white lines despite the road being clear. Something not quite right, to Mickey's eye. Too many unexpected variables. A threat profile forming quickly. And even as the thought formed, a flicker of motion caught his eye. A black-clad figure climbing out of the van's side door on the pavement side. Looking bulky, and camouflaged by the dark garments, barely visible even under streetlights. Vanished behind the van, walking quickly around its front. Mickey keyed his mike.

'SEG One, possible threat, coming round the front of the van, debus and—'

The dark figure reappeared at the van's offside front quarter. The Jag's brake lights flared as the driver hard-stopped the car. Doors opening as the crew prepared to go into action. And then, with a blast clearly audible inside the car as a monstrous bang, the dark figure simply ceased to be. The Jag momentarily vanished in a gout of black smoke and dust that punched out from where he had stood. A fierce blink of light at its heart.

An instant later the shock wave slapped the Sentinel. Rocking the heavily armoured vehicle even at a hundred yards' distance. Followed by the metallic pinging of shrapnel impacting armoured bodywork and bulletproof glass. Kev dropped his bike and staggered across the road clutching his chest. Making no more than half-a-dozen steps before he collapsed in a spreading puddle of blood. Recovering his wits, Mickey snapped out an instruction.

'Emergency egress rear!'

Wade slapped the drive selector into reverse. Accelerating backwards rather than trying to turn the big car round. SEG Two copying the move, windows rolling down and machine pistol barrels protruding to either side. Mickey keyed his radio.

'Romeo Control, Four Six, urgent assistance! IED detonation, south end of Fulham Palace Road, multiple casualties—'

He stopped talking momentarily, for two reasons. First, the hammer of an automatic weapon, something heavy duty, heard faintly through the thick glass to their front. Joined by another an instant later. Second, the squeal of rubber from behind the convoy. As the flatbed's driver pulled his steering wheel over and came to a stop behind them. Parked across the road, completely blocking it. Leaping from his cab and running. SEG Two's crew refrained from shooting an unarmed man. Faces appeared at house windows with expressions of amazement. Doors tentatively opened as the braver of the street's inhabitants nervously investigated the explosion.

Momentarily nonplussed, processing events and considering options, Mickey released the mike trigger. Maisie's voice sounded in his ear, her tone harsh and urgent. A series of pops underlaid her comms – 9mm going downrange, Mickey guessed. Pissing in the wind against automatic weapons though.

'Working Two, taking fire from the east! Three or four shooters! Working One is down, repeat Sean is down, multiple GSW! Request urgent rein—'

The words stopped, cut off by a grunt that could only mean one thing. Simultaneously Mickey heard the short burst that silenced her. And realised that the only way to break the ambush was by driving past the wreck of SEG One. Risking automatic weapon fire and the likelihood of running over fallen riders. Risks, given the lack of options, that had to be deemed acceptable.

And then the last part of the trap closed. The loitering van, having accelerated across the roundabout, braked to a halt alongside the wreck of SEG One. Turned at the last minute, putting its nose over the pavement and wheel against the kerb. Preventing it being pushed backwards by superior horsepower. And thereby closed off the only remaining escape option.

Wade looked at him questioningly, selector in Drive, ready to floor the big V8. But lacking any clear exit from the ambush's box. Mickey's attention was caught by a flurry of motion on the Sentinel's right-hand side. Both men watched helplessly as another black-clad figure emerged from the cover of a bus stop and sprinted at the two remaining cars.

SEG Two's crew alert and ready. The two remaining outriders with their Glocks drawn. Four expert shots opened fire on the attacker before he could even get into his stride. Hitting him with a hail of 9mm. He staggered and fell. A wire trailing from his right hand to the bulky bomb vest encircling his torso. Dead man switch.

The slabs of explosive strapped to his body detonated. The blast slamming into the Sentinel like an open-handed blow from an angry god. A storm of shrapnel raked the street, the blast blowing in every window for fifty yards.

The last two outriders went down instantly. The Jag was battered sideways, landing on deflated tyres and bursting into flames. Its occupants either dead or beyond assistance. The Sentinel's offside windows were suddenly milky and opaque, bludgeoned by a dozen shrapnel strikes and more. Mickey and Wade abruptly barely able to see the burning car to their right.

As the explosion's pall of smoke and dust cleared, Mickey knew what the attackers' plan was. Trap the convoy, preventing the target from escaping. Creating a kill box for the suicide bombers to scour with flying metal. While the shooters waited around the corner in Fulham High Street. Ready to close in for the coup de grâce. Sustained fire into the Sentinel at close range to defeat the armoured glass that was its weakest point. That, or perhaps an anti-tank rocket or limpet mine. Delivering a shaped charge warhead that would punch through the armour and incinerate its occupants. And without an escape route, their options were down to one.

Attack.

He nudged Wade with an elbow. Pointing to the ruins of the bus stop.

'You go round the back of the car and set up to shoot down the pavement. I'll go forward and close the range. Put out some smoke so they have to come to us.'

He turned back to Cavendish and the minister.

'Stay in the car. If they start shooting at the glass, get below window level. Met Control will have armed response on scene in minutes, and this vehicle is bulletproof.'

'So why are you getting out, if—'

Cavendish, perplexed, Mickey cut him off.

'Because even this glass won't stand up to sustained fire at close range. We have to hold them off until Trojan can get on scene.'

Mickey grabbed a flimsy plastic document wallet from the glove box, Shaking out the papers. Then looked at Wade and nodded. 'Find cover, stay low, give me covering fire.' He patted the Rattler. 'I'll do the rest.'

They both opened their doors at the same moment, slipped out and pushed them shut. The lock mechanisms clicked over, securing Sir Patrick against the people seeking his life. At least for as long as the armoured glass could hold against full auto at close range. Mickey looked around, wincing at the damage to the houses to his left. Casualties a certainty. Looked down at Kev. Eyes shut with the pain. Still breathing but struggling. He knelt, talking quickly into his radio.

'Romeo Control, Four Six. Second IED detonation. Convoy immobilised, and under automatic weapons attack. All SEG officers casualties. Four Six and Seven Seven deploying on foot towards the junction with Fulham Road. Multiple civilian casualties likely. Estimate two zero seriously wounded.'

Talking while he undid Kev's jacket and ripped his shirt open. Put the plastic over the shrapnel entry wound and placed his friend's hand over it.

'Hold this in place. It's a sucking chest wound; this will keep you alive long enough for assistance to get here.'

Ignoring the look of disbelief in Kev's eyes, he patted his shoulder and stood up. Put the Rattler back to his shoulder.

Trying to work out how the hell he and Wade were going to hold off a determined attack with automatic weapons.

Not much cover to be had. A park on the road's right, with a line of trees whose trunks looked pretty attractive as protection against assault rifles. But separated from the road by a high fence of iron railings, topped by spikes. Not sharp, but enough to delay him crossing the obstacle. And the last thing he needed was to still be climbing over it when the assassins came around the corner.

'Four Six, received. Trojan units ETA your location in two minutes.'

He momentarily considered falling back to take cover behind the Sentinel with Wade. Use its bulletproof armour for protection. But instantly rejected the idea as abandoning any shred of initiative they had left. Looked instead at the battered wreckage of SEG One. Seventy yards or so distant. And his best chance of putting something hard between him and the threat. Bent low, he moved down the road. The carbine raised and ready to fire.

The street was eerily quiet, the occupants of the houses on its left side presumably shocked into immobility by the two massive explosions and gunfire. That, or casualties of the twin hails of shrapnel. As he got closer to the vehicles, the sheer violence of the suicide vest's explosion became clearer. The van's paint work was pocked with shiny craters, where hot metal had vapourised paint in an instant. SEG One was a charnel house, its bloodied crew lolling lifelessly in their seats. Of the bomber himself, there was nothing to be seen other than a booted human foot lying in the road.

Sirens were sounding from all sides now, still distant but getting louder by the second. Mickey grinned mirthlessly.

Let the bastards who'd just slaughtered close to a dozen officers know that their mission time was running down fast. Moving south towards the roundabout, he looked back without breaking pace. Seeing Wade hunkered down behind the Sentinel's rear end.

Looking forward again, he saw Maisie trying to get back to her feet from behind the dropped bike that had been her cover. She raised a pistol in her left hand and fired unsteadily down the street. Her other arm hanging uselessly, blood dripping from the fingers as she engaged whoever it was she could see around the corner. A violent hammer of automatic fire answered her shots. Mickey flinched as the rounds sent her sprawling to lie motionless. The weapon's racket sounded dangerously close, as if its wielder was about to come around the corner.

He went down on one knee. Holding the Rattler roughly on target with his left hand. Using the other to pull a smoke grenade from his belt. Cocked his gun hand's little finger to grasp the pin. Pulled it out, let the lever fly, then hurled the slim canister over the wrecked Jag. A plume of grey smoke gushed out. Jetted across the junction and filled the air in seconds. In for a penny, he decided. Threw the second grenade a little shorter. The street was suddenly filled by an absence of vision, the streetlights' illumination ghostly and flickering as the cloud thickened.

Downside: the opposition now knew there were still officers in fighting condition between them and the target. Upside: they wouldn't be able to do what Mickey would have tried in their place. Fire and move, advancing in bounds with a gun ready to shoot at the slightest movement. Suddenly flushed with adrenaline, he was barely able stop himself from bellowing a challenge into the chemical fog. Knowing that whoever had set up such a well-planned ambush wouldn't be giving him any clues as to where they were.

'Contact front!'

And the bang, bang, bang of 9mm from behind him. Wade engaging with his Glock. Presumably at targets that had emerged from the smoke in front of him. A grunt from the other side of the van. A hit? A brutally loud clatter of full automatic answered from behind the shrapnel-peppered van. Two long bursts. With no return fire. Something snapping in Mickey's head as the implications of that hit him.

He heard the clatter of an empty magazine hitting the pavement. Behind the van. Dangerously close. Backing away from the wreck of SEG One, he pivoted to his left, dropping onto one knee. A militaristic figure stepped out of the van's cover, slotting a fresh magazine into an assault rifle. Smudged urban camouflage, black belt order and combat boots. An integrated helmet and face mask. Faceless and anonymous. Wearing a webbing harness laden with armour plate. Presumably what had stopped Wade's pistol fire dead. The olive drab tube of a man portable anti-tank rocket slung over the figure's back. Presumably to be used on either the Sentinel or the first responders.

Assault rifle's barrel pointing at the Sentinel, the attacker strode purposefully towards the battered car. Mickey took up the trigger's slack, tracking the unsuspecting target. Unexpectedly, the assassin suddenly spun towards him. Some battlefield instilled instinct, perhaps. A mix of bloody experience and trained peripheral vision. Reacting to

Mickey's presence with near-divine speed. Swivelling with an almost feline grace. But too slow.

Mickey squeezed off a single shot. Close enough to ignore the gunman's bulky armoured torso and take the head shot. Spattering the house behind his target with blood. The shooter's corpse sprawling over the low wall behind him. Mickey held his on-target stance. Ready to put more rounds into the dead or dying gunman. And then he was moving, without really knowing why. Instincts overriding the conscious thought process.

He went for the van's cover. Dived forwards, knowing he was too slow. A reaction triggered by a fleeting glimpse of movement in the smoke to his right. A fraction of a second too late. A second gunman had simply walked out of the grey veil behind SEG One. Snapped up his rifle and triggered a burst at Mickey. Whose instinctive evasive move saved him from taking the bullets centre mass, but something agonisingly hot plucked at his side.

The impact was hard enough to physically tumble him as he fell into the van's cover. Recovering from the sprawl, ignoring battered knees and elbows, he reached for the Rattler. Realising that his side was wet with blood, and already going numb. It would only be a matter of a minute or so before he went into shock. Before he lost the will to fight. And floated away into the quiet place where serious gunshot wound victims went to die.

Except, on reflection, Mickey decided, fuck that. He'd fight while he could and die on his feet. He struggled up onto one knee. Using the Rattler's butt as a prop to hold himself vaguely upright. Knowing he needed to get the barrel horizontal and pointed toward the enemy. But not sure if he was capable of making such a complex move, under the circumstances.

And then, to make matters worse, the attacker who'd shot him came around the van's right front wing. Wearing the same face-masked urban camo as the man he'd just killed. Raising the barrel of his weapon the final few degrees needed to put it on target. After which a short centre-mass burst was going to tear into Mickey's body and finish his struggle to stand up permanently.

In the brief instant between finding himself looking straight down the rifle's barrel and the trigger being pulled, Mickey looked into the other man's eyes. Finding nothing there. No anger. No emotion at all. Just professionalism. Mickey the only thing between him and the kill. And so just collateral. Something hit the gunman hard in the chest. Rocked him back. A familiar bang from behind Mickey announcing that 9mm was being used. Wade?

The bullet had hit Kevlar plate, at a guess. Staggering the assassin, but not putting him down. Probably leaving one hell of a bruise, but nothing worse. Another bang, with no discernible impact. A miss. Mickey absent-mindedly unsurprised, given the shooter sounded like they were thirty yards back. The first shot pretty damned good in itself.

Another bang from behind Mickey, with more spectacular results; 9mm still a lethal calibre even at that distance. If the gods of shot placement and target topography were favourably minded. The gunman's face mask growing a third eye hole. A perfect head shot, extraordinary at that distance. His body slowly toppling backwards onto the road surface. Rifle clattering to the ground beside him.

Mickey twisted painfully and looked back. Not Wade. Cavendish. With, he presumed, Wade's Glock in both hands. The approved special force's gunfighter stance, when a pistol was all there was to be had. His point of aim swinging fractionally, to a new target, Mickey presumed. Then staggering back and collapsing, his shoulder seeming to come apart in a spray of blood.

Mickey snapped his attention forwards. Having raised the Rattler without conscious effort and thumbed the selector to automatic. Emptied the weapon's magazine in a long burst that hurt like hell. Knowing that a man protected with titanium-backed Kevlar plate wouldn't be stopped by a single shot. Saw the gunman standing over his dead companion stagger back. Arms thrown wide as the stream of heavy .300 rounds chewed through his armour and killed him instantly.

Three down. Instinctively knowing there'd be a fourth assassin, Mickey slumped sideways back into the van's cover. Fumbled with numb fingers to eject the spent magazine. Managed, after two attempts, to pull the other from his pocket. Got it seated and pushed it home. Thumbed the bolt release to reload the weapon with a loud clack.

Stalemate? Mickey at one end of the battered van. Shooter four presumably at the other. Neither of them with anyone else to assist. But Mickey, gunshot, was quickly losing his tenuous grip on the situation. Knowing that he had to get on his feet and change position. That he was dead if he stayed where he was. The other man only having to come around either side of the van to find him on his knees.

If he hadn't just been hit by a high-velocity round, he

could have countered that move easily enough. Fallen back, weapon raised and ready to fire. Reducing the other guy's chance of a first-round hit. Improving his own ability to put the assassin down with the Rattler on full auto. With a hole in his side, however, that wasn't going to happen. Because hydrostatic shock, for one thing. And blood loss for another.

Which left him with only one possible course of action. One that only worked if he'd guessed the rifleman's next move correctly. Knowing that if his opponent chose differently he'd come round the right-hand side of the van instead. And find Mickey neatly laid out for the kill.

Knowing that standing was going to be well-nigh impossible, he allowed his body to slump to the ground. Rolled onto his left side and put the carbine to his right shoulder. Barrel pointing, not entirely steadily, at the letter-box gap between the van's underside and the pavement's edge behind it.

Perhaps an inch of clear space through which a bullet could fly. If he didn't fuck it up and put the shot into the kerb's concrete. And waited. Intently focused on an inch of open air, ignoring the risk of his unguarded back.

A wave of detachment washed over him. The inevitable consequence of having a metal projectile blast through his body at 900 metres a second. Shock sinking sharp teeth into his limbic system. His vision was starting to tunnel, peripheral detail vanishing. Sounds softer, less crisp.

Events seemed to drop into slo-mo, as a booted right foot appeared in the gap, in front of the van's nearside front wheel. After a moment's pause, another step taken behind the van's wheel, the same boot came down again. Urban combat footwear, rubber soled for stealth. Moving quickly, but with exaggerated care. Rolling the foot from heel to toe to move silently. Another pace forwards, balancing stealth with the need for haste.

Mickey leaned into the Rattler's butt. Knowing that shooting was going to hurt. Gritted his teeth. Tensed his body as the next step put a boot down in his sight picture. A split-second alignment of rear sight, front sight and the bottom inch of his opponent's left foot. He fired, the weapon's report thunderous in the narrow space beneath the van. An aural assault that blasted his hearing back to almost nothing. A tinnitus roar in his ears like a jet engine spooling up twenty feet away.

The gunman screamed with pain, barely audible, and fell to the pavement. His head and face were bare. Helmet and mask discarded for better use of his senses, perhaps. A nondescript face, vaguely Slavic in appearance. His rifle skittered away across the slabs. He lay facing Mickey, his face a hate-filled snarl as he reached for the pistol strapped under his left armpit. Tiredly, without any conscious effort, Mickey fired again, putting a bullet into the fallen assassin's chest. Centre mass. Lights out. Too much damage done for anything more than one last, autonomic spasm.

After a moment Mickey rolled onto his front. Considering whether to try getting to his feet. Body and mind taking a quick vote and deciding by a majority of two not to bother. His hearing was starting to return. The screams and pleas for help of the bombs' civilian victims audible over the approaching sirens. Emergency services perhaps only thirty seconds away. Leaving him feeling disposable.

Used up and ready to stop doing anything whatsoever. Job done, thank you and goodnight.

He slumped down onto the road's wet surface, as consciousness deserted him.

64

Mickey woke up in discomfort. With an ache in his head that carried the promise of greater pain to come. And a soreness in his right side that was already worse than discomfort. Combined with a mouth dry enough that even the thought of swallowing felt like a bad idea. He opened his eyes experimentally. Blinked at the soft light from above his head. Looked around for a way to summon assistance. Found it after a moment inventorying the room. Bed. Chair. Drawers. Various machines with lights and diagnostic screens. Metal stand holding the blood bag that was emptying its contents into his right arm through an intravenous line. A clock, telling him it was 05.18. An armed SCO19 officer standing in the corridor beside the open door. And a call button lying by his right leg. He pressed it and waited.

After a minute or so a nurse put her head around the door. And smiled warmly.

'About time too. We were starting to wonder if you were going to sleep all morning. Want a drink?'

Mickey nodded, sucking gratefully at the tube she offered. Cool water. His mouth lubricated, he managed to croak a word. 'Hurts.'

'Really hurts, or just uncomfortable?'

'Bit of both.'

She nodded, passing him another control. 'Press this button once to get a small dose of the good stuff. Press it every five minutes until you feel OK. After that don't press it again until it starts to hurt again. You came back from surgery about an hour ago, and you'll be pleased to know that the bullet that hit you went straight through without hitting anything too important. Nicked your bowel, which has been sewn up and carpet-bombed with antibiotics. Hungry?'

Mickey shook his head, pressed the button, lay back and went back to sleep. Woke again with the same discomfort. Pressed the button again and waited for the pain to ease. Felt the soft pleasure of opiates caress his body and smiled.

'Well I'm glad you can find something funny in this fucking awful mess.'

He opened his eyes to find Roz by the bed. The clock telling him it was 08.39. Her expression somewhere between concern and exasperation. He pointed to the water bottle on the bedside cabinet. 'Drink?'

The water was warmer this time, but no less welcome. Mickey would have happily gone back to sleep, but Roz had other ideas.

'Apparently you've got a fucking great big hole in you, and everyone thinks you're lucky to be alive.'

Mickey nodded tiredly. 'Assassination attempt.'

'Well duh! It's all over the news channels. Cars blown up, police dead. Civilians too. There were suicide bombers!'

'Yeah. I remember something like that.'

Roz stared at him for a moment. And all Mickey could

do was smile wanly back at her, his mind too frazzled for anything better.

'And there's you. Almost the only survivor, apart from Kev Smalls and some army bloke. And that politician prick, obviously. Smiling like it's a fucking great big joke! What about all those dead coppers? What about their families?'

'They will be looked after, Mrs Bale. The Met always cares for its own.'

They both looked over to the door. Jasmine Chen, in full uniform. Career hard woman incarnate. She looked tired and, to put no gloss on it, pissed off.

'If you could see your way to allowing me a minute or two with your husband, Mrs Bale? I promise to get out of your hair as quickly as possible.'

Roz snorted derisively, turning for the door.

'Have him for as long as you like. I'm done with him.'

AC Chen, recognising a kindred spirit, stepped aside with a tight smile. Then advanced into the room under full sail, a hard-eyed suit in her wake. Mickey vaguely recognised the man, a DCI. Her current bag carrier. Hand-picked, hatchet-faced. Known to lack any sense of humour. The perfect match for Our Jasmine. He closed the door.

'Good morning, Sergeant. You'll have to forgive me for not waiting until you're a bit more compos mentis, but this really won't wait that long.'

Mickey nodded wearily. 'Get the story straight before the press start digging?'

A firm nod of her head. 'Press coverage of last night's incident will be on the Met's terms.'

'A dozen dead officers. How do you control *that*?'

AC Chen looked down at him for a moment. Her regard

not quite as friendly as might have been expected, under the circumstances.

'We couldn't stop the footage that was shot by a small number of witnesses to the attack from going viral, of course. Thankfully they were sufficiently far away and shit-scared that it isn't too graphic. Although the camera phone film of Constable Blake returning fire and being cut down is powerful stuff. When the Trojan units got to the scene they managed to stop any further recording, and got the bodies covered up. And since nobody managed to get any footage of what happened in Fulham Palace Road itself, we can present the press with the best version of events.'

Mickey nodded, wincing at the pain. 'The sanitised version.'

She shot him a jaundiced look. 'Well of *course* the sanitised version. You saw the mess that those bastards made of the Special Escort Group. The commissioner is determined that the press will be fed only the images we want them to see. Wrecked vehicles. Constable Blake's bike riddled with bullet holes. The damage caused by two suicide bombers. But not the men and women who died. Dead heroes will be mourned, but their bloodied corpses will not be put on display by the media. And everyone will breathe a sigh of relief that by some miracle no civilians died. Although there are still seven of them in hospital. Three of them in ICU.'

'Who were they?'

She shook her head. 'We have no idea. The best guess the forensics guys have come up with so far is Chechen. Perhaps we'll know more once their DNA's been properly analysed. Their clothing and equipment had been sanitised. No labels, no extraneous DNA, no nothing. There are no serial numbers on their weapons and the ammunition is probably untraceable as well. Probably imported illegally. No fingerprint or DNA matches in the Interpol database, nothing from face recognition. Nothing to link them to any cause or country. And of course the government will be scrupulous in seeking proof before accusing any third party. Although I think it's fairly clear who they're looking at as being their paymasters, behind the smoke and mirrors. Although if MI5 have any clue who it was, they're not sharing them with us mere mortals.'

Mickey looked up at her. Already pretty much knowing the answer to the question he had to ask. Unable to put it off any longer.

'Wade?'

'Constable Harris was declared dead on arrival at Charing Cross Hospital. He was hit three times.' Her expression softened, just for a moment. 'My commiserations, Sergeant. I know how hard it is to lose a partner.'

Mickey closed his eyes, seeing his friend's face. Opened them again. 'Kev?'

'Sergeant Smalls suffered multiple shrapnel wounds. One of them a sucking lung perforation. He should pull through. And he's already telling anyone who'll listen that you saved his life.'

Kev was alive then. Small mercies.

'Cavendish?'

'He's still in surgery. Reconstructing his shoulder. Seems from what the bystanders told the investigating officers that he saved your bacon.'

'No doubt of that. Sir Patrick?'

'Not a scratch. At which point it would be easy to be

cynical, given he lived because of several brave officers' actions. But to be fair he insisted on continuing to the embassy immediately, once the situation was under control. Whatever it was that was so important, he carried it through. And he's suitably grateful to you and your colleagues. I believe he's already decided what decorations he's putting you all in for. Constables Maisie Blake and Wade Harris will both be awarded a posthumous George Cross.'

Mickey nodded. 'Justified. They went down shooting, both of them. Maisie delayed the shooters long enough for us to get deployed.'

The assistant commissioner nodded.

'On that, at least, we can agree. Whether you're quite as deserving is yet to be proven.' She shot Mickey an indecipherable look. Identifiable as less than friendly. 'But the decision has been made not to stand in the way of the award, given your pivotal role as described by Sir Patrick. Oh, and the major will be awarded a George Cross as well. The most he can get given the attack wasn't carried out by a recognisable enemy. Everyone else will be awarded a posthumous George Medal. So we'll bury our dead with full honours, and pin medals on the survivors.'

Mickey closed his eyes, suddenly tired again. 'If that's all, ma'am, I could really do with pushing this button again.'

Opened his eyes when the silence drew out well beyond the point of just being uncomfortable. To find the assistant commissioner staring down at him with a distinct lack of sympathy.

'Wound hurting you, is it, Sergeant? Seems to me that you've been lucky to make it this far without *someone* putting a bullet in you.'

'Prot's not that dangerous, ma—'

'I'm not talking about your Protection Command duties, Sergeant Bale. As we *both* know all too well.' She held up thumb and forefinger with a few millimetres between them. 'I'm this close to having the proof I need that you've been a very naughty boy.'

'I see.'

Mickey was not inclined to offer her any help. Firstly because of the fact she wasn't sharing whatever evidence she had with regard to his extra-curricular activities. And secondly because his wound was doing a fair impression of having a hot poker sticking out of it.

'I'm sure you do.' Jasmine looked pitilessly down at him. 'Which is why you're not denying it. And why I'd be a good deal happier if you'd done the decent thing and bled out on the Fulham Palace Road. Right, I need a cigarette. Push your magic button to your heart's content. You'll keep for a few days.'

65

'Professional Standards interview with Sergeant Michael James Bale of Protection Command. Interview to be carried out by Deputy Assistant Commissioner Michael Haskins and Detective Chief Inspector Martin Irving of Professional Standards.'

DAC Haskins paused. Clearly wanting to make something of a point.

'And in the advisory presence of Assistant Commissioner Jasmine Chen of Specialist Operations Command.'

The big guns were out in force for him, Mickey mused. Haskins, the Met's Grand Inquisitor. Wielding the service's bell, book, candle and disciplinary code. The man sitting to his right was his bag carrier, a detective chief inspector barely out of his twenties. Destined for greatness. Ticking an important career box with Professional Standards. But, beyond that, known for his uncompromising stance on corruption. Having come to Haskins' attention by shopping several of his own officers for accepting favours from local "businessmen" as a young DI.

Mickey had waited on the street outside New Scotland Yard from two hours before his allotted interview time. Watched the traffic with a close personal interest. And noted the arrival, with half an hour to spare, of a prisoner transport vehicle. Recognisable as such by its tiny armoured windows and, in this case, the Trojan escort vehicle. No prizes for guessing who'd be making the journey to Pentonville in that later. If, that was, Mickey found himself excommunicated with extreme prejudice.

He wondered momentarily just how hard Jasmine had had to push to get in on the interview. She certainly wasn't a necessary component. Professional Standards had whatever they had against him, and her presence wouldn't add to the case. He also suspected that DAC Haskins would have resisted the idea of her attendance robustly. Perhaps mistakenly believing that she would attempt to defend her officer. As if.

He was, nevertheless, delighted to see her present.

'Firstly, allow me to congratulate you on your recovery, Sergeant Bale.'

Mickey nodded to the superintendent.

'Thank you, sir. It's good to be up and about again.'

Noting that Haskins hadn't mentioned his Commissioner's Commendation. Or the George Cross. Haskins not mentioning his awards because, presumably, they wouldn't have been bestowed on him with quite such haste if Jasmine had had her way. Or if the evidence that Haskins was about to lay out had been complete at the time?

'This is not an interview under caution, Sergeant Bale. But it may result in further interviews, disciplinary action, a caution, or even your arrest on criminal charges. Do you understand the serious nature of the matters you've been asked here to discuss?'

Mickey looked across the table at the DAC. A known

hard man. The scourge of the corrupt copper, meting out justice even-handedly. Or with both fists, depending on your perspective. White haired. A kindly grandfather in his private time, more than likely. Wearing demi-lunette reading glasses that were, fairly obviously, a cosmetic affectation. Allowing him the theatrical conceit of staring over them with a wide range of expressions. Disbelief, astonishment, even the full-on Paddington Bear if needed.

Haskins was an actor playing the swan song role of his career. And looking for the Oscar with this one. Likely to put him in the papers. And then in the Old Bailey, if Mickey went for trial on numerous counts of murder, GBH and firearms offences. With the potential for a tabloid career after retirement, if he played his cards right. Although prosecuting a decorated protection officer would be an interesting minefield to navigate.

But in one matter he was right on the money. The issues he'd been invited to discuss were about as serious as you could get without being nicked. Nicked, and then flushed down the criminal justice system's big shitter. Life, in this case, likely to mean exactly that.

And Mickey, who knew just how the game would be played, kept his face admirably blank. Playing Haskins' opening delivery with a completely straight bat.

'Given the lack of any forward briefing? No sir, I do not understand the seriousness of whatever questions you're planning to ask me.'

The DAC wrote something in his tablet. Adding to his grocery shopping list, perhaps.

'And you've chosen not to be accompanied by a federation representative?'

'Yes, sir.'

'Might I enquire as to why you feel you don't need the federation in your corner, Sergeant? Given you profess to have no idea what it is you've been called here to discuss?'

'When I understand what it is that you feel might be the problem, I'll decide if I want a fed rep to help me answer. Sir.'

Jasmine looking across the table at him with an expression that was one-third professional reserve. One-third insincere concern for her officer. And one-third poorly disguised glee.

The likelihood being that Mickey would have refused a fed rep in any case. Even had he been formally warned of what he was about to be accused of. Knowing that with those sorts of charges a fed rep would be about as much use as a warm toffee dildo. Flying solo on this one being very much his best chance of averting the wrath of an enraged Met.

'Very well. Let us proceed.'

Haskins opened his evidence folder.

'Sergeant Bale, there are a few things I'd like you to help me with.'

'Sir.'

The DAC nodded to his DI – Irving, overweight, northern and gruff. A known devotee of the sausage sandwich and therefore never likely to chase down a running perpetrator. But, by reputation, a fiendish bastard when building a case.

'Sergeant Bale. You live in Monken Park, do you not?'

'Yes, sir.'

'We can lose the "sir" from here on. A simple yes or no will be good enough.'

'Yes.'

'And on the 17th of April last, a drug dealer by the name of Warren Margetson was murdered in Monken Park. In an alley just off the High Road. At more or less the same time you arrived in the nearby Carpenter's Arms to drink with three former colleagues.'

'Yes.'

'This dealer... Warren Margetson... was shot. In the head and at close range. With this weapon.'

Mickey watched as evidence item one was produced. Looking an awful lot like the .22 automatic he'd killed Warren with. Enclosed in a sealed evidence bag. He leaned over to look at the gun. Making a show of examining it like it was his first viewing.

'If you say so, I can only take your word for it.'

Irving smiled thinly. 'It's not my word we have to consider, Sergeant. Ballistics have made a close enough match to the bullet removed from the victim's cranium to be reasonably sure this was indeed the murder weapon. It was a bit touch and go, apparently, given the state of the bullet, but modern science will usually find a way.'

Mickey pursed his lips and nodded. Disappointed that Martin's "unrecognisable bullet" theory had apparently been proven to be nothing better than sales patter.

'The firearm being presented in evidence here was recovered in the course of a raid on a known firearms dealer. Under the auspices of Operation Broom.'

Mickey nodded again. Guessing that Broom was the sort of major initiative that was kept under duck's arse levels of security. Until the time came for a series of doors to be smashed in at 05.00 one morning. Keeping the knowledge that gun dealers were being tagged and set up for simultaneous arrest to the favoured few. Wisely, given the tendency for bent coppers to provide warnings to the criminal underworld. And, of course, dawn raids were media-friendly to boot. Op Broom doubtless just about to be the subject of a major *Clarion* exposé. "Dealers in death", or some such. And right up Jasmine Chen's career path, given her responsibility for Specialist Operations.

Jasmine butted in. 'The dealer in question was talking before we could get the interview recorder started.'

Her interruption drew an unreadable sideways glance from Irving. Her poorly concealed smirk flashing like searchlights from her eyes. Mickey guessed that it was her supervision of Broom that had given her the right to attend the interview. Given she effectively owned the evidence.

'And he was very quick to name an associate of his as having borrowed this pistol. On the morning of the 17th of April, funnily enough. A favour to a "fellow professional", apparently. And the fellow professional he named was previously unknown to us. A man called Martin Hyde. Does that name ring a bell to you, Sergeant Bale?'

No point in lying.

'I went to school with a Martin Hyde. I don't recall him wanting to be an arms dealer when he grew up though. And what he ended up doing for a living was a bit more down to earth. But presumably you already know that?'

'Yes, Sergeant, we do.' Irving retaking control of the interview. Jasmine coiling back into her chair, temporarily at least. 'Martin Hyde worked as a local authority refuse collector. And seems, on the face of it, to have lived a blameless life. No abnormal financial patterns in his bank account…'

No, Mickey thought. Martin always having been cute enough to keep his business funds completely separate. Under a different name and identity, of course.

'And presumably you arrested him and searched his flat? Did that shed any light on this gun dealer's accusations?'

'No. Although we did find a hiding place under the floorboards which contained traces of gun oil and traces of gunshot residue. Prints, of course, but mostly Mr Hyde's, plus a good few glove marks. But that's not all we didn't find. Were you aware that Mr Hyde had left the country?'

'We haven't spoken for weeks. Perhaps he's on holiday?'

'It would seem not. His neighbours say he left home the same day you fought off Sir Patrick's attackers in Fulham. And hasn't been seen since.'

Mickey shrugged. 'Three weeks. That's not too long for it to be a holiday.'

'And his bank account hasn't been touched in all that time?' Jasmine back in the hunt. Unable to help herself, he guessed. 'What's he doing for money, I wonder?'

'Can't help you there.'

Mickey pretty sure that that was a dead end for the Martin angle. Given there was no CCTV evidence of his visiting Martin. And Martin's weapon store having been cleaned out by Joe. While the Friday Night Boys had bleached and scoured the Bren and then dumped it in the River Lea after its final outing.

'So you're telling us that the hard fact that a suspected arms dealer known to you borrowed this murder weapon, on the same day your dead sister's drug dealer was found shot, is pure coincidence?'

Mickey shrugged again.

'Martin knew Katie well enough. Perhaps he chose to take revenge? Although the idea that he was some kind of weapons dealer is frankly amazing. Especially without any hard evidence.'

Nice try. Is that all you have? Irving, perhaps reading his thoughts, moved on. Taking the bagged pistol off the table.

'Very well. Let us turn our attention to another event. Soon after Warren Margetson's murder. The fatal shooting of five members of a North London crime gang. You might have heard about it. They were a cash collection crew working for the Castagna family.'

'I saw it in the papers. Caused all sorts of excitement.'

'The killings were performed with a Heckler & Koch MP5 machine pistol. A weapon you're familiar with, I expect?'

Mickey saw the freshly baited trap that had been placed before him. Clumsy, but still effective. The opportunity to deny ever having handled or fired an MP5SD. A slip now and they'd charge him with five murders. The fact that the weapon had been silenced never having made it to the media.

'MP5? Yes, I'm familiar with it. Noisy little thing in such a confined space.'

'Indeed.' Haskins shooting him a hard stare that Mickey returned levelly. 'And where were you, at 16.00 on the 25th of April? You told your wife you were on duty, but there's no sign of you having worked that day.'

'No. It was a lie.' Mickey allowed the silence to build. 'What, you want to know why I lied to my wife?'

'In this instance, Sergeant? Yes, we do.'

He nodded. Sighed. 'I was struggling somewhat with the

aftermath of the Margetson killing. It brought the whole matter of my sister's death back to me. I told Roz I was going to work. But I spent the day on the South Bank. Wandering around. People-watching. Relaxing. I needed some time to myself. And it was very therapeutic. Check the CCTV, if you've still got the footage on file. You'll find me more than once. Wandering about, eating an ice cream, getting some sun.' *Before I got on a tube train north to go and meet a Polish delivery driver*, he didn't add. 'You think that I was the Car Park Killer?'

'It had crossed our minds. The machine pistol in question having been ballistically linked to several gang murders over several years. Clearly a weapon for hire. Possibly owned by Martin Hyde. And eventually surfacing in the possession of a recently deceased London gang boss by the name of Giuseppe Castagna. Known to his fellow criminals as Joe. Can you see where this is taking us?'

'Not really. Gun dealers. Gang bosses. It all sounds a bit far-fetched to me.'

Mickey raised an eyebrow, inviting Irving to elaborate.

'Two of the murderers who used that weapon have since been convicted. And, as you can imagine, they were both keen to provide any information that might contribute to their parole hearing's outcome being favourable. They both told us they rented the MP5 from a man they contacted through the dark web. Going by the name of Steph. A man matching Martin Hyde's description, it seems. And we've discovered that Hyde had an aunt who went by the name of Steph. Leading us to wonder if he was continuing an established family business.'

Mickey nodded. 'OK, I can see the angle. You're presuming

that Martin, being from a long line of gun dealers, procured a weapon for me to murder Margetson with. And then lent me an MP5 that he rented out to criminals. Which I then used to attack the Castagna gang, having first established an alibi.'

And shut up again.

'So, where were you at 16.00 on the day of the Car Park Massacre?'

Irving, boring in for the kill.

'Just wandering about.'

True enough. And Mickey secure in the knowledge that when he stopped wandering about there was no CCTV of him ducking into London Bridge tube station. Thanks to a reversible jacket, a wide brimmed cricket hat and a quick image change in a camera-free section of Borough Market.

'How did you get home?'

'Taxi. I couldn't face the tube. I paid cash.'

And there's a dead end for you, he thought. *You've got the weapon identified and that's it.* And was promptly proven wrong.

'Moving on. Item of evidence two is a video clip. Showing the moment that five members of the Castagna gang were killed. We obtained this from Joe Castagna's laptop after his spectacularly violent demise in what appears to have been a gang turf war that went nuclear on him. It was confiscated as part of a wide-ranging investigation into his death. Mr Castagna seems to have had sources inside the Met.'

Irving picked up a remote control. Pressed the play button. And there he was, climbing out of the Astra all those weeks before. Rendered anonymous by the balaclava. Going into action without any hesitation. Putting down the four gang members inside a ten-count. Irving paused the video.

'The killer looks about the same height and build as you, Sergeant. Excellent marksmanship too, well up to your proven abilities. No spray and pray, which is what you'd expect from a gang banger. Four precisely placed three-round bursts, which killed four men. Two immediately, one soon after the police arrived, and one before he reached hospital. And then…'

He pressed play again. And all present watched Mickey make the fifth kill. The reluctance with which he waited until he had no other choice.

'And that's not in keeping with a gang hit either. Is it?'

Mickey looked across the table. Raising his hands in bafflement. 'I wouldn't know, not having ever seen a gang killing. Or had any professional exposure to contract killing, which is what that looked like.'

'You can take it from me, Sergeant, that—'

'I'm happy to be told what you think it looks like, Chief Inspector.'

Mickey sat back, resisting the urge to smirk at Jasmine. Or even look at her. Irving looked at him, blank-faced, for a moment. Then resumed his line of attack.

'That last kill was reluctant. It would be easier to shoot the sort of thugs Joe Castagna employed than putting three rounds into a child, I suppose.'

'A child? He had a beard.'

'He was seventeen. Which would have been obvious enough, if you were looking at him over the barrel of a machine pistol from six feet away. And then, of course, we have the younger brother.'

Irving was watching him intently. As was Haskins. Mickey's instincts told him there was a twist coming. The DAC took up the running.

'We've met the child. We requested permission to speak to him, once the dust had settled on Joe Castagna's somewhat spectacular murder.' Here it came. Professional Standards' ace-in-the-hole evidence Mickey had been waiting for. 'Samuel claimed that the Car Park Killer spoke to him. Which is corroborated by this video footage. It seems Castagna put him on a retainer. Which his mother discovered when he came home in box-fresh Nikes. She reported it to us; we interviewed him again. It seems that Castagna planned to use him to identify the Car Park Killer, if he came up with a suspect.'

Mickey kept a straight face. Wondering where this was going.

'Let me guess. You played him my voice?'

'Yes. And he positively ID'd that recording as being the Car Park Killer.'

'Really?' Mickey looking from Haskins to Irving. Putting his best bemused face on. 'This is what you're planning to charge me with? Knowing an alleged arms dealer who now can't be found? Being about the same height and build as the Car Park Killer? Being proficient with the weapon he used? And being voice-ID'd by a twelve-year-old, who was probably scared out of his wits when the Car Park Killer spoke to him? It doesn't sound like CPS will be all that keen to prosecute on that evidence to me.'

And waited. Wondering what else they had on him. No mention of Number 37 yet. Surely they'd have questioned Tamara on that subject? Wanting to know how she came to be on the spot at just the right time. And nothing on Lewis's death either.

'That's not all. Although it's a decent enough circumstantial case in itself.'

Yeah, thought Mickey. But where's the hook to hang it off?

'Here's how this plays out, Sergeant.'

Jasmine, leaning forward across the table. Revealing her true colours, apparently to Haskins' surprise.

'I think we'll have you charged with the murder of Warren Margetson. Just to be going on with. I'm pretty sure we can persuade a jury that you were in that alley with that pistol. You had the means. You had the motive. And you clearly had the opportunity. I think a jury will put you away for it. As long as your previous record isn't allowed to blinker them to the facts. And as for the Car Park Massacre, I think we can afford to wait, don't you? At some point your friend Mr Hyde is going to come to light. Want to know why?'

Mickey nodded equably. Happy enough to let the senior officer talk.

'He's going to get homesick. That's why. Wherever it is he's run to, he won't last a year. Because he's just another North London boy. And wherever he's gone, it'll be too hot. The food won't be to his liking. And he'll run out of money too.'

Hah. Mickey doubted that money was ever going to be the problem. Not that he could afford to provide any clue on that score. Jasmine sat back. Looking triumphant. Having, Mickey presumed, misread whatever minute facial signal he'd given out on that last point.

'You can still make this easy on yourself. By not having

your reputation dragged through the courts and the media. And on your wife, for the same reason. She seems like a good person. Do you really want to put her through that? And then there's Ms Egerton, of course.'

Now that last point was interesting. Mickey made the "go on then" face.

'We're pretty sure that it was you who raided a Castagna property on the 2nd of May. Number 37 Walcott Road. Actually a pretty good night's work, if it was you. Whoever it was rescued several female prisoners from a deeply unpleasant future. And gave an almighty kicking to the bastards who were holding them. In and of itself, I'd be more than happy to ignore it. Even give whoever did it a pat on the back. Except whoever it was made the huge mistake of involving the press. Grandstanding, perhaps? Doesn't fit with the previous kills, but hey, we've all got egos.'

Yeah, don't we? Mickey shot Jasmine a pitying look.

'Anyway, the long and short of it is that I think Tamara Egerton knows exactly who hit Number 37. Because she was tipped off and waiting.'

'Which seems to have worked pretty well for you. Career wise, I mean?'

Her jocular tone was promptly replaced by something a good deal more authoritarian.

'You can display the appropriate respect, Sergeant. You're so deep in the shit that you're breathing through a straw, right now, whether you realise it or—'

'Of course that's quite possibly not all Tamara Egerton knows.'

Mickey made the statement bluntly. No longer interested in any idea of respect. Left the hook dangling. But not a fishing hook. A meat hook. With Jasmine's career hanging from it, whether she knew it or not.

'What do you mean?'

He looked pointedly at Haskins and Irving. Telling Jasmine that she might not want to share the details of what he had to say to her with any other officers. He raised his eyebrows, silently telling her how close to the edge of the ice she was. And Jasmine, whose instincts had always been strong when it came to self-preservation, nodded.

'Very well. If you believe that there are aspects of this that might be on a need-to-know basis, I'm willing to speak privately in the first instance.'

Haskins shot her a disbelieving look. And got a significant percentage of his safe radiation life dosage in reply.

'Very well, ma'am. We'll be outside when you wish to resume. DAC Haskins and DCI Irving leaving the room.'

Haskins and Irving rose from their chairs. Making, Mickey noted, no effort to stop the recording. With the two of them alone, Jasmine played a calculating stare on him.

'If this is some kind of attempt to bargain your way out of this, it isn't going to work.'

Mickey folded his arms. His body language deliberate: *I have no desire to help you*. Then started his counterattack.

'You're pretty good friends with Anthea Hall, aren't you?'

Not bothering to "ma'am" her. Because, as of this moment, Mickey knew that the Met was in his past. And was just a little broken-hearted. Just a little elated.

'The *Clarion*'s news editor? We've broken bread a few times.'

'So I gather. But you've never passed her any stories?

Unofficially, I mean. We're not talking about your routine virtue signalling in the media. I mean personal information. About serving officers. And not necessarily *true*.'

Jasmine started to bridle at the very suggestion. As if unable to believe that he was asking the question. And then realised that Mickey was staring at the recorder. And in the space of a couple of seconds, her face flushed scarlet. Mickey nodded slowly. Oh yes. *It's every bit as bad as you've suddenly realised.* She reached out and put a finger on the recorder's stop button.

'Interview temporarily suspended by AC Chen.' And stopped the recording. 'What do you mean?'

'Let's level with each other, Assistant Commissioner. Me first. After all, confession is supposed to be good for the soul.' Mickey nodded. 'Yes, it was me. I killed the drug dealer who poisoned my sister. I am the Car Park Killer. It was me who raided Number 37. I also killed a Castagna enforcer by the name of Lewis Dearlove, but you probably haven't got me in the frame for that. And, when Castagna threatened my family, I mounted a raid on his hideout. There was no gang war. Just me. Although that last one needed help from some people you'd be *very* wise not to go looking for. Which you'll already know, if you've recovered CCTV of the attack.'

He leaned back in the chair.

'And I can confidently predict that you'll never prosecute me for any of it.' Smiling in the face of her incredulity. 'How do I know that? We'll get to that in a minute. Because that's not all I know.'

She leaned back in her chair. Her panic of a moment before on the back burner. Too busy digesting his confession.

'Go on then. What else do you know?'

'I know that you're going to recommend my *honourable* early retirement from the Metropolitan Police Service. With a payoff and a disability pension for PTSD.'

She started. Shot him a disbelieving stare.

'Are you fucking *mad*? You're a mass murderer! You've just told me everything I need to have you jailed for the rest of your life!'

Mickey shrugged. 'Nobody else heard it. And you'd better pray it stays that way. Because if the next thing I'm going to tell you ever gets out, you're done.'

'Done?'

'As in also retired. But dishonourably. In disgrace. Am I really worth that much sacrifice? I mean, full marks to you if I am. And to me, I suppose. But really?'

Jasmine stared at him for a moment.

'I think you're bluffing. What can you possibly have—?'

'You briefed the *Clarion* against me. You called Anthea Hall, on a video link. You told her some things that should have remained secret. Officially secret, I'm guessing. And then some things that you'd invented, to make me look bad. Leading to an article in the papers intended to make me persona non grata across government. A small-minded act of personal revenge for my not rolling over and telling you everything when I got back from Belize. And you got away with it, despite the fact that the source must have been fairly obvious. Because it suited more than one agenda. Covered up the participation of ex-military contractors in the minister's protection, for one thing. Made it look like all my own work. After all, I had been sacked. No smoke without fire, eh? Weren't those the words you used? On your call to Anthea?'

She visibly relaxed. 'Let's assume that what you're saying is correct. And that someone you know managed to witness it. Just for the sake of argument. Yes, it would be a difficult thing for me to step out from under. But here's the thing, Sergeant. You can't prove any such thing. So I can charge you with the Margetson killing in the certain knowledge that you did it. Thanks.'

Mickey grinned at her. And held the expression for long enough that he could see her confidence starting to crumble. Then fished out his phone.

'Before I show you this, let's think about one more thing. Specialist Operations has a leak. You know it. I know it. How else could whoever it was that hit us in Fulham have known our route? We only logged it with the control room just before leaving the Hall. One of a small number of people leaked that information to the hit team, and whoever was controlling them. Who used it to ambush us, and to set up the hoax bomb alert in the Cromwell Road to divert us down the secondary route. Which means that the deaths of a dozen of our own and numerous wounded civilians is on your directorate. And you, Assistant Commissioner, have form for leaking. Just saying.'

Gave her a moment to consider that before continuing. Adopting a cheery tone as he put his phone in front of her.

'Here you go. Just watch this. Amazing the quality of video that a decent digital SLR will record these days. Complete with metadata showing the date and time, there on the screen. And there you are, less than four hours after you forced me to make you look stupid in front of your management team and the commissioner. The audio is dubbed over it, obviously. I had to pay a lip reader to tell me what it was you were telling Ms Hall. And I had to pay quite a lot to get a proper expert-witness-level job done of it. But it was *so* worth every penny.'

She looked at the screen. Seeing her own face, unmistakable in high definition. And listened to the accompanying voice-over.

'...and then Bale told a government minister that he was a cunt and to fuck off. He'll deny it, of course, but he has been sacked by the man in question. And there's no smoke without fire, as the old saying goes. Quite shocking behaviour for a serving protection officer, and one that has to call his career into question. I'm not saying that he wasn't provoked, of course, but we expect better of our—'

Mickey stopped the recording.

'And for the avoidance of doubt, if I fall under a tube train later on this afternoon, that recording will be released to all UK news media. If Ms Egerton gets any – *any* – comeback from the *Clarion*, that recording will be released to all UK news media. Which, incidentally, will also wreck your friend Anthea's career. And if I don't receive a medical discharge on a pro-rata'd pension, in the grounds of enduring psychological and physical trauma? That recording will be released to all UK news media. I'll take my chances in court if I have to, but you won't be there to see it. You'll be in free fall. Wondering where your career went. And why the ground's coming up so fast.'

He shrugged at her.

'Your choice. Your move.'

66

Mickey walked out of LX and into the early summer drizzle. Tamara was waiting for him, sheltering under a golf umbrella.

'It worked then?'

Not an unreasonable guess. Given that he'd walked out of the front entrance.

'Yeah. It worked just about as well as it could have. You shouldn't get any come-back either.'

She smiled wanly. 'I couldn't give much of a toss if I do, to be honest. If that evil cow Anthea says anything to me on the subject I'm going to break her fucking nose. As will also be the case if she says "people go missing all the time" to me just one more time. Heartless bitch. I think I'd rather be back in the army.'

Mickey nodded sympathetically. Knowing the degree of disgust in which Tamara held her editor. Horrified at the lack of interest the *Clarion* had taken in the fruitless hunt for her colleague Mark, after a few days of high-profile concern.

'You do know he's dead, don't you?'

She nodded. Unable to meet his eye.

'And you'd like to blame me?'

Another nod. 'You for involving us. Me for being so keen to be involved. Your assistant commissioner for being so keen for the *Clarion* to lean on Castagna. And Anthea for not giving a shit about the fact the poor bastard got disappeared.' She shook her head. 'But mainly I blame Castagna. You're absolutely sure he's dead? Don't tell me to look at the news reports; we both know they can be fixed.'

'He's dead. I put a remote-detonated shaped charge on the underside of his car. He drove off, laughing at me for letting him go. When he got far away enough to be safe from the machine pistol I was carrying he stopped. Shouted the odds out of his car window about how he was going to kill us all. Me, you, my wife. So I pushed a button and the bomb punched a jet of molten copper through the bottom of his driver's seat. What was left wasn't identifiable as a human being, by the time the fire was put out. Most of him having been blown out through a hole in the roof in tiny pieces.'

'That sounds too quick to be real justice.'

'Yeah. But it's what I had.' Mickey guessed she'd swap a dozen dead Joe Castagnas to get her colleague back. 'Mark didn't deserve to die. But he did, and I took revenge for him.'

'Revenge.' She seemed to consider the word. The concept. 'It was revenge for your sister that started this all off, was it?'

'Yeah. And it felt good. At the time.'

Although the first kill, the most important one of them all, now seemed as meaningless as all the others. As seen through the filter of what had followed.

'You and your wife…'

'That's over. She's not the type to take prisoners. Or

forgive the sort of things I've been up to. It's amicable enough, but it's final.'

'Like with the Met?'

He laughed sardonically. 'Like with the Met? The Met's even more implacable than Roz. The Met would have put me in solitary for fifteen years, given the chance. Or possibly sent me to Broadmoor. I was lucky that you gave me what I needed to fend them off. And put the Met over a barrel. I showed her that video and it was interview terminated. I'm out early. Nothing signed yet, but Jasmine doesn't really have a lot of choice, thanks to you. Medical discharge, full pension rights. And I keep the commendation and the Christmas tree ornament. Should be handy when it comes to job hunting.'

'Job hunting? Why would you want another job?'

A question Mickey had been asking himself. A lot. Because he undoubtedly didn't need to work. Not with his share of Joe's money available from Shaw whenever he chose to call it in. If he could bring himself to touch it.

'Good question. And the simple answer is that I'm just not done with what I do for a living yet.'

It was a subtle blend of factors. And Mickey's self-knowledge was good enough to have worked that out. One part the satisfaction he got from taking responsibility for other people's safety. Whoever those people were. One part the buzz of operational tension. Like a trickle charge of adrenaline. And, he was forced to admit – to himself, if no-one else – there was one more thing. The feeling of invincibility that came from being the best at what he did. From holstering a pistol and knowing he was pretty much unbeatable one on one.

'So where will you go? Now that you've irritated the police badly enough for them to cough you out?'

Mickey shook his head. 'I genuinely have no idea. But I do know there are a lot of people out there who need protecting.'

67

'Call to order, ladies and gentlemen.'

Albie stopped gobbing off to the man next to him. His new focus of irritating chatter since Joe's unexpected demise. And showed the appropriate respect for the meeting's chair. In this instance, Sammy Chin. Who, having called his colleagues to the Bosphorus Cafe, got to set the agenda.

'There are two items to discuss. Regarding the division of Castagna family assets and territory.'

He looked down at a single piece of paper.

'Firstly, it is proposed that the immediate legitimate assets willed to Joe's beneficiaries be allowed to proceed through probate. Joe's wife and kids can inherit a legit business, with the appropriate supervision to ensure no move back into our field of operations.'

'What if his son decides to come looking for payback, ten years from now? Might be better to remove that possibility?'

Sammy shook his head at Albie. Having expected the suggestion. And already canvassed the alternate point of view.

'No. The collective has already made this decision. We're

not animals, Albie. And we don't have to live by the old rules when it's not necessary. With the right guidance, which Julie Castagna realises she would be wise to provide, that won't be an issue. Joe wasn't killed by any of us. And besides, his family get a fully functional business empire. They won't be coming after us. So the Castagna family are off limits. Do I need to call a formal vote?'

Off limits being the gangs' code word for "repercussions will result if this is ignored". Something Albie knew all too well. He shook his head.

'No need to vote, I agree.'

'Secondly…' Sammy looked back at the paper. 'It is agreed that Castagna turf will be split between those present in the proportions and geographic boundaries laid out in our revised detailed territorial plan. We will now express ourselves content or otherwise.'

Four solid days of territorial negotiation had been needed. Street by painful street. But the gang leaders, as all had known would be the end result, were collectively agreed as to the new normal. Smart enough to know that a good negotiation left everyone a little disappointed. Peace in our time the order of the day.

Chin looked around the table, one person at a time. All present nodded in turn, and said 'content'. Even Albie, who would probably have loved an argument just for the sake of it. The meeting started to relax. Body language speaking of relaxation from a peak of tension. Muttered side conversations starting between individuals.

'There is a third subject for discussion.' Pitching his voice loudly enough to overcome the growing babble. 'A renewed peace agreement.'

All present looked at Sammy. Wondering what the fuck he was on about. Especially as there was no third item on the paper in front of him.

'My friends, I have a confession to make. I have broken our agreement. I was instrumental in the downfall of our associate.'

All present stared at him, mostly without expression. Too used to holding in their emotions under any and all provocations. Waiting to see what he was going to tell them before deciding what to do about it.

'I formed the opinion about six months ago that Joe's overly hard-line approach to the business was going to cause problems. The fact that the Metropolitan Police Service were going after him was only part of it.' He looked around at them. 'How many people have your people killed in the last year? With me it's two. And one of them was an accident. It's a handful between us, right? Not Joe. He'd offed at least half a dozen in the last twelve months. He was drawing attention. Too flash. Too brutal. You get away with that shit for so long, then you're suddenly a modern-day Ronnie Kray. And we all know what happens then. We *all* get it in the neck.'

Nods around the table. A little grudging, but agreement nonetheless. Nobody wanted to arouse the establishment's ire. Knowing that when it came to wars, the golden goose usually gets caught in the crossfire. And becomes early collateral damage.

'I recruited an insider. Someone who could provide the sort of detail I would need.'

Albie shot him a calculating look.

'Who? Eddie, I bet.'

Some of the attendees nodded knowingly. All present knowing the full details of Nigel's murder on Joe's terrace.

'No. Richard.'

'The geezer's lawyer?'

Chin nodded at Albie. 'He was shit-scared of the man. And happy to help. Especially when I intimated to him that Joe's demise would get him out from under. And with enough money to retire on. Then I went looking for someone to do the dirty work. And an associate of mine, a small-time gun dealer, knew just the man. A friend of his. A policeman. And very well motivated to want revenge on Joe.'

He waited for the general outrage to die down before continuing. Facing them down with the outward confidence of a lion tamer in the middle of the cage. He raised a hand to forestall Albie's question.

'No. You don't need to know who. It wasn't easy, of course. The man in question had to believe he was acting of his own free will. But we gave him the information and weapons he needed. One hit at a time. And he did the rest. Like some sort of fucking Terminator.'

'What, so all that was your doing? The dealer. The car park. His safe house?'

The older of the two women on the council asked the question with a look of disbelief. Chin shrugged.

'Yeah. The man was better than I could have hoped for. He even took Lewis off the board.' That got a moment's silence. 'It nearly went wrong at the end. My associate was unwise enough to get captured by Joe.'

'And he grassed your shooter up, right?'

'Of course. Wouldn't you have? I reckon I'd have been

talking double-quick. We can be grateful that he had the sense not to mention our arrangement. Or Joe would have come at us like a blood-crazed wolf. Of course what we didn't know was this policeman had some high-end military contacts. Deniable assets, I think they call them. Special forces nutters.'

'You mean the raid on Joe's arches was...'

'Yeah.' The second-generation Chinese kept his face straight. 'A government death squad. They killed anyone who even looked at a gun. Did Eddie. Did Joe. Took his contingency money and disappeared.'

'What, back to the LA underground?'

Albie smirked. 'This isn't the A-Team, Albie son. These are some proper nasty people. First thing you know about it, if they come for you, is when you realise your throat's been cut. Which you know because your fucking head's on the floor and you're looking up at yourself.'

The older man nodded. Knowing where this was going.

'Which is why you're about to propose that we leave it there. And don't try to silence your man the gun dealer.'

'That won't be necessary. He's gone for a long holiday, under an assumed identity. And with all the money he'll ever need, if he uses his head.'

'And the shooter?'

Sammy nodded at Albie. Knowing where his thought process was going.

'We especially don't need to go after the shooter. He has no interest in the rest of us. He's had his revenge, done and dusted. All he wants now is to get on with a quiet life, I expect.'

'But you've kept him in your pocket? In case you need a special job doing?'

'In a manner of speaking. He has no idea he's been used. Or that he might need to be used again. But I'm keeping a nice close eye on him. After all, who knows when we might need someone like that again?'

Acknowledgements

In making this unexpected leap from historical fiction to contemporary thriller writing (unexpected to me, at least, when the idea came to me in a Brisbane hotel bedroom at two in the morning), I have found myself grateful to a number of people. To Robin Wade, both for his initial encouragement as my agent, and then for his impeccable taste in picking out a replacement agent with the experience and skills to maximise the opportunity presented by *Nemesis*, when he decided to pass the baton. His generosity in making that move in such good spirit leaves me both in awe and in his debt. I am of course indebted to Robin for his calm and sensible guidance of my writing career across the first twelve books of the Empire series, and the Centurions trilogy, and the way in which he facilitated my move to Sara O'Keefe at Aevitas Creative was textbook Wade, drama-free and expertly managed. Thank you, Robin!

Sara has quickly proven herself to be (as Robin intimated would be the case) exactly the right agent to take on a book that was very different to my previous work, both in terms of content and style. Her suggestions were subtle but went straight to the heart of the matter, inspiring a transformation in *Nemesis* that turned it from a good book to something even better and, I am absolutely certain, pushed it across the line into being publishable. My gratitude is considerable, both for that invaluable advice and for managing the process of finding the right publisher with the essential blend of determination and good humour, given the challenging circumstances in mid-2020.

Nic Cheetham and Holly Domney at Head of Zeus/Aries both showed the sort of enthusiasm and expertise that inspire an author to place their work in the hands of fellow professionals, and I am grateful for their commitment at a difficult time for the industry. Let's hope that *Nemesis* can repay that trust! And while we're talking about editors, I'm also grateful to Carolyn Caughey at Hodder for her patience at this unexpected distraction from my other genre.

I must also mention someone whose insights were a large part of painting Mickey Bale's backstory, not to mention his pointing me in the right direction when it came to my characters' fashion and firearm choices. Dan Monisse, you're golden!

And lastly but most importantly, as ever, I am eternally grateful to the chance meeting that teamed me up with one of life's good people, the woman whose firm hand on the tiller of our lives has gifted me with the stability and encouragement needed to combine a day job with a two book a year writing habit. Thank you, Helen Riches. For everything.

**Read on for an exclusive preview
of the next Mickey Bale thriller,**

TARGET ZERO

Prologue

Somewhere in the back of his mind, Darren Pearce was still playing catch up.

Not in terms of the ground reality. His team had responded to the scramble call like the pros they were. Following the drills they'd had trained into them over several years. Endless preparation for something unlikely ever to become real. Now they were closing in on the appointed point on the map as directed. With not much more than a minute or so to spare, from the sound of the radio chatter.

Sergeant Pearce and his team had been patrolling the airport, ground side. A routine gig for the Essex force's Field Support Unit. Equivalent to the Met's SCO19. Two teams of two, one officer facing forwards, one facing backwards. Still working coppers, of course. Looking amenable. Fielding questions. Giving directions. Swapping bantz. While all the time alert for anything out of the ordinary. High focus, energy sapping, but low drama. The sight of a rifle having the tendency of smothering drama at birth, in a country still unused to heavily armed police. Making the job a bit boring, truth be told. Although, as a specialist firearms officer, boring – as the cliche went – was a good thing. True, Pearce occasionally dreamt of getting a chance to do the exciting side of the job. But knew at the same time that dream could become nightmare in the blink of an eye. Be careful what you wish for stuff.

And then, without warning, an urgent radio message had turned it all upside-down. No warning. No 'this is a drill'. Punters gawping as the sergeant and his three constables legged it from the far end of the busy concourse to their carrier. Driver waiting, engine running, blue lights already flickering. Red-lining it to the M11. With directions to head up the motorway to as far as the unmarked turn off at Wicken Water. Under the carriageways and back on, southbound. Pearce and his team getting their breath back as they were briefed on the move. Their duty inspector on the radio from the other side of the county, filling in the detail. Sounding as jealous as fuck. Suspected Islamic terrorists heading for London from the north. Their route clearly taking them down the motorway past Stansted. And on, presumably, into the target-rich jihadi mecca of London. One vehicle, four suspects. Pearce's team's mission being to stop and detain. Standard rules of engagement. Arrest if possible. Use of firearms authorised if necessary to preserve life.

Pearce watched his troops as they kitted up. His own preparation so practised as to be on auto-pilot. Securing kevlar 'Fritz' helmets, ballistic goggles ready for use. Helping each other strap on heavy plate carriers over black boiler suits. Swaying in the moving vehicle, but getting it done quickly and without fuss. Belt kit going on last. Everything needed for a variety of circumstances. Spare mags, trauma kit, restraints, smoke grenades and flash-bangs. He talked them through one last weapon check. Loaded mags, rounds chambered, safeties off. Condition one, fingers off triggers. All four of them equipped with Heckler & Koch G36C carbines. 5.56mm, serious military firepower. Big boy stuff. Everything falling into place, the way they'd rehearsed it time after time. A machine. But something was still nagging.

The van was slowing, and looking through the windscreen he could see a motorway spec X5 on the hard shoulder two hundred metres distant. X marks the spot, his mouthiest officer joked. Her face pale, fight or flight kicking in. The driver pulled in in front of the BMW, leaving a fifty-metre gap between the two vehicles. Braking distance, for a stricken target vehicle.

'Listen in!'

An army cliche, he knew, and one his people constantly ripped the piss out of him for. But old habits die hard. And Pearce knew the adrenaline would be fizzing in their veins. That commands would have to be crisp and clear.

'We de-bus! We stay in the cover of the carrier! Keep it low, avoid being seen! The Road Policing boys will deploy the Stinger, then *we* do the heavy lifting!'

Which got him some smiles. The radio interrupted before he could continue.

'Foxtrot Sierra Uniform from Whiskey Two Four. We're the Romeo Papa crew at your six. Target vehicle sighted, estimate forty-five seconds to contact.'

Pearce's response was immediate.

'Roger Two Four. Call out Stinger release, with a countdown please. All stations, clear channel, clear channel!'

That got a series of clicks in response. Nobody was going to talk over an operation like this. Pearce knowing he had a few seconds to finish his orders.

'You know the drill. If you have to shoot, go centre-mass!' Nodded to his most experienced officer. 'Richie, you're lead! I'll be right behind you, then Jenny, then Karl! Once we're out of cover we go echelon left! I want maximum firepower if it kicks off! Right, let's go!'

Richie pulled the carrier's side door open. Climbed out and moved forward, staying low and close to the vehicle's side. Crouching in the cover of the van's left front wing.

'Whiskey Two Four. Stinger in thirty seconds.'

The Road Policing officer sounding as calm. As if there was nothing more exciting than a sit down with a cuppa in the offing. Pearce mentally doffed his cap to the man.

Richie crouched by the front offside lights, putting a padded knee onto the tarmac. Raised a hand and shouted the expected statement of preparedness.

'Ready!'

Pearce echoed the shout. Looking back at the other two as they replied. Both on one knee behind him. Weapons pointing at the verge. A good team. No, a great team. He instinctively knew they'd do him proud.

'Stinger in twenty seconds.'

Still something at the back of Pearce's mind. Something he'd lost in the rush to embus and kit up. Richie looking back at him, waiting for the go order.

'Stinger in ten, nine, eight...'

And Pearce realised what it was that was bothering him.

'Six, five, four...'

Too late to ask the question now. He exchanged a last-minute nod of respect with Richie.

'...two, one... Stinger deployed!'

The suspect vehicle whipped past them with a howl of

protesting rubber. Tyres already deflating as the hollow spikes allowed their air to escape in a rush. The driver's foot hard on the brakes, barely controlling the car as it skewed into the outside lane. Coming to a halt forty metres past the carrier.

'Go! Go! Go!'

Richie led them out onto the empty motorway, carbine raised. Pearce a pace behind him and to the left. Carbine held on target with one hand. The other keying his mike back to the control room in Chelmsford.

'Control, FSU. Suspect vehicle stopped. Interrogatory: is there an explosives risk? Urgent response please!'

Still moving forwards, hearing the mosquito whine of a drone in the air behind them. Pearce waved the other two further out to his left. Wanting more than one rifle on target if the suspected jihadis had the means of going loud.

'FSU, Control–'

The doors of the battered looking Vauxhall opened. Four men in the act of getting out. And anything that control had to say was suddenly way less interesting than the situation to hand.

'Armed police! Down on the ground!'

Richie amping up the volume to a roar. As trained. Intimidate the person you're looking through the sights at hard enough and you might not have to shoot them. Or so the theory went. Jenny and Karl were shouting too. Still advancing. Pearce drew breath to reinforce the bellowed commands. And a single word in whatever control were trying to tell him broke through the cognitive chaff that was swamping his ability to process their message.

EOD.

Explosive Ordnance Disposal.

Shit.

He looked up, close enough to see the suspects' faces as they lowered themselves onto the motorway's tarmac. One just scared. Not really realising the depth of the shit he'd stepped into until this minute. Another frankly terrified. And looking like he'd already pissed himself, or worse. One with the beatific smile of a true believer. Which was heart stopping enough in itself. Bespeaking the expectation of imminent martyrdom. And the fourth... Pearce felt the adrenaline surge. His animal brain making the decision to kill the fourth man before his conscious thought processes caught up.

The fourth man was grinning hard enough that his face was almost a rictus. Teeth bared. The grin turning into a snarl even as Pearce put his hand back on the carbine and lined up the shot. Putting the death dot on his forehead and his finger onto the trigger. He fired, the gentlest squeeze of his index finger unleashing the terrible power of the 5.56mm round chambered and waiting.

Just a tenth of a second too late.

1

Monken Park Boxing Studio. Fashionably bare brick walls, tiered rows of punch bags and speedballs.

Outside, cold rain on the streets, leaves whipped by the wind. Commuters scurrying home with their hoods up. Eager for central heating and oven ready. How was your day, or just telly's solitary embrace.

Inside, warm and aromatic with sweat, liniment and grim determination. Half a dozen paying punters pounding bags, a couple more skipping with their personal trainers. And in the ring, two men. One past his prime in fight terms, one yet to reach it. But Mickey knew the kid had him in deep trouble the moment the fight started.

Grizzler gestured for the two men to get to it. And the shit promptly hit the fan. To be fair, it wasn't like Mickey hadn't been warned. The kid had strolled across the ring towards him nonchalantly enough. Gloved hands down by his hips and a knowing smile that set his instincts jangling. Leaned in, as if to say hi and thanks for offering to spar. And delivered the good news through his Irish flag gumshield. Flat stare, flat monotone.

'My Da says you're filth. Says you smacked him, good and hard, one Saturday night. On the High Street back in the 90's. Says you knocked him spark out. So I'm gunna make you my bitch, right? When I'm done with you, they'll be doing the ten-bell salute.'

Slight overkill with the final ten-count thing, but effective enough as threats went. He'd looked Mickey up and down with the expert eye of a butcher considering a side of beef. Cleaver in hand. Seeing, Mickey knew all too well, a slightly creased and dog-eared former copper in his forties. Gym toned, minimal body fat, bullet-hole pucker in his right abdominals. Muscles, poise, and the scar to match. Fit, and known to be double-hard. But still well past his sell-by for the ring. Ready to be battered, likely to be deep-fried, by the right fighter. Kid gave Mickey one last disparaging look, then turned and walked back to his corner. Kid was this year's bright prospect, a potential super-star in the making. Not wholesome like Joshua. Not a dancing joker like Fury. A wild-eyed animal of a fighter, known to idolise Connor McGregor and his ilk. And a product of the club Mickey had been exercising at for the last three decades. Already tipped to be at least a finalist in his weight class at Amateur level inside the year, despite only being seventeen. Runner up for the National Youth championships a month before. Unlucky to have lost to a split decision that still had the fight fraternity exchanging knowing glances. And champion at Junior and Youth levels for the past three years. A red-hot prospect with fast feet, a granite jaw and the full deck of offensive options. A potential world champion, with the right management. Which management was sitting ringside, accompanied by suitably hench minders. Watching his new boy work out against a disappointingly thin succession of mobile punch-bags. With the kid's da sitting next to him, looking daggers at Mickey. Who didn't know him from Adam. But then he'd decked a few lairy geezers on the High Street in the nineties, so go figure. And now the kid was intent on reducing his da's one-time persecutor to a lumpy paste.

Grizzler had wandered across, raising an eyebrow. Good instincts, Grizzler. Probably picking up the vibe from the kid's father.

'You owight, Mickey son? Was good of you to offer up when he put his last partner to sleep early, but the little bastard's like a junkyard dog when he gets started. No shame in changing your mind, eh?'

Last chance to bail on the whole stupid idea. Make his excuses and climb back out through the ropes. Rather than be carried out through them.

'I'm fine mate. Happy to help the kid out.' Mickey almost unable to believe his own bravado. Other descriptive nouns being available. Grinned at the gnarled old trainer through his gum shield. 'What could possibly go wrong?'

'D'you want a *list*?' A shrug. 'Your funeral son. Just don't say you wasn't warned. And watch his left. He uses the right to intimidate, but the left hook's the killer.'

And walked back to the centre of the ring. Getting ready to usher them both forward. Leaving Mickey to ponder just what the fuck he'd got himself into. Mickey Bale, ex-copper, current geezer. Moderately respected around his own manor. Yes, he was a copper - because once a copper always a copper. But he was always straight, innit? Which was what Mickey liked to think was the consensus of opinion. Knowing he was probably being optimistic. Recently returned from abroad, a few months away to get over the events that had made him an ex twice over. Ex-copper and ex-husband. Fit as fuck from all the recreation he'd indulged in, true enough. But in fight terms as ring rusty as a fifty-year-old Lancia.

The bell rang, and Grizzler pointed to the centre of the ring. And Mickey walked out to take his twenty-year-deferred spanking.

The first ten seconds confirmed the likely degree of punishment. And took Mickey straight to full-on red alert. Kid came in fast and hard. Throwing combinations from the get-go. And nothing trivial. Inside the first minute he'd landed a dozen tidy body shots. The professional boxer's go-to blow of choice for the early stages of any encounter, unless an opponent left their chin hanging out. Only so much punishment a man can take before it starts to hurt. And Mickey, with a proper six-pack and the full muscle jacket to match rode the blows easily enough. But knew he was taking damage. Imagining his health bar starting to dwindle. Tried an experimental jab, leaning in to get the shot away. Missed, the little bastard's lightning reflexes taking him around the punch like trying to hit smoke. Then paid for the pleasure of watching his gloved fist go nowhere that mattered. Took a short right to the face that staggered him back blinking. Had the kid's dad, manager and hangers on roaring approval. Kill the filth, nail the prick, yadda yadda yadda.

Taking strength from their hatred Mickey raised his gloved fists and went back to basics. No way he was going to last if he stood up and tried to box with the kid for the remainder of the three rounds. Fell back on the two most simple defensive tools he had to hand. Taking the beating on his hands and running away. Blocked and shuffled backwards in a circle, feeling no shame and giving no shits for the abuse he was taking from the audience. Made it to the end of the round intact and went back to his corner with an inward sigh of relief. Rinsed his mouth out and spat in the bucket Grizzler offer him. No blood. Yet.

'He's got you pinned, Mickey son. Got any ideas?'

Mickey looked up at the ancient trainer. Who'd already been middle-aged when Mickey's stepdad Terry had brought him in to the gym for something to do. And delivered him into the arms of redemption. Grizzler, named for a one-off shedding of tears. Prompted by an alumni of the gym's brief success on the pro circuit in the early 80s. Before Mickey's time, but still the stuff of legends. And Mickey, still breathing hard, knew exactly what he had left in his locker.

'Thought I might run away for the rest of the fight. Give him some practice unpicking locks.'

A grim headshake.

'You ain't got the wind. He ain't got the patience. Think again son. Take another three minutes, eh?'

Thanks, Mickey thought, nodding and standing back up. The usual Grizzler opinion, terse, pithy, invariably correct. It was a quirk of fate that the old man had never had a Lewis or a Benn walk through his doors. Leaving the club under-regarded by the cognoscenti. But like Arsene, Grizzler knew.

Kid came out under full sail. Look on his face that said he was minded to close out the fight quick. Telling Mickey that he'd have to offer more than being a bag on legs to survive the next one hundred and eighty seconds. So Mickey fell back on the endless repetitions of his youth. Moving up from running away to moving sideways. Not exactly dancing, not at his age. But up on his toes, taking random lateral steps to throw the kid's aim off. And taking his blocking game up a notch. No longer just letting the kid smack his hands to a pulp, but actually parrying. And trying the odd shoulder-roll, smiling inwardly as the kid's impatience started to show. Took another shot to his face when he rolled instead of parrying and the kid second-guessed him. But found himself able to grin back, giving it the old 'that all you got?' eyebrows. If round one had been a straight beating, round two was still a points loss. But better. Grizzler held the bucket up, grimacing at the blood washing around against the white plastic.

'He's gonna have you this round. Come out with the big one ready to throw. *You* be ready, eh?'

And walked away. Mickey shook his head in dark amusement. Gnomic being a word specifically invented for Grizzler, he reckoned. But he knew exactly what the old man was telling him. Time to die, so to speak, unless he had something more to offer.

In a boxing movie the kid would have said something at the top of the third. Something spiteful, or goading. This being real life he just gave Mickey the stare and got down to business. End game stuff, storming in with a raging flurry of combinations. One eye constantly on teeing Mickey up for the big one. Just as advertised. Manoeuvring Mickey round the ring with one thought, to put that golden punch through his crumbling defences. Deliver on his promise to the pack baying for blood behind him. And Mickey notched his defensive game up again, slipping to left and right. Channelling what was left of his energy to proper boxing. The years momentarily washed away on a last-gasp wave of adrenaline. Even the gym punters were watching now. One or two nodding respect that the old guy had made it to the third with more than just rope-a-dope left in him. And the kid's da, inflamed at the thought that his one-time persecutor might yet escape punishment, made the fatal mistake. Brushed off the kid's manager and jumped to his feet.

'Fucking *hit* him!'

The roar enough to give Mickey a millimetric, fleeting moment of opportunity. The kid's attention spilt, for one beautiful, yawning instant, between opponent and instruction. Better yet, caught extended, right arm out feeling for the chance to unload his left. A chance, the only chance of the fight, on offer. And Mickey took it. Stepped forward and counter-punched properly for the first time in over five hundred seconds of fighting. Fired his trademark right hook in from low. The punch finding the kid wide open and liking what it found. Inch perfect, straight to the on-off switch. Lights out. Kid went down like the proverbial sack of shit. Eyes rolling to show the whites, mouth falling open to spill his gum shield. Mickey turned away as he hit the canvas. Winked at a simultaneously disgusted and secretly delighted Grizzler and then grinned down at the kid's da. Raising his gloves and making the universal gesture for 'you want some?'. Sending a message, loud and clear. Have some class, step up or shut up. Watching as the famous manager's goons went round confiscating phones and deleting camera files. Knowing there was no way they'd get them all. Uncrimp that, motherfuckers. Mickey Bale most definitely back in town.

About the Author

ANTHONY RICHES, coming from a family with three generations of army service, has always been fascinated by military history, psychology and weaponry – which led him to write the Empire series set in ancient Rome. The idea for his first contemporary thriller, *Nemesis*, came to him under the influence of jetlag at two in the morning in a Brisbane hotel room, after a chance text discussion with a police officer. He lives in rural Suffolk with his wife, two dogs the size of ponies and a bad-tempered cat.

www.anthonyriches.com
@AnthonyRiches